D1548501

NO ONE SHOULD SUBSTITUTE THE CONTENTS OF
THIS BOOK FOR EITHER A DOCTOR'S ADVICE OR HIS
TREATMENT. THE FOLLOWING IS A SPIRITUAL WORK
TO BE USED IN CONJUNCTION WITH, AND NOT IN
OPPOSITION TO, MODERN MEDICINE. SO USED, IT IS
COMPLETELY SAFE. THE RELIGIOUS BASES OF ILL-
NESS AND SUFFERING DISCUSSED HEREIN ARE
ULTIMATE CAUSES AND, AS SUCH, THEY DO NOT
PRECLUDE THE EXISTENCE OF THE PROXIMATE
CAUSES WHICH ARE THE REALM OF MEDICINE AND
PSYCHOLOGY. SINCE WE SHARE THE GOAL OF THE
ALLEVIATION OF SUFFERING, THERE IS NO REASON
WHY RELIGION AND THE HEALTH SCIENCES SHOULD
NOT WORK HAND IN HAND. IT IS TO THIS GOAL THAT
THIS BOOK IS DEDICATED.

The Book of Life
by
Rōshi P.T.N.H. Jiyu-Kennett
and
Rev. Daizui MacPhillamy

Illustrated by Rev. Gyokukō Kroenke

Shasta Abbey Press
P.O. Box 478
Mt. Shasta, CA 96067

First Edition — March 1979
First Printing — March 1979

Printed in the United States of America.

ISBN 0—930066—04—9

To our True Master Shakyamuni Buddha, Who was gracious enough to teach us these things.

ACKNOWLEDGMENTS.

The authors wish to thank the following people who have contributed their time and effort towards the preparation and publication of this book:—

Editorial and legal consultation:—
Rev. Jishō Perry.
Typing, layout, and proofreading:—
Revs. Gyojin Cherlin, Meian Elbert, Myōhō Harris, Saidō Kennaway, Rokuzan Kroenke, Kōmei Larson, Meiten McGuire, Jiryu Parkinson, Shikō Rom, Isan Sacco, and Teijō Stimac.
Production:—
Revs. Ekō Little and Kōmei Larson.

Special thanks are due to Rev. Gyokukō Kroenke for the illustrations and the cover and to Rev. Mokurai Cherlin for translation from the Chinese.

We wish to express our deepest gratitude to those students of the anma arts who have so selflessly shared with us their knowledge, to the authors referred to herein whose books have provided a foundation, to the Zen monks of the Far East who have passed on the tradition of the Zen of harmonizing body and mind, and to many of the monks of Shasta Abbey who have proved for themselves the truth of the contents of this book.

CONTENTS.

Book One.

The Third Law of the Universe,
The Law of Karma is Inevitable and Inexorable.

Book Two.

The Harmonization of Body and Mind
through the Cleansing of Karma.

BOOK I.

THE THIRD LAW OF THE UNIVERSE, THE LAW OF KARMA IS INEVITABLE AND INEXORABLE.

by

Rōshi P.T.N.H. Jiyu-Kennett

INTRODUCTION.

This book is *not* intended as a substitute for conventional medical treatment: it is something to be used in conjunction therewith. What is spoken of here will enable the reader to recognise in himself the signs of possible sickness and enable him to do something about it *before* he actually becomes physically ill. Should he already be ill, he should continue with the course of treatment his doctor has prescribed whilst using the mudras and meditation to discover the *true* cause of his illness. The doctor's medicine will prevent the illness from becoming worse whilst, by taking charge of his life through meditation and mudras, the patient brings about not only his own cure but the prevention of a recurrence of his symptoms. Doctors know *how* to deal with symptoms, some even know the *superficial* reasons for those symptoms, but it is only the patient who can find the *true* reason as to *why* he is ill: only by taking full responsibility for his life, loving and caring for his body, studying its needs and bringing it into harmony with his spirit, will a man be able to find the *true* cause of his sickness.

We have divided this book into two sections which may be roughly described as theory and practice respectively. There is no way that the theory of this vast subject can be fully covered in any one book—indeed several volumes could be written on *each* of the Five Laws of the Universe. In many respects what is written here is a dissertation on the Third;

1

the payment of karmic debts is inevitable since the Law of Karma is inexorable. But it is not possible to write on the above without some mention of the other four. What is written in this book is going to amaze some, worry a few and relieve many. It is the result of putting Buddhist teachings into *practice* without fear of what Buddhist theoreticians may say or think. The information given here concerning past lives (klesa) has all been *experienced* by persons personally known to me and whose characters are unimpeachable; such information revolutionises karmic theory as it is usually taught although, if a person is persistent in his studies thereof, *all* of what is written here is either spoken of, or depicted, openly, or described in somewhat flowery language, throughout the Buddhist Scriptures, so there is nothing 'invented' or 'imagined' in the pages that follow. I personally, when in the East, witnessed the use of acupuncture, acupressure and moxa burning for the alleviation of tension and pain,—Holmes Welch[1] speaks much of the spiritual properties of the last named,—it was there that I became acquainted with what I *thought* was acupressure. Through its use upon myself during meditation I was able, at first hand, to experience its great value when done in mudra form. What is described here is *not* the same as acupressure, being a spiritual exercise in which the person on whom it is done is completely in charge of what is happening to him since, except in exceptional circumstances, he is doing it upon himself. Acupressure is something that a second party does upon a patient in which the former is in charge rather than the latter. As I understand it, both from my reading and from what I was taught, acupuncture, moxa burning and acupressure are all somewhat corrupted forms of the spiritual exercise here called mudras, the corruption probably coming about, centuries upon centuries ago, as a result of persons wishing to hand over responsibility for themselves to others out of worldly curiosity or, quite simply, because the mudra system does not bring about the alleviation of *symptoms* in anything like so short a time as the other three. Thus our ancestors sacrificed *genuine* cure, both spiritual and physical, for quick relief.

Man is body and spirit; there can be no separation of the two without sickness occurring. Although Book I is the theory behind Book II, it is also a blue-print for the future prevention of the need for Book II. In other words, it is an attempt to describe the ideal conception, birth, upbringing and adult life-style of a human being so that separation of body and mind shall not occur, previous karma be cleansed and rebirth in the Womb of the Tathagata[2] made possible at the time of so-called death, thus this volume is called *The Book of Life*. Life lived as described here will make possible the appearance in this world of the Five Laws of the Universe as the *norm* for human behaviour rather than the exception thus leading man to a higher quality of life, both physical and spiritual, and a higher morality.

CHAPTER I.

THE FIVE LAWS OF THE UNIVERSE.

Law 1.   The physical world is not answerable to my personal will.

I am not the Cosmic Buddha[3] and there is nothing in me that is not of the Cosmic Buddha. I am not God and there is nothing in me that is not of God. Thus no Zen Master ever says he is either enlightened or unenlightened.

Law 2.   The Law of Change.

There is no such thing as a separate, individual soul that goes to a God or a Buddha to live unchanged in its individuality at the time of physical death. The physical body parts from the *seemingly* individual part of the Buddha Nature[4] (or Holy Spirit) which man mistakenly calls his soul or spirit at the time of what is presently described as death. The body in its present form is unplugged, as it were, from the apparent life force and disintegrates into various components which turn again into other life forms or life-sustaining forces, e.g. worms, maggots, compost, water, etc., nothing whatsoever being wasted, all being recyclable.

Law 3.   The Law of Karma is inevitable and inexorable.

The so-called individual soul or spirit which a being, male or female, has thought of as himself returns to the Source, called herein the Buddha Nature (the third Body of the Trikaya[5] or Holy Spirit), in its entirety *only* if *all* past karma, both of the life-existence just ended, and those life-existences prior to it, has been purified. For example, a person who has lived an exemplary life during *this* lifetime may *still* not become one with the Buddha Nature if he has not looked deeply within himself and purified the karma he inherited from former lives.

That part of the karma that *is* purified, however, returns to the Buddha Nature and becomes one with it, so that which is being thought of as an *individual* soul becomes divided up, like returning unto like: the purified part of the spirit returns to the Buddha Nature and the unpurified part is reborn into whatever is a suitable form for its presently unpurified state. It should be noted that spirit, however uncleansed, is still spirit and herein lies its ability to bring life into existence no matter how debased the form may seem. Thus, a person who kept all the Precepts[6] except the prohibition against carnal lust would find only the lustful nature of himself reborn as we know life, probably, but not necessarily, in animal form or as one of those unfortunate humans who are always in trouble for carnal acts they have not committed, the purified karma of his former life returning to its rightful home in the Buddha Nature.

For centuries the argument against rebirth has always been statistical, i.e. if a person dies another must be born in his place, so why is the world population always changing? However, rebirth does not work this way. The physical body disintegrates and becomes recyclable material for use by the as yet unpurified karma-carrying sparks of spirit. These sparks become living organisms exactly in ratio to their own unpurified karma and are thus again given a chance to transcend that karma by purification, thereafter returning directly to the Buddha Mind, sometimes called the Buddha Nature.[7]

Because of the above it is impossible, and even stupid, to expect a baby human to be born every time another human dies. *Anything* can be born as the result of *any* death, whether human or animal and, because every being in the world has done totally different things from everybody else, there is *no* formula that can be laid down as to what will happen specifically to anyone. *Only* the individual can do something about that, *for himself*, through meditation. All that can be *truly* said is that *certain* acts will have adverse effects on new life and other acts will have beneficial ones. The Buddhist Precepts are the nearest a person can get to a working formula for this purpose.

Nor is just *one* being likely to result from the death of a previous being. An unconverted carnal lust *may* be reborn in animal form, an unresolved confusion at the time of death *may* be reborn in a muddle-headed human and a secret and hidden evil act may cause the birth of a fixed or wandering ghost, just to give a few examples. Thus the death of *one* human *could* result in the rebirth of an animal, a human and a ghost all out of the unpurified part of that human's karma which will then become purified in its *own way* to become a beautiful part of the Buddha Mind. Such unpurified karma becomes a karmic debt which the new-born creature inherits (more concerning this later).

Thus Buddhism says with absolute truth that that which is reborn is not the same soul or spirit as that which died nor is it different from it. No being keeps his soul or spirit intact at death unless he has purified every karmic jangle within that soul or spirit from the time that it was part of the original Buddha Nature before the universe began to the present. At the time of the death of such a being his or her spirit returns in its entirety to the Buddha Mind, for it is indeed the whole of that Buddha Nature, and loses its individuality therein leaving nothing whatsoever to be reborn. Thus the Zen Master can say with truth that enlightened action leaves behind it no speck of dust and the fully enlightened man is truly free.

Very occasionally a person may be the inheritor of all the karma from one particular previous existence and it may seem to him that he has inherited the equivalent of a whole previous personality. This is the main cause of the belief in reincarnation, however one should know that however much karma a person may inherit from one place, he still will *not* inherit an individual soul since that which was purified in the former being will have returned to the Cosmic Buddha.

Law 4. Without fail evil is vanquished and good prevails; this too is inexorable.

Periodically it is necessary for the Buddha Nature to give more of Itself to a new-born being than is usual, otherwise there is no way in which that being will have sufficient purified spirit to be able to cleanse its present load of karma. For this purpose there comes forth from the Buddha Mind that which is termed a Bodhisattva[8] who works for the

6

conversion of the unpurified karmic stream in order to bring it to the Bodhisattva state. The following is a typical example. A person whose nature alternates between extremes of cruelty and compassion in his or her present existence begins to meditate deeply. He finds within himself two distinctly different natures and longs to be undivided. As his meditation deepens he experiences past lives wherein he has been sadistic time and again down the centuries starting with little acts of excessive love which eventually, several lives later, became cruelty. In his last existence this person was a vicious Nazi. For such a person the next step would be to be born mad had it not been for the fact that, at the hour of death, he had begun to doubt the wisdom of his actions. This doubt, constituting the equivalent of his saying "I could be wrong," is sufficient to cause the Buddha Nature to pour out compassion; thus there issues forth a stream of pure spirit which picks up the impure stream and converts it from within. Herein the truth of the Fourth Law is proved:—without fail evil is vanquished and good prevails. No matter what a being has done, either in this life or in a past one, if he truly repents, or so much as even doubts, the wisdom of his evil acts as late in life as the moment of death, he opens the door to freedom. If, however, he willfully persists in his evil there will be born some unfortunate being who will carry that karmic stream and, unless it is converted cither from within by a Bodhisattvic stream, or by meeting a priest or doctor who possesses such a stream, that unfortunate being will be born mad and remain mad, and continue to be born mad, until such time as the karmic debt which he has inherited is paid in full.

Law 5. The intuitive knowledge of Buddha Nature occurs to all men.

All beings have the intuitive knowledge of the Buddha Nature—hence the creation of religions and Precepts down the centuries. When man does not heed this intuitive knowledge body and spirit separate and the cycle of birth, old age, disease and death becomes as a binding cord from which he cannot be free until he again decides to heed the still, small Voice within which is the voice of that intuitive knowledge which comes directly from the Buddha Nature. As a result of modern thinking man educates his children away from this between the ages of five and seven and, with the spread of materialism, man is increasingly looking for the cure of physical and mental illness outside of himself rather than within and the young become steadily more confused at an earlier and earlier age. The purpose of the following chapters is to show people how to bring body and spirit back into harmony from within and bring up future generations without this split ever taking place.

CHAPTER II.

HOLY CONCEPTION.

That which comes forth from, and indeed is, the Cosmic Buddha is called variously the flow of immaculacy, love, Mu, Buddha Nature, Buddha Mind, etcetera. When beings know nothing of duality, nothing impedes this flow between them and the Cosmic Buddha; this state is called enlightenment. As man has evolved, his egocentric self has come into existence and duality has gradually taken the place of his original unity with the Buddha Nature; the resultant disharmony of his body and so-called soul or spirit, called herein the disharmony of body and mind, has clouded man's knowledge of his rightful state.

Because man is no longer in active touch with his rightful state, his True Nature, which is also the Buddha Nature, he relies more and more on his own opinions and the skills he is learning to develop, i.e. on the *external* knowledge that intrigues his physical brain, and listens less and less to the still, small Voice that all of us hear within our hearts in our childhood and turn away from at about the age of seven, i.e. the Voice of what Keizan Zenji calls the Lord of the House, the Buddha Nature.

When a man listens to himself and not to the Voice of the Lord, he turns outward from his centre and wastes his precious energy on useless, external things in order to amass wealth and power none of which can help him at the time of his physical death. When he listens to the Voice of the Lord his energy is not wasted, he lives from his centre, and the flow of immaculacy, the Buddha Nature, flows from the Lord to him and from him to all beings and back to the Lord.

Man is not the Lord of the House and there is nothing in him that is not of the Lord of the House. Therefore when a man wantonly wastes that which is the Lord's he beckons to sickness and death; when he preserves it he is immediately one with eternal life, i.e. the Cosmic Buddha.

It is because of the above, and not out of any moralistic thinking, that the Precept against the misuse of, i.e. *indulgence* in, sexual intercourse was formulated. There is nothing whatsoever wrong with sexual intercourse when it is used advisedly and sensibly for the procreation of children. Likewise there is nothing wrong with love and physical affection between people. However, when sexuality is used to create more karma of attachment and suffering, it becomes both physically and mentally harmful for reasons explained below. This is sexual indulgence, and it is just as much indulgence whether the people involved are old or young, married or not, heterosexual or homosexual, or anything else. The sexual act has, as its highest purpose, the union of two people before the Lord and with the Lord in order that the karma of sentient beings may be cleansed. To turn it into an act which creates further karma and suffering is the true meaning of perversion.

Beings developed reproductive organs for the purpose of bringing into existence other beings, each according to its kind. This reproduction provides an opportunity for the cleansing of the karmic jangles or knots created by previous beings which remain behind to hinder the flow of Buddha Nature. Thus beings are born human to cleanse human traits, animal to cleanse animal ones, etcetera. As explained in Chapter I the death of one being can result in the rebirth of several.

At the time of death a being is asked to judge his own life and actions and is not judged by the Lord Who is a Being of Pure Love—there is no judgementalism where there is Pure Love—and, according as a being judges himself on seeing his life in review, so he is shown the place and state of rebirth that is about to take place for the *largest* number of his karmic jangles that *he* believes separate him from the Lord, i.e. a person with mainly human failings will be clearly shown a future *human* state, a person whose animal traits were in the ascendancy will be shown a suitable animal one. For example, I know of one lecherous wino that was reborn as a dog partly because his animal traits had been in the ascendancy during his lifetime and partly because a dog was the last creature to give him physical companionship as he lay dying in the gutter (it is necessary for all beings to have both a spiritual and a physical being embrace them at the time of death, see Chapter IV for full explanation of this, and there is a slight tendency to be reborn in the *last physical* form seen prior to death although this is greatly conditioned by the inherited karmic jangles).

The parent beings of an about-to-be-conceived being are also deeply involved in the karmic jangles of the unborn-being; there is no such thing as accidental parentage. A being is shown his parents prior to his rebirth and the reason for his rebirth with them is clearly explained to him. He is then free to accept or reject such a future rebirth for the Cosmic Buddha, Who is Truth Itself, does not insist; karmic jangles, since they are the result of our own judgement of our own actions, i.e. the result of our opinions, must be given up by us as a result of our own free will, not of coercion; the cleansing of karma must come about as a result of a desire to be re-united utterly with the Lord.

Because of the above it is of grave importance that parents shall think very seriously upon these matters before sexual intercourse takes place. They should meditate deeply and ask the Lord how best they may help their soon-to-be-conceived child cleanse his karma and in what way that child can help them cleanse theirs. Only when this has been done soberly and with great reverence should intercourse take place. The attitude of mind should be utterly respectful and gentle in the sense of the marriage vow, "with my body I thee worship;" intercourse is a holy act; orgasm a sacred unity.

Because humans have not understood the *true purpose* of sexual intercourse and turned it into a pleasant game to alleviate the boredom that has resulted from their living externally from their centre rather than internally, they suffer from guilt and embarrassment concerning sex and the whole matter is moralised over and either hidden behind closed doors as a taboo or flaunted in an unsuccessful attempt to pretend that the guilt does not exist. If the true purpose were understood the sacredness of the sex act would be fully comprehended and the guilt would immediately vanish. The child born of such a union would be wanted and understood from the moment that it stood before the Lord and was asked if it was willing to accept its new parents and there would be no separation of body and mind at the age of around seven (see Chapter VI).

The best time for conception should be chosen according to the body instincts of the woman. During the months of pregnancy both parents should spend much time meditating with the unborn child so as to enable both them and it to cleanse their karmic streams as soon as possible. By this means they will quickly be able to be free of karmic debts and live in unity with the Lord for eternity, i.e. both in this life and the next—the cleansing of karma does *not* result in *physical* death although, when all the karmic stream is cleansed, the Lord *will* ask what one's *purpose* for living is and one had better *know* when the question is asked! At the time of death there will be no shadows in the great, round mirror in which a being sees the accrued karma of his former life and therefore, since he will have nothing with which to judge himself, nothing will stand between him and the Lord. This is the state of Mu; even immaculacy is not adequate to describe it; the absorption in Eternal Love.

True conception is an offering up to the Lord of oneself, the unborn child and the sex act itself; the body must be thought of as the temple of the Lord and treated accordingly. When all is offered up to the Lord the seed of life descends in purity; when that seed is snatched in lust the chances of *all* the karmic jangles being cleansed in that lifetime are not good. Parents should know well what their mental attitude can do at the time of conception. It is because children are born out of their parents' lust that guilt comes into being and children are forced to bear a karmic jangle that rightfully belongs to their parents. There is no such thing as a child *born* in sin; there *are* children conceived in lust as a result of their parents trying to rob the Lord of His Seed. Such parents rob themselves of their unity with the Lord and, if they persist in the misuse of sex, put off that unity for countless ages. The sex act is the act of the Lord when it is undertaken to free an unborn being from his karmic jangles, i.e. former judgements of himself. Thus man stands between heaven and earth as the highest of physically living beings, free to do the Lord's Will or turn away from It; animals do not have this choice—man does; unremitting *indulgence* in the sex act can result in spiritual death in this life and confusion at the time of physical death.

All of the above must be considered carefully before conception takes place.

CHAPTER III.

THE SACRAMENT OF CHILDBIRTH.

The birth should take place in a slightly dark and very silent room otherwise both mother and child will be traumatised and the seeds of tension will already have been sown in the child. It is essential that the father be present, not as an observer but as the defender of mother and child: the mother is the queen of the birthplace wherein she brings into existence the son or daughter of the Lord, the father is the defending general, their chief and chosen warrior who defends the peace, silence and sanctity of the birthplace: the rôles are totally different and absolutely co-equal. This sanctity of the birth should not be violated, even by the doctor or nurse, unless the mother becomes fearful or complications set in. This is not to say that the parents should deny themselves and their infant the finest of prenatal and obstetric care available from modern medicine. Such care need not conflict with maintaining the peace and sanctity of the birth if both doctor and parents respect each other and fully appreciate the religious importance of birth. With understanding and cooperation they can arrange a plan whereby the doctor's skills are immediately available yet his presence does not intrude upon the birth itself. Light, if the birth takes place at night, should be kept to a minimum; the mystery of birth should not take place under fluorescent strip-lights under any circumstances for these fritter away at the spirit of the new-born being.

When the contractions begin the mother should lie down on a firm but comfortable bed with her knees drawn up and her legs open. The bed should not be more than a foot above the ground. She should relax as much as possible and begin to meditate upon the joy and honour of bringing new life into the world. If she keeps the mind of meditation the contractions will synchronise naturally with the inhalation of the breath and relax with the exhalation; pain, which will in any case be kept to a minimum by this means, will become something above which she will sit; just she will watch it arise and depart as she meditates. The father should sit still in meditation also but be highly alert so that absolutely *nothing* shall disturb the mother. Much of a mother's pain during childbirth is caused by fear of disturbance.

As the contractions get quicker the mother's body will tend to flow rhythmically and she will find that her hands are coming ever closer and closer to the orifice through which the child's head will appear. They will not reach there until the head actually emerges when they will receive it and, as a result of the natural arching of her body, the rest of the child's body will be born quickly and easily, slipping into the mother's waiting hands and arms. Holding it at the shoulders encupped in her hands she brings it up the front of her body, never allowing it at any time to leave contact with her trunk and massaging the top of its spine and neck with her fingers as she does so. She lets it rest upon her belly until the umbilical cord has stopped pulsating, at which time it is right to sever it. In ancient times this would have been done by the mother with her own teeth. Today it may be done by the father using sterile materials according to the plan the couple has worked out with their physician. The child is then brought by the mother up her body to her face, where her natural instinct is to begin to wash it with her tongue. Most couples at present do not follow this instinct and so the child must be washed by another means. After kissing her newborn, the mother passes it to the father, who welcomes his son or daughter into his arms and brings the child to his (preferably naked) chest. Holding the infant gently to him, he takes it to its first bath, setting it down gently in body-temperature water. Each nostril must be thoroughly cleansed of mucus and the breathing encouraged by gently massaging its chest and spine downwards. The child's eyes (if still closed) are washed, followed by the mouth, ears, arm-pits, between the fingers, groins, private parts from front to back, and between the toes. In this way every part of the child's body is stimulated, welcomed and cleansed and every orifice is, as it were, opened. An excellent and detailed discussion of the process of washing and caring for the child at birth can be found in *Birth Without Violence* by Frederick Leboyer (Knopf, 1975).

When the navel is cared for and the bath completed, the child should be given back to the mother who offers it her left breast so that it may be closest to her heart during its first meal. By this time the afterbirth will probably have come forth, and the suckling of the child should help it to do so if it has not. Once it has been removed the father may now relax his vigil and enter into the joy of the child's first meal by stroking its head and spine. These physical strokings of *both* mother and father are vital.

When the meal is over the father should hold the child whilst it sleeps so as to give the nurse, who should only now be called in, a chance to change the bedding and make the mother clean and comfortable.

It is this guardian duty of the father which marks the difference between the human and the animal at the time of birth. Details may vary slightly from the above since it is a blue-print, as it were, for the perfect birth: however, with the exception that, in some cases, the father may need to physically soothe the mother by stroking her should she become anxious, they will vary only very slightly so long as there are no complications.

CHAPTER IV.

THE SPIRITUAL CAUSE OF PHYSICAL ILLNESS.

In presenting the following information I am not making a medical conclusion or diagnosis of anyone, nor should you use the information given here to do so. I present it to show you the possible serious physical consequences of spiritual mistakes in order that you may avoid suffering in the future for yourself. The tables found in this chapter should be understood as a spiritual explanation of what can happen as a result of not keeping the Precepts and not be regarded as in any way diagnostic.

Every living thing is born with some one or more seemingly inexplicable physical weaknesses or propensity to weakness. These weaknesses are actually karmic debts that have been inherited as a result of ignorance of the Five Laws of the Universe on the part of that spark of the soul or spirit of a dead person now found within the new-born being. This uncleansed karma causes, as it were, a jangle in the ribbon of immaculacy that flows from the Lord of the House to us and, from us, back to Him. These jangles cause the disharmony of body and mind which leads eventually to physical illness.

The causes of some of these weaknesses are clear and obvious. For example, a baby may be born with a hole in its heart as a direct result of a person being executed by a firing squad or stabbed to death. Executions can account for serious illnesses which afflict children at *birth* as can karma inherited from murder victims. Persons who die as a result of war wounds do not inherit karmic debts. This is because there is not, at the time of death, a *deliberate* turning away from a particular individual by the whole human race. Let me make this clearer.

When a person is executed he is powerless to help himself and society will not lift a finger to help him. If beings are to be reborn without serious physical defect (see list hereunder) two things are absolutely essential at the time of death:—1. They must know that the Cosmic Buddha, or God, does not, and never will, turn away from them no matter what they may have done and, 2. They must *know* that man does not turn away from them either. (In the case of both an executed person and a murder victim man, as represented by the executioner and society and the murderer, turns away; thus, the last *human* act of which a person who is executed or murdered is aware is one of violence committed against him personally as an individual, by the only representatives of humanity present. The killing of a soldier in battle is an impersonal act.)

The first of these is, or should be, dealt with by the priest present at the bedside of the dying and, I hope, by prison chaplains at the time of execution. The second, however, is much more difficult to come by. In the old days a person died with his family and friends around him. Nowadays doctors and nurses provide a better-than-nothing substitute in many cases but the condemned man or woman is turned from absolutely by society—the witnesses are there to punish and see so-called 'justice' done. There is no love, no compassion and, above all, no attempt to keep the person from dying.

Because of ignorance of the Law of Karma and its attendant ignorance, the knowledge of skhandic[9] memory, the new-born being who inherits karma from an executed person or a murder victim is usually born sick. This causes its parents to cry out "Why? What has my child done?" when they should beat their breasts in repentance for supporting a social system that turned away from, and judged, another being; all beings are one—he who turns away from another turns away from the Lord and from himself—he who judges another judges the Lord and himself and inherits the karma of that judgement. Thus a society that advocates judicial murder begets children that suffer the consequences of their parents' ignorance; should a person be against capital punishment in this life, and have such a child, he should look carefully at his former lives. Although blameless in this life, he may very well have been an executioner in a former one, the horror of his acts of judicial violence having come home to him at the time of his death. In order to bring the Truth fully home to him, and to give him a second chance, he has been given the gift of a sick child that he may turn that which was judgemental punishment into holy love and acceptance of a being which he may well have harmed in a former life, to which he now owes a debt and of which it is his duty now, as his child, to take loving care. He and his child may well be karmically linked, the former having inherited some of the karma of the executioner, the latter some of the karma of the victim. These two karmas have been reunited in this lifetime because hatred, violence, punitive thinking, vindictiveness and judgementalism *must* be converted into love and acceptance of the Lord's Will before one's own skhandas can be cleansed of their karmic debts. As at the time of death a being needed to know he was loved both by the Lord and by his fellow men, so when cleansing the skhandas of karmic debt it is necessary for both a priest and another human to love the former being so that the flow of immaculacy may return freely to the Buddha Heart and the being that inherited the karmic jangle be free of the karmic debt. The following list shows types of executions with their attendant skhandic memory debts:—

Type of Violent Death by Execution	Inherited Weakness
Firing squad	Holes in the heart and other organs
Electrocution	Serious nervous disorders, multiple sclerosis
Hanging	Spinal deformity, weak neck vertebrae
Gas	Asthma, serious lung problems
Burning alive	Sinus problems and serious lung problems
Decapitation	Brain defects due to oxygen starvation at time of birth

There are numerous others as a result of middle ages tortures that have not yet been cleaned from the skhandas of people alive to-day but these are too numerous to be catalogued here. They can be recognised by an experienced Zen Master and dealt with accordingly.

In modern medicine doctors have rationalised the "how" in the cause of many birth defects so that the spiritual reason "why," stated here, has become obscured. Whilst it is necessary to employ the services of doctors to sew up the holes in the hearts, for example, and provide material medical care for such unfortunate babies, it is important *not* to pay attention to their superficial explanations as to *why* such things occurred, cleanse the child's skhandas spiritually in private, according to the methods prescribed in this book, and thus ensure that no further being shall be born with that particular karmic debt. The medical doctor does have a useful function but it is a physical and not a spiritual one. Do not allow him to usurp the job of the priest; he knows how; he does not know why. It is a fact that although 'life-saving' techniques in hospitals are often unsuccessful they can, if done with a pure heart, help a lot in smoothing the karmic jangles for the inheritor of the karma of a dying person simply because they imply love on the part of the human race. However, techniques that are applied out of a desire to show off one's medical skill are worse than useless in this respect and only cause misery to the dying.

Some organs of the body seem to be weaker in some people than in others. This is because the skhandic memory of the disharmony of body and mind, due to character traits that were not properly dealt with during the life-time of a dying person, results in uncleansed karma. Although medical help should be sought for relief of the immediate physical symptoms and to prevent the loss of life, it is imperative that the skhandic memory be erased by the cleansing of the karmic debt and the correcting of the character trait. The following is an incomplete list showing basic causes of seemingly inexplicable weaknesses in human organs. These may occur as a result of a former being not having dealt with a certain character trait, as stated above, or they may flare into actual physical illness as a result of a person continuing certain inherited character traits unchecked; or they may start up fresh in this life as a result of over-indulgence in any of the activities mentioned in column two below.

Organ	Cause of Weakness	Resulting Illness
Heart	Grief and loneliness	Heart diseases
Stomach	Worry	Ulcers
Intestines	Excessive grief and worry	Serious bowel problems
Kidneys	Fear and disappointment	Urinary problems and eventual kidney failure
Pancreas	Lack of security, peace, quiet and privacy	Diabetes, hypoglycemia
Liver	Anger and frustration	All liver disorders
Circulation	Allowing the head to make decisions rather than the heart	High blood pressure
Lungs	Feelings of ostracism and loneliness	Various lung diseases
Brain	Overwork for which the brain is unsuited caused by believing in oneself instead of in the Lord: i.e. relying on one's own puny mind instead of living in the Lord and allowing Him to make all the decisions	All diseases in this list since the brain can trigger any of the causes in column two; the *complete disharmony* of body and mind
Sex Organs	Sexual indulgence	Inability to feel at peace within oneself leading to mental illness
Bladder	Failure to deal with fear	All bladder illnesses
Gall Bladder	Failure to pay attention to the needs of the other organs	Gall stones

The real *cure* in all cases is *not* the physical medicine which removes the symptoms, and is *said* to "cure" the physical illness, but the removal of the root cause. For example, a man may have his ulcer removed but, if he does not stop worrying, he will get another one. He has to do a lot more than just have surgery performed on him. An executive can take all the blood-pressure pills under the sun; his condition will not cure itself until he gets rid of his pride and gives the Lord the credit for his achievements, as well as asking His advice, instead of terrifying his brain by trying to do everything without help.

We can, as I said, *inherit* any of the above weaknesses, along with many more, in which case we not only have to deal with our tendency towards the certain trait in this life but cleanse the karma of a former one, or we can start something new going for ourselves and those who follow us. For example, a man can pass on a liver weakness both by drinking whiskey and/or by having a lousy temper. It is up to the one who inherits that weakness to find out which and avoid both. He may, however, start the first as a result of inheriting the second! If such is the case, the being who inherits such a double, or compound, karmic debt from *him* may be born with a seriously diseased liver.

There is no way in which I can give *explicit* instructions for dealing spiritually with *every* illness and karmic debt; the above is a general but, nevertheless, accurate *key* as to where to look in one's character for the *cause* of the disharmony of one's body and mind usually called physical illness. In ordinary life such disharmony usually goes on for some time before actual physical illness results, and may have been carried over as a karmic debt from a previous life, the latter making the resultant illness appear in a severer form than it otherwise would. One must study oneself in detail and meditate deeply if one would cure oneself of the *potential* for illness and expect, as a result of centuries of past, uncleansed karma, the information given in this table to be several times compounded. Thus the clearing of one karmic debt may uncover another, one having one illness potential and the next a different one. The wearing out of the physical body is inevitable but the harmonisation of body and mind will slow down the aging process and absolutely remove the fear of death thus making the transition from what we call 'life' to Life Eternal easy, natural and joyous.

When surgery is performed a lot more has to be done than merely the removal of the affected part. This is because, although man is *not* the Cosmic Buddha, there is nothing in man that is not *of* the Cosmic Buddha and any violence, however well meant, inflicted on the skhandas of a being is violence inflicted upon the Cosmic Buddha. Unless the patient can find someone to spiritually seal the wound, the scar will retain a skhandic memory of the violence done to it and interpret it as a skhandic insult thus leaving a weakness proclivity to be inherited by an, as yet, unborn being. Although a person can do a lot to help himself in this respect, another person *is* necessary to perform the sealing. Just as man, in the person of the surgeon, did physical violence to the skhandas, so man must apologise for that violence to those skhandas. The ideal person to do this, of course, would be the surgeon but his training in "how" rather than "why" may make this not practicable. It would only be effective if he believed utterly in what he was doing and had his ego completely out of the way whilst doing it.

A surgical scar that is not spiritually sealed to prevent leakage of spiritual energy will appear as a mole or other blemish in a new-born child. If the mole is then excised the skhandic memory is compounded. For this reason all skin blemishes should be spiritually sealed against leakage and loved and caressed by a competent person at the time of birth to prevent their turning into something more serious and possible re-occurrence of the original illness. If a mole or blemish is diagnosed as malignant, or possibly malignant, this should be regarded as reason to remove it and the spiritual sealing should be done, and an attempt should be made, to find out its original karmic cause.

Persons are occasionally born without certain organs. The cause of this is the removal of organs by surgery from which the patient did not recover. Since the wounds are not spiritually sealed prior to death, and the last memory of both the patient and the organ skhandas is one of violence and trauma, the spiritual energy of the removed organ leaks out and the inheritor of the karmic debt, an innocent child, is born with an organ missing.

Wounds which cause persons to die in battle are also the cause of moles and other similar blemishes in new-born children but such blemishes do *not* become malignant;

they do, however, require love and spiritual sealing since they are a potential source of weakness. Blemishes may also be caused by psychic injury which can date back thousands, or even millions, of years but these blemishes do not show up until several weeks or months after birth. The treatment is the same although the sealing may be somewhat more difficult requiring considerable skill.

CHAPTER V.

THE SPIRITUAL CAUSE OF MENTAL ILLNESS.

In presenting the following information I am not making a medical conclusion or diagnosis of anyone, nor should you use the information given here to do so. I present it to show you the possible serious mental consequences of spiritual mistakes in order that you may avoid suffering in the future for yourself. The tables in this chapter should be understood as a spiritual explanation of what can happen as a result of not keeping the Precepts and not be regarded as in any way diagnostic.

Physical illness, as we saw in the last chapter, is caused by the acts of *others* which create tensions in our various organs as a result of the mental states that those acts have engendered in *our* minds. In other words, *purely* physical illness is primarily the result of our *passive* acceptance of what others do and the frustration (felt in the gall bladder which is, as it were, the harmoniser of all the other organs) that we have bottled up inside ourselves. Physical illness is primarily caused by passivity; mental illness by *willful* activity that is turned outwards from the Lord instead of inwards towards Him.

If a person *willfully* persists in smoking twenty cigarettes a day, the likelihood of his getting lung cancer is far greater than that of a person who only smokes one, and the latter's chances, although much more remote, still greater than those of someone who does not smoke at all. (There is always the possibility of a lung cancer victim being a non-smoker in which case the disease will be a karmic debt from a past life; this should not be allowed to cloud the issue— my purpose here is to illustrate the heightened propensity for illness brought about by *willful* action when a person knows that an act is harmful and persists therein.) If a person *willfully* persists in breaking the Precepts he will succeed in making his various organs so sick that he will eventually cause *actual* organic lesions in some of them in this life, according to which Precept he is constantly breaking, and a *potential* weakness in the organs of an, as yet, unborn being. If such willfulness is persisted in down the karmic chain from rebirth to rebirth a kind of negative emptiness, called herein reversed Mu, impregnates the ever larger karmic jangle. This is the moment when the physical organ can take no more sickness in its physical state down the line of rebirths and its spiritual body is threatened. Deviation from normal behaviour begins to show in a person after this and, in its final stages, the person becomes completely and totally mad. Interestingly enough, when this negative emptiness hits the karmic jangle, the result is to cleanse the karma completely of that jangle; thus a mad person, by his very madness, has his karma cleansed for him.

So-called madness is the Lord's answer to a refusal on the part of the inheritors of karma to take the responsibility for their lives and cease to be willful. It is one of the reasons why the Fourth Law of the Universe is as it is—*without fail* evil *is* vanquished and good prevails. We are given chance after chance until our bodies can take no more. In other words, we destroy ourselves physically and, if we still persist on the road to destruction, we next proceed to try to destroy the Lord. It is then that we lose our free will, as a result of our willfulness, and some being who never did wrong as far as we can tell with our limited knowledge, pays the price of thousands of lives of turning away from the Lord. Man may turn away from man but he cannot escape the Lord; should he try to destroy the Lord's work he will suffer physical illness; should he try to destroy the Lord he will go mad.

Madness is the eventual result of willful breakages of the Precepts that are *persisted* in from life to life; it is the *immediate* result, if not in this life then definitely in the next one, of *willfully* turning away from karmic debts that are *recognised* as such, of *deliberately* refusing to take *heed* of the Law of Karma once one knows its truth for oneself either by *deliberately* clinging to old opinions or not caring because one believes oneself to be above such laws.

The following is a table showing the various willful acts and their effects on the physical organs of the body as well as the type of so-called madness resulting from negative emptiness: —

Organ	Willfully Persistent Evil Act	First Signs of Disease	Type of Madness
Lungs	Lying	Panting and inability to breathe well	Paranoia
Heart	Murder and all forms of killing for food or other purposes, turning away from the Lord (i.e. attempting to kill the Lord), being tired of life	Palpitations, valve weaknesses, heart attacks	Schizophrenia
Gall Bladder	Any act that causes tension in any other organ	Pain in area, insomnia	Manic-depression
Liver	All forms of violence and anger, including violence to the teachings of the Lord, i.e. evil willfulness	Hardening of the liver, insomnia	Manic-depression
Pancreas	Insulting behaviour, (pancreases empathise with each other— someone who is persistently rude to others will upset not only the other's pancreas but his own too)	Digestive problems due to malfunctioning of pancreas	Paranoia
Stomach	Speaking against others and puffing oneself up, doing others down in business, meanness	Ulcer tendencies, insomnia	Paranoia
Intestines	Coveting, jealousy, greed	Bowel malfunctions, constipation	Paranoia

Brain	Clinging to one's own opinions after knowing the truth, deluding oneself and others	Headaches, feelings of hyperactivity in the head that are most unpleasant, harshness of speech	Schizophrenia
Sex Organs	*Indulgence* in sexual activity, thinking that the sex act is all there is to love	Lassitude, loss of intelligence, flaccidity, inability to enjoy *real* pleasure and to distinguish between pleasure and pain	Any of the known forms, depending on what else was done to arouse the sexual desire, i.e. sadism, masochism, etcetera
Kidneys	Every evil act engenders fear thus the kidneys take the *brunt* of *everything* that is done on the physical level whilst the gall bladder takes it on the spiritual	Backache in the lumbar area, water retention, (last organ to be healed should a person take charge of himself)	Paranoia in its worst form

A person can "mix and match" evil acts and this compounds both the disease signs and the resultant madness.

To my mind a good psychiatrist or psychologist should not attempt to do anything with a patient before he finds out if the person has any wish to try to sort out his karmic jangles. There is great danger in both behaviour modification and drugs since they tend to cloud the karmic jangle and coarsen the person as to what is really needed to be done. Behavioural modification can help greatly if there is any sign of the person *wishing* to be different but not *knowing* how to change; however, it would have to be used by a doctor with the heart of a saint. Drugs are valuable in that they can buy time for a person who may be ready, later on, to handle his karmic jangles; but shock therapy should never be used. Frontal lobotomy should *never* be used under *any* circumstances since it is likely to force a person to be *unable* to deal with his karmic jangles in this life and leaves a psychic scar in his brain for the person who comes after him. It has the added disadvantage of compounding the doctor's karma since he has undertaken to usurp the prerogative reserved for the Lord of the House, a willful act which can have far-reaching consequences if the motives are not utterly pure.

The most important thing in all forms of mental illness is to remember that it does not exist as an 'illness' but is, instead, the consequence of a refusal to take responsibility for past acts by *willfully* repeating them again and again. Mental illness is the result of setting oneself up in defiance of the Lord of the House. A good doctor, to my mind, will not think himself a doctor but rather regard the patient and himself as two beings who are trying to find the key to life and unity with the Lord and use his skill for that purpose.

The kidneys are not only the seat of deep fear, they are also the seat of *positive* (as opposed to *willfully evil*) will, so it is in this area of the body that the first peace and harmony of mind should occur.

The following is a chart showing the cut-off line of sanity and its attendant higher and lower states:—

5.	*Full Enlightenment or Cosmic Buddha*	
4.	Wisdom	States resulting from
3.	Love	unified harmony of
2.	Compassion	body and mind

So-called normal human state of sanity containing usual amount

1.

of instability, greed, hate and delusion.

-2.	Paranoia	States resulting from
-3.	Manic-depression	dualistic disharmony of
-4.	Schizophrenia	body and mind
-5.	*Madness incurable in this life-time*	

The black wavy line, 1, shows the normal fluctuations in intensity of the greed, hate and delusion of the average, so-called sane, human being. -2 shows the sanity line of the average nation during war-time; 2, 3 and 4, the graphs of persons who have experienced first, second and third stage kenshōs respectively (see *How to Grow a Lotus Blossom,* chapter on kenshōs), and -2, -3 and -4, their attendant opposites.

Deviations from the so-called norm such as homosexuality and lesbianism are not mental illnesses but the result of karma. A being is reborn male or female down the chain of rebirths and does not stay as one or the other. At times of change, for karmic reasons, one has a tendency to stay with the former sex mentally, whilst moving physically, and a homosexual is the result. Once this is understood, compassion and love, rather than censure, are the result as is also the case with the understanding of so-called mental illness.

CHAPTER VI.

THE PREVENTION OF THE DISHARMONY OF BODY AND MIND OR THE PREVENTION OF DISEASE.

This chapter is concerned with the bringing-up of children for their education is the key to the prevention of the disharmony of body and mind. Because of social pressures, popularly known as 'keeping up with the Joneses' or maintaining one's so-called standards of living and social position, a child is educated to regard outward things as important and inward ones, at best, as secondary and, at worst, as unnecessary.

All beings are *born* in harmony with, i.e. have an intuitive knowledge of, the flow of Buddha Nature; this is the Fifth Law of the Universe. Unless there are grave problems in a child's home such as constant parental quarrelling and/or an absolute lack of loving direction, the disharmony of the body and mind of a child will *not* take place until around the age of seven. Seven is, however, a very arbitrary figure; whilst *no* child is ever *born* in a disharmonised state, inherited karma *can* begin to work upon the child through the aegis of its parents, doctors or nurses within hours, or even minutes, of its birth and, although it takes some time for the child to actually give in to the pressure that such karma exerts, the resulting tension *can* cause the child to disassociate itself from its *natural* state of oneness with the Buddha Nature simply to avoid the pain, both physical and mental, that the tension produces.

Because the new-born child has no *remembered* experience in this life upon which to fall back, its *only* hope of knowing what to do is to observe its parents and other adults with great care; if those parents are in a state of disharmony, a conflict will occur in the child who will then feel that it is being forced to choose between an instinct or feeling inside it, i.e. the Buddha Nature, which it clearly knows is in disagreement with what is going on around it, and the pressures exerted by parents, doctors and, later on, teachers which tell it to follow *their* ways rather than the ways of the Lord. Depending on how heavy these pressures are, the child will retain its rightful harmony for a longer or shorter time. For example, a child that is both loved and completely wanted by its parents will probably *not* experience disharmony until about two years *after* entering the public school system although, even in this case, inherited karmic debts can cause it to happen earlier; a child who, from the moment it is born, is made to feel a nuisance will, after trying everything it knows to communicate its dilemma from crying to making itself ill, become disharmonised at the age of two or three. I have not yet met a child that did not hold out against such pressures for the first two years. Disharmony of life-style in marriage, quarrelling parents and feelings of inadequacy on their part are all factors that can cause early separation of body and mind in a child. This is because the parents stand in relationship to the child as the Lord of the House does to its parents although few parents either know or understand this. If the parents are out of harmony with the Buddha Nature the child feels the tension of being pulled in two by his parents because of his own *certain* knowledge of the Buddha Nature. This tension causes him to cry and fret until he gives in to his parents in order to be relieved of the tension. In so doing he rends the harmony of his own body and mind—he buys ease in his present physical situation at the cost of dis-ease for most of his spiritual life. At the time of death and rebirth he is given another chance in the form of renewed communion with the Buddha Nature but the pattern continues to repeat itself until one day he finally *decides* to do something and actually *does* it.

When *this* rebirth comes the following happens. The child holds on, against all odds, to a remnant of the Buddha Nature which becomes, for him, a seed of faith in something greater than himself. During his teens he nurtures it in secret and heeds the still, small voice of conscience; this latter, later on, becomes for him the loving and all-embracing Voice of the Lord of the House. Such children have an extraordinarily rough time at school, usually being avoided by their fellows as somewhat odd or to be pitied; they tend to be quiet and seemingly uncommunicative (for fear of being laughed at), they are untroublesome and seemingly withdrawn; they do not follow popular trends because of their determination to do something about themselves. Because of their resistance to social pressures and attempts to draw them out of themselves to find out what is going on, they excite the censure of their teachers and are then in a very dangerous situation.

Whenever a being decides to *really* deal with his inherited karmic debts everything that *can* go wrong for him seems to do so. *This is because he is going in the opposite direction to most of his fellows and* **not** *because some nameless god is making him pay for past wrong-doing.* This is a very important point. Guilt is a very dangerous thing and is *not* involved here. Everyone knows that it is easy to swim with the current but that it is a lot harder to swim against it. A child who wishes to follow the Voice of the Lord rather than go mindlessly along with his fellows faces temptations far greater than they do, not least of which is the doubt which constantly assails him as to the wisdom of his actions which is, of course, a doubting of the Lord and of his original decision. Every time he doubts, disharmony comes nearer; every time he overcomes the doubt, his faith is strengthened. Some adolescents relieve the peer group pressure by doing something wrong which they regret for the rest of their lives; they are frequently caught and then branded as 'bad' owing to the lack of understanding of their actual situation when nothing could be further from the truth. Because they are so much closer to their centre than their fellows their feelings of guilt are greatly magnified; if there is no understanding person available to put things into their correct perspective such a child *may* embark upon a life of crime simply because it feels itself to have fallen so far from grace as to be irredeemable. I have already spoken of the danger of creating guilt as a result of judging others and here is another case of that same danger.

If a person makes it through childhood and adolescence to adulthood without getting caught in the above predicament he will possibly cleanse his karmic inheritance although sex will rear its head for a few years and somewhat hinder his efforts at least until he reaches his mid-twenties. There *are* cases of full reharmonisation prior to this age but they are rare indeed and the person usually dies very young.

Parents who wish to *prevent* the disharmony of body and mind in their children must take great care with their own personal lives and life-styles as spoken of in chapters two and three. They must *cherish* their children and make certain that those who educate them understand the Law of Karma as well as the rest of the Five Laws of the Universe. They must provide as fine and comprehensive an education as possible but take great care that it is *not* in the present public school system because of its insistence upon dualistic thinking, materialistic competitiveness, externalisation of outlook, desire for gain and ignorance of the Law of Karma. Buddhism has *always* taught that a parent *must* give his child a better education than he himself received and, if this education includes a practical, working knowledge of the Precepts and the Five Laws of the Universe, it is a significant factor, i.e. man's contribution, in speeding up the Fourth of the latter:—without fail evil is vanquished and good prevails, simply by the responsibility for the cleansing of the karmic debts that it engenders.

It is a parent's duty to meditate with his child from the moment prior to its conception and continue to do so *formally* at a regular time *every* day after birth. It is his duty to study every blemish on the child's body and to help the child find the cause of any weakness in its organs through meditation so that illness may be avoided and an end to the passing on of the karmic debts be found. It is a parent's duty to see that adequate medical treatment of symptoms be given to a child whilst searching for the true cause of its illness through meditation. The Catholics had a saying when I was young, "The family that prays together stays together," —change the word 'prays' to 'meditates' and you have the ideal Buddhist family.

A child should be encouraged to find the causes of character traits in himself and be helped to overcome them if they tend to disharmony; he can be rewarded when successful, consoled when he is not and lovingly punished when he willfully persists in going against the Lord's Will. As soon as he is old enough the cause of the seeds of sickness should be explained to him so that he may know, for example, that every time he lies he makes the possibility of lung weakness a little greater. At all times he must be treated with respect by his parents who must not think of themselves as his creator and that he is, therefore, their property, but as beings who wish to share their experience with another being who, because he has but recently re-appeared, has less experience of life as it is *presently* lived than they do. The parent/child relationship creates duality; beings who are trying to find the key to life by helping each other through their own experience, and thereby return to their oneness with the Lord both in *this* physical life and in all future lives, are free of duality.

The above style of education is a recipe for a long, full and healthy life at the end of which, if daily meditation is maintained, a being is united with the Lord wholly and with all karmic debts cleansed; *all* learning is good and should be used to do the Lord's Will—there is *no* skill or knowledge, however humble or great, that He cannot use for all knowledge comes from Him in the first place—it is only our abuse of His gifts that has made some knowledge seem evil.

Above all remember that a child is a full-time job for *both* parents and *no* short cuts can be made either in its education or upbringing. A parent who is *not* willing to sacrifice his or her career to take time to meditate with, and study the karmic debts of, both his or her child and marriage partner just does *not* have the right to be a parent and should give up their children for adoption by parents who *will* take the time because *they* know that the *purpose* of life here is to make themselves fit to return to the Lord. A parent is entrusted with a child by the Lord for the purpose of helping that child; the Lord is thus asking the parents to help Him in His work and giving them a quicker way to return to Him by so doing. What greater opportunity could there be—and what greater love than that of the Lord Who trusts us so much again and again with that which is His.

CHAPTER VII.

THE VISITATION OF THE SICK OR MORTALLY ILL.

[The following should be done *only* when a sick or mortally ill person has requested that you visit him or her for the purpose of teaching them how to practise Buddhism during their illness or how to prepare for death. It should not be done when simply paying a social call on a sick person. If the person requesting to be instructed in religion during his illness is not mortally ill, please take care not to do anything which will imply to him that you might think otherwise.]

The sick and mortally ill should be taught to meditate properly, using the Fukanzazengi[10] as a basis for study and paying special attention to the proper method of breathing for turning the Wheel of the Law (see *How to Grow a Lotus Blossom*, Appendix A) and assisting the sick person with the Harmonising of Body and Mind (see Book II) if he is too sick to move the spiritual blocks for himself. The sick person should meditate in 'corpse pose'[11] unless his sickness is not heavy. Anything whatsoever that the sick person may reveal of his past actions during the cleansing of his karmic stream must be regarded as having been uttered in the strictest confidence and the priest must understand that no such communications may ever be alluded to, either in company or in private, except at the *express* wish of the sick person. The sick should be exhorted to study true spiritual humility and the importance of asking the Will of the Lord of the House with a view to learning all acceptance. His faith should be strengthened by teaching him the meaning of the Kanzeon Scripture[12] as well as that of the Sandokai[13] and Hōkyozammai,[14] and the meaning of the Scripture of Great Wisdom[15] should be explained as soon as his faith is strong enough for this to be of real value. He should be taught to recite the Litany of the Great Compassionate One[16] and the Makura Om Dharani[17] as well as the importance of repeating these any time he feels sleepy since they will ensure his turning of the Wheel during sleep and thus enable him to make the right decisions subconsciously should he die whilst sleeping. All questions should be answered but doctrines that bring up doubt and/or fear should neither be insisted upon nor discussed.

CHAPTER VIII.

VISITATION AND EXHORTATION
OF THE DYING.

When it is established for *certain* that a person is terminally ill the following eight exortations should be read and carefully explained to him or her. If the person still has a life-expectancy of a few months, or even a few days, he or she should be taught to meditate as described in the 'Visitation of the Sick and Mortally Ill,' and the Plates of *How to Grow a Lotus Blossom* should be explained with a view to the obtention of a pre-death kenshō for *nothing* will ensure that a person will make the right decisions at the moment of death better than the certainty that a kenshō can give. Should there be time for this, it should be pointed out that the steps of a pre-death kenshō are in reverse order to those of the post-death kenshō which *every* person experiences after *clinical* death if he has not had a kenshō prior to it; to ensure the right decisions on the part of the dead during this post-death kenshō is the reason for these eight exhortations. A person, or priest, who has not experienced a full kenshō should *not* attempt these exhortations since he or she will not *know* what they are describing from their own *certain* knowledge, and *absolute* certainty is necessary if the dying person is to make the *right* decisions after death; the slightest doubt or reservation on the part of the person with the dying one *can*, but not necessarily will, cause the latter to make a wrong decision. If someone in attendance on the dying has had no kenshō, he or she should *love* the dying person with all their might and, if possible, keep one hand at least in physical contact with the dying until clinical death has actually taken place; such a person should not try to force the dying to stay alive but keep in mind the latter's right to make his own decision as to the right *time* for a dignified death; this right time will be the moment when the person is most likely to make the *right* decisions afterwards. The person with the dying, if he does not know how to meditate, should hope and pray for the dying to choose the *right* moment and make the right decisions. The reasons for this will be apparent in the exhortations. The attendant must not pussyfoot around in order to keep the dying person from knowing that his end is near; he or she must face this fact squarely, holding out his or her certainty of the post-death kenshō as a light-beacon for the dying.

The exhortations which follow are those which I have learned from various Buddhist priests. Tibetan Buddhism has, it would seem, an almost identical practice which has been described in Evans-Wentz's translation of the *Tibetan Book of the Dead* and summarized in Edward Conze's *Buddhist Scriptures* (Baltimore: Penguin, 1959). Because of the degree of similarity between the Tibetan text and what I learned, and the excellence of the above translations, I have borrowed freely from them in creating the exhortations given here.

Exhortation I. (To be read and explained when clinical death is imminent but has not yet taken place.)

I, (Name), Transmit to you that which I received from my True Master, Birushana Buddha,[18] the Great Dharmakaya,[19] Dharma Itself, who Transmitted it to all the True Masters, the Nirmanakayas,[20] before me and from whom, as (Name of own master), I learned it in detail. Pay attention, be still, calm, clear-headed. Do not allow your thinking to wander or you will not hear the Voice of the Lord! Be very mindful of what you hear! Do not succumb to a restful oblivion from pain and suffering for they will return in your next life if you do not face them now and know that they are as a dream; FACE THEM AND GO STRAIGHT TO THE LORD! Do not look from side to side, do not look DOWN! LOOK UP! SEE THE LORD WITH OPEN ARMS AWAITS YOU! BE ALERT! BE READY TO SAY **YES, I AM WILLING** when the moment comes. KNOW that NOTHING stands between you and the Lord except your own opinion of yourself. Do not give in to forgetfulness. Go right through

the pain and suffering to That which waits. BE AWARE!
BE ALERT! The skhandas which comprised (name of dying
person) are now disintegrating; spirit is separating from
physical matter and entering into the tunnel known as the
place between life and death. LOOK UP TO THE LIGHT
AT THE END OF THE TUNNEL! Gather your energy for
you must go through this tunnel in full consciousness of
spirit, in full control of your will. Say the Litany of the
Great Compassionate One with me with ALL your being.
(Here follows the Litany of the Great Compassionate One
recited by all present including the dying. The attendant—
or priest—should not worry if the dying seems to be making
no sound; if the Litany of the Great Compassionate One is
uttered truly the dying will hear, join in, in spirit, and make
the *right* decision; do *not* doubt this no matter what the
dying person may have done in the past, no matter what he
or she may have confessed to or what he or she may be
thinking of themselves at the time of death.)

Exhortation II.   (To be read at the moment of clinical
death.)

As lightning, appears the luminescent splendour of the
Great Dharmakaya, encompassing you in Its glory on all
sides, thrilling throughout your entire being. *Submit* to Its
embrace for It is *Pure Love.* Do not, through feelings of
unworthiness, try to flee because of your past actions, do
not judge yourself before the Lord for in Pure Love there is
no judgement; in this Pure Love your past actions are but
dreams. Love is Love; do *not judge* Love by your standards
of yourself for this is to cling to a separate self which is pure
illusion. Submerge yourself gladly and willingly in the
Splendour of Light which is the Splendour of True Love,
beyond all human dreams, the Great Dharmakaya. Cry, with
a *great* cry, **I AM WILLING** and you *are* saved for eternity.

Exhortation III.   (This should be read to the dead *before* the
first memorial ceremony but *after* the funeral. The funeral
should take place this same day.)

If, as a result of terror at the time of meeting the Great Dharmakaya, you were shocked out of salvation by the memory of your past deeds which you believed to have been perpetrated by the *real* you rather than the illusory one, you will now be in the world of dreams. Whether these be pleasant or not they represent a second chance to enter the Great Dharmakaya so remain alert in meditation and do not be pulled away from your True Centre by fantasies. To-day there will have emerged the 'mind body' which is permeated with all your past karma and former senses; it can pass unhindered through all former physical hindrances such as walls, rocks and mountains and encompass any distance of time and space in the twinkling of an eye. You will see and know, although your physical body is no more, since, because you judged yourself, your old karma will still work upon you. BUT *KNOW* THIS! He/She who did these things is *not* the *Real You*; these *dreams* are all illusion; they are *not* reality; they cannot harm the *Real You;* none of these things exist. **FEAR NOT! DO NOT BECOME ATTACHED TO DREAMS!** (Utter a kwatz[21] here then continue the exhortation in a quiet voice.) Remain still in meditation, neither holding on to any of these things nor pushing them away, no matter how beautiful, desirable or horrible they may appear. This meditation is Itself the Great Dharmakaya.

Exhortation IV. (To be read three days after death before the memorial ceremony for that day.)

If you have not yet entered the Great Dharmakaya to-day you will meet with the benign, peaceful Buddhas and continue to do so for seven days. Do *not* be afraid to look at them for they are the emanations of the Great Dharmakaya; do *not* fear their brightness. Enter serenely into their radiance without fear or attachment, desire nothing, push nothing away. Say I AM WILLING and let the Pure Love of the Great Dharmakaya encompass and bathe your very essence for It has come to greet and embrace you in this Form which It feels will be more familiar to you than when It first appeared and thus cause you to fear It less. It will appear as any God, Buddha or Bodhisattva in Whom you truly believe for, as Pure Love, It *longs* for you with a Great Longing in which there is *no* earthly desire. WHAT COMPASSION! *GO ON!* These emanations have come to receive you into the Buddha Realms. In true faith and humility pray with all your might, enter the rainbow halo, *become* ONE with the Great Dharmakaya, dwell for *ever* in one of the realms of the Buddhas. Here, for SEVEN MORE DAYS, the Lord holds out His arms to you in *familiar* and loving form for It is True Compassion, the True Father/Mother Dharmakaya and It *waits* for you with longing and outstretched arms unto eternity if need be.

Exhortation V. (To be read one week after the previous exhortation before the Memorial Ceremony for that day.)

If you missed salvation during the previous seven days you will, from to-day, be meeting the angry deities and demons and these will continue to threaten you for the next seven days. Because you have *not* yet entered into the Great Dharmakaya through familiar, loving emanations, It now shows you the confusions of your own mind so that you may be driven by your own fear to abandon your false views of self and merge with the True Self. These deities and demons, with their numerous followers, threaten you on all sides. Animals you have never before beheld appear with them. In the multi-coloured light they cry, "Beat him/her! Kill him/her!" and these things appear because *you* caused them to. It is *you* who, so far, have preferred dream forms to True Reality; all of this *you* have created for yourself and brought upon yourself because your mind does not yet know that there is *no* separate self. These deities and demons are the result of your *own* confusion of mind; *all* are unreal! Remain still in meditation, do *not* try to run away from, or towards, them. FEEL NO FEAR! DO NOT FEAR THESE CREATURES! DO NOT FLEE! It *is YOU* who have changed the benign Buddhas and Bodhisattvas into these seeming evil forms by your false views of yourself and your confusion. *IN YOU* is the *power* to turn back to the Great Dharmakaya.

42

The reflection of the contents of *your own mind*, which *continues* to judge itself by its own standards rather than the Lord's, is appearing to you in the Mirror of the Lord. Do *NOT* mistake the reflection for the reality! It is you who have turned the five wisdoms into the five poisons and you alone who can, by saying, **I AM WILLING**, turn them back again into the five wisdoms. Should you do this, so great a change will make you unconscious, your 'mind body' will disintegrate and you will become One with the Great Dharmakaya. **TURN! NOW IS THE TIME!** (utter a kwatz.) There is still time! Turn round! Fear not! Become One with the Dharmakaya, enter the rainbow halo of paradise!

Exhortation VI. (This exhortation is read one week later before the Memorial Ceremony.)

If you did not turn back to the Lord before this time you are now about to be reborn in a dualistic state as a result of your mistaking the reflection in the Mirror for the Reality. You have clung to a separate existence and turned away from the Great Dharmakaya out of your confusion of mind. You are now appearing before the Judge of the Dead whom you yourself have created. Hell hounds hold you, bound and helpless, before the mirror of Karma, which is the mirror of your own memory, into which *you* project the doings of your past for you are still mistaking dreams for realities. The judgment of the Judge of the Dead is *your* judgment of *your* self; it is *not* the judgment of the Great Dharmakaya: Love is Love; in *Pure* Love there is no judgment for then Love would not be *Pure*. *You* pronounce your own *judgment* of yourself and *sentence* yourself to your next rebirth. The Great Dharmakaya, being *Pure Love*, does *not* sentence you; your *self* is not Its problem. The hell hounds who carry out the punishment to which you sentence yourself are the creation of your own mind as is this court and its sentence; *you created* the Judge of the Dead, the gods and the demons with your own karma. **KNOW THIS! A-WAKEN TO THIS! GO STRAIGHT TO THE GREAT DHARMAKAYA! BE FREE!** (utter a kwatz.)

Exhortation VII. (This exhortation is read one week later before the Memorial Ceremony.)

If you have not yet returned to the Great Dharmakaya you now know that you are dead for the first time and do not know what to do. Since you clung to a separate self you know that that self must have a body for it to feel comfortable and safe. You are tossed hither and yon, squeezed between rocks, burned on red-hot coals as the flames of your karmic debts drive you on. You *must* know that it is *you* who created it and *you* who sentenced yourself to it. All of this is *YOUR* doing. Upon the dark horizon there now appear the six lights of the six worlds of rebirth. The light of that world to which you have sentenced yourself will shine brightest. These lights will seem safer than the first blinding flash of light of the Great Dharmakaya but they are still part of It in a Form you are prepared to accept for Pure Love will appear in whatever Form the beloved desires and will never desert the beloved how ever many times the latter may turn away. According as you have sentenced yourself you may go to a heaven for a little while should you have done some good; if you judged yourself as jealous or ambitious your lot will be among the asuras;[22] you may have sentenced yourself to be a human as a result of clinging to your erudition or to being an animal as a result of your believing that you do not have the Buddha Nature; perhaps you have sentenced yourself to be a ghost or to enter the hells. However, the Great Dharmakaya is in *all* these worlds; it was Its Light that guided you to the world to which you have sentenced yourself. **THINK ON THE GREAT DHARMA-KAYA! ALL THESE WORLDS ARE UNREAL!** Abandon your false, separative self. Stay still in meditation! Love all worlds and all beings. *You* are the source of all these worlds. Do not move from your true centre! *Love* the Great Dharma-kaya! Say **I AM WILLING TO GO TO THE GREAT DHARMAKAYA** and you will *immediately* be **FREE EVEN NOW! DO NOT FEAR! BE STILL IN MEDITATION!**

Exhortation VIII. (This exhortation is read on the forty-ninth day after clinical death before the final Memorial Ceremony.)

If you have not turned back to the Lord **LISTEN WITH ALL YOUR MIGHT!** Your desire to be reborn is becoming overwhelming since your false view of self needs the physical organs of sense to give it expression. Because of this desire you are as in an arid desert, longing for water and finding none. There are no resting places here for fearful shapes from your former unconscious self rear up to drive you on with screams, threats and torments. The wind of karma hurls you through the scorching air and you *long* for a body. All the beings around you are copulating and, according as you have sentenced yourself to be male or female, so you will hate the sex you have chosen for yourself and love the one you have not. If you did not *choose* a specific sex you will have no particular hatred or love for either and may be born as a homosexual. Do not try to interfere between the copulating couples, or to become part of one of them; one of them is your parents to be. Allow their intercourse to take place naturally, do not interfere, allow yourself to be reborn; accept the state of physical rebirth. In whatever world you have sentenced yourself to be, the Great Dharmakaya is to be found; willingness and humility are the key to becoming One with It.

(Here end the Exhortations of the Dying and Dead. A relative or friend may undertake a forty-nine day Sesshin[23] with a dead person in this way if he or she so wishes, loving them deeply and meditating and/or praying that they make the right decision. This forty-nine day Sesshin is always undertaken by trainees in a monastery when their Abbot or Abbess dies [see Funeral Ceremony of a Priest[24]], and the body is not buried or cremated for a week so that they may spend the first seven days actually sitting with the remains.)

CHAPTER IX.

SPIRITUALISM, DEMONS, GHOSTS AND VISIONS.

Theories abound throughout the religions of the world with regard to spiritualism, demons, ghosts and visions. All the great religions, including Buddhism, view the first three with displeasure and the last with caution. Buddhism, however, categorically states that the first is to be absolutely eschewed and even goes so far as to admonish Zen priests against it in the "Secret Papers." The following is what I have personally found to be true and which many Buddhists believe although there may be some schools which will think differently on these matters.

If the reader has understood the foregoing pages clearly, he will know that past life experiences are but ghostly perfumes to be cleansed and washed away in the Water of the Spirit of the Cosmic Buddha. However, there are people, especially in the West where past life experiences, owing to the teachings of Western religion, are not believed in, who, by accident, come into contact with bits and pieces of their own or other people's past lives. Owing to their lack of understanding and belief therein they consider these splinters from the past to be spirit guides sent from the world of the dead to help them in this present life or to assist them in making contact with their departed loved ones.

Because the experiencing of past lives is extraordinarily real, it is very important to have someone easily available who understands what to do when they occur: if a person knows nothing whatsoever about past life experiences, a karmic spark *can* become so terrifying that the person feels he is possessed by demons. Worse still, he can become so fascinated by it that he gives it the dignity of power over him as a spirit guide. When the latter is done, the person actually permits what is only a ghostly perfume to take shape and substance. Since this ghostly perfume was an originally uncleansed piece of karma, only reappearing in order to teach the person what *not* to do, the person who does not cleanse it now becomes a medium for the expression of that unclean and spiritually sick karma which continues to spread the wrong ideas which originally led to its destruction. If the medium persists in what he or she is doing, it is likely that they will be destroyed by their "guide" since the spark gains momentum and energy from the medium and, wishing to be cleansed even whilst persisting to the contrary, frequently kills that which will not do what it truly wants, i.e. to be reunited with the Cosmic Buddha. The "dead relatives" and "friends" that such sparks "contact" are other karmic sparks that are eager to find earthly homes, hence another reason for the death of genuine mediums during trance states. No spark, or even whole past life, can kill unless it is dignified with eager acceptance *and* a desire, on the part of the person experiencing it, to continue its existence. During exorcisms in the East such sparks are embraced joyfully as jangles in the karmic stream that need cleansing and sending back to the Cosmic Buddha; they are not embraced as long lost friends or relatives whose lives are to be perpetuated and no attempt is made to drive them further into duality by ordering them into *permanent* separation from the Cosmic Buddha in a hell. Buddhism is a religion that transcends Unity; transcending duality is but the first step in that direction. Just being an uncleansed karmic spark is sufficient of a hell in itself without a priest being so lacking in compassion as to force the spark to stay that way by offering it no comfort whatsoever. In so doing such a priest continues karma, makes the jangle worse than it was before, and does a disservice to the Cosmic Buddha Whom he has sworn to serve. The "Secret Papers" contain explicit ceremonies for helping such sparks.

The more spiritually mature a person is in the mystical sense the more likely he is to pick up stray pieces of karma. Because of the fragmentation of karma, owing to there being no permanent and unchangeable ego at the time of death, it sometimes happens that stray sparks of karma are left floating, as it were, in the atmosphere and people who

have done much meditation, or who are naturally spiritually inclined, can unwittingly pick them up. It is important
to know that such things, whilst being very scary if they are
not understood, are completely harmless if properly handled.
One does not need to get a third party to "cast out" one's
"demons;" any person, with a belief in God or the Cosmic
Buddha, who believes he has become "possessed," has only
to show these sparks compassion by cleansing them and
sending them back to the Cosmic Buddha. I have explained
how this is done in *How to Grow a Lotus Blossom.* There is
no such thing as possession by demons unless one is ignorant
of the above. *Everyone* has the capacity to deal with such
things by himself so long as his belief is strong. A lady visited
me recently saying that a religious teacher with whom she
had been studying was causing her to be possessed. My
disciples and I were able to prove to her that she, and only
she, was in command of herself and that all she had to do
was to believe in the Cosmic Buddha and order the voices
that were speaking through her to be silent. This she did and
the voices ceased. The problem came back again several
months later when she let herself doubt in the Cosmic Buddha's ability to help her. If once a person gets to that stage of
spiritual growth at which such sparks can be comprehended,
it is impossible for him or her to lead a normal, productive
life without maintaining a highly active faith in the Cosmic
Buddha. Only by so doing has a person a means of cleansing,
and therefore freeing themselves from, the karmic sparks
which, since he or she has trained themselves, are clutching
desperately at them for help. I have often said that one
should not meditate unless one intends to continue for the
rest of one's life. This is because one is not only beckoning
to the Cosmic Buddha; one is also attracting all the karma
that is longing for help and reunion with That Which Is. In
Marlowe's "Faust" hell is described as "being separated from
God;" if a person meditates, all that uncleansed karma that
longs to be with Him again rushes to get help. There are no
such things as demons; only despairing karmic jangles.

The above information on spiritualism and demons is
not a recommendation to hang out a shingle for the purpose

of performing so-called "past-life therapy," karmic-jangle removing or exorcism. Whilst it is true that any person *can* help himself if his faith is strong enough, it is equally true that *no* third party can help him *safely* unless that third party has undergone the proper training for so doing. For such a third party skill is a necessary adjunct to faith and such skill can *only* be obtained by proper training under a genuinely licensed Zen Master. It is also true that the above remarks *only* apply to *genuine* mediums. I am not speaking of, nor do I have any patience with, bell-ringing, table-rapping frauds and fortune-tellers. I am only speaking of what are commonly called "gifted spiritualists"—and the word "gifted" is a misnomer. Fake mediums belong in jail; genuine mediums, if they do not understand the desirability of cleansing jangles rather than causing them to materialise, face, at least, the possibility of madness and, at worst, sudden death.

The reader is doubtless wondering what substance such sparks are made of. I have heard that Tibetan Buddhism states that they are wrongly used energy and, since the only matter that we are composed of is pure energy, these sparks desire greatly to be reunited with us. Zen takes this a step further. In our True state we are one with the Cosmic Buddha Who, when transcended, is Pure Love, therefore there is no such thing as *a* Cosmic Buddha and no such thing as *I*. Karmic sparks are the result of wrongly used, i.e. egotistical, love and may therefore be properly called slightly dirtied, or saddened, love which is longing for a return to its pure state which can only come about if it is assisted by a being somewhat similar to that which originally sullied it. By cleansing such karma a person turns the stream of compassion within to do his or her small part in helping the Cosmic Buddha instead of always greedily grabbing from Him. Compassion for the Cosmic Buddha is the beginning of Pure Love. In the Vimalakirti Scripture it says, "After initiation into the non-dual Dharma had been expounded, five thousand Bodhisattvas at the meeting were initiated (Transmitted) into it, thereby realising the patient endurance of the

Uncreated." In this chapter of the Scripture, the Bodhisattvas all give their personal explanations of non-duality. When Vimalakirti finally expounds to them its True Nature in silence, they all realise the incredible patience of the Cosmic Buddha Who was willing to let them go on and on in their dualistic discussions of that which lies beyond Unity until they found the Truth.

Arguments as to whether or not ghosts are the figments of over-stimulated imaginations or something more have abounded for centuries. Zen, along with the necessary ceremonies, has the following explanation. Any violent acts that cause persons to die in states of fear or terror are likely to leave behind in the places where they were perpetrated such colossal karmic jangles that years later even spiritually coarse persons will at least sense that something is wrong in these particular areas. I dislike using the term "negative karma" to describe such jangles but it is the only apt description of which I can think. Simple delusion, doubt, fear or terror that is non-volitional at the time of death will cause karmic jangles resulting in catchable sparks and past-life experiences. Acts of violence, doubt, fear or terror that are *deliberately* (i.e. volitionally) created, as well as delusion that is deliberately spread, will leave behind such huge jangles that "haunting" of certain places may result from both the terror of the victims, who understood nothing else at the time of death and meeting the Cosmic Buddha, and the evil of the perpetrators who were directing that terror. As far as Zen is concerned such "hauntings" are no more real than is the ego of the average person. However, like the ego, they produce some very real-seeming effects and therefore must be dealt with in a real manner for, just as with past lives, which are ghosts that we carry about with us, so also hauntings are a reenactment of past karma manifesting as ghosts of past persons and activities that are rooted in a particular place. The "Secret Papers" explain how the cleansing of such places is carried out and Zen priests deal with such things frequently and successfully. The reader is advised to leave such procedures to the professional priest. Such large jangles need a lot more attention and skill than do the small sparks;

amateurs, even presuming that they could get hold of the "Secret Papers," should *never* attempt the cleansing of such large jangles.

Visions are the positive side of the foregoing but should be regarded with caution and great respect for the following reasons.

Just as deluded karma will produce karmic sparks to teach us the advisability of *not* repeating our mistakes as well as showing us characteristic tendencies that we have developed from life to life that we would do better to cleanse, so visions are a prediction of *possible* future life but *not* a guarantee thereof. Let me make this plain. The main reasons why *Zen* is cautious about visions are as follows. Visions that occur *before* genuine conversion *may* be the result of wishful thinking on the part of the new monk or merely the result of using wrong posture. Hence the Zen Master tells the pupil to neither push them away nor grab at them. His advice is always to "just sit." After genuine conversion, however, and the cleansing of all karmic jangles as a result of seeing Suffering's Cause, visions are frequent and become an example of what the future joy of Union with the Cosmic Buddha is going to be like *PROVIDED* that the person concerned continues his training in the same state of purity of heart that he has now reached by cleansing his karma and that he does *not* return to his former deluded state by creating more karmic jangles. It is for this reason that Zen Masters never say that they are enlightened. There is a time of climbing the mountain to be with the Cosmic Buddha; after descending it one must live in the world as if in the sky. The Zen Master is *not* released from all future karma resulting from his actions as a reward for ascending the mountain; he is just as much bound by karmic consequence as is everyone else. Should he commit acts that result in bad karma he will enter real hell for he knows the joy of Union with God from the visions and has turned his face away thus placing himself in the same position as Marlowe's Mephistopheles whose hell was not to see God.

The reality of the *pictorial* side of visions of the future is as real as the *pictorial* sides of both our past and our present existences. Our future with the Cosmic Buddha is assured so long as we keep the Precepts and turn the stream of compassion within. To have a vision of future life in which one sees the means by which one will die is to see the logical result of continuing as we are now. It is possible to change this by doing something different for we have free will at all times. Whereas past lives are a statement of what *has* been, future lives are a statement of what *can* be if we continue the way we are going but no guarantee of what *will* be. It all depends on us. Whether or not cleansed energy, or unsaddened love, takes form and shape after Unity with the Cosmic Buddha has been transcended (see *The Book of Universal Law*) matters not at all.

BOOK II.

THE HARMONIZATION OF BODY AND MIND THROUGH THE CLEANSING OF KARMA.

by

Rev. Daizui MacPhillamy

CHAPTER I.

HISTORY.

The origins of *anma* (the practice of touching points on the body for the purpose of enhancing well-being) lie hidden in the prehistory of northern China. Tradition relates that the art was first set down in the time of the Yellow Emperor (2697-2596 B.C.) in a text known as the *Nei Ching*. The earliest written record of this work of which we have certain knowledge dates from around 200 B.C., and the oldest extant copy of the complete work comes from the Tang Dynasty. Compiled by Wang Ping in 762 A.D., it exists at present in both Chinese and Japanese editions and was recently translated in part into English.[25] Today there is a whole family of related arts derived from these ancient practices: acupuncture, moxibustion, *anma* massage, *shiatsu*, *G-Jo, dō-in, Jin Shin Jyutsu,*[26] and *Jin Shin Dō.*

When Buddhism came to China in the first century A.D., it encountered the anma arts, which were by then well developed and fully integrated with the traditional Taoist cosmology of the interplay of yin and yang. While not necessarily accepting the Taoist explanation for the phenomena of anma, the Buddhists recognized the ability of the practices to bring well-being to people and assimilated them into their religious tradition. We reproduce as Appendix B a chart and text illustrating points to be used for the alleviation of both spiritual and mortal illness from the *Taisodaisokyo* (The Chinese Mahayana Buddhist Canon), Volume 78. The association of anma with the Zen sect has been dated (Masunaga and Ohashi, 1977)[27] at least to the time of Hakuin Zenji (1686-1769 A.D.), who is believed to have combined the practice of self-anma with directed breathing and simple seated Zazen (formal meditation) to overcome the disquieted mind produced by his previous excessive use of asceticism and kōans.[28] This association continues today with various of the anma arts being part of the practice of Zen in temples around the world. In temples of the Chinese tradition acupuncture and moxibustion are the forms more often to be found,[29] while in those of the Japanese tradition moxibustion (Sato and Nishimura, 1973;[30] and Suzuki, 1972),[31] shiatsu (Masunaga and Ohashi, 1977), and the simple holding of points are more frequent.

In addition to using these arts for the prevention of disease, Zen temples follow the example of Hakuin Zenji in employing them to assist the trainees in their religious practice. When Rōshi Jiyu-Kennett was a trainee in Sōjiji Temple in Yokohama, it was the tradition for the Chief Junior trainee to distribute the moxa herb to all monks once each term for use in moxibustion for the relaxing of physical and mental tensions prior to and following the week of intensive meditation (*sesshin*), in order that their meditation might be more peaceful and deep. She also observed some of the old monks holding various places on their bodies in some of the mudras given in this book. It was explained that this was the natural way to ease tension.

The importance of the state of one's body and mind to the state of one's meditation has long been known to Zen; in fact, Dōgen Zenji (1200-1253 A.D.) went so far as to say that the harmonization of body and mind was the essence of Zen.[32] Dōgen also gave us one of the best descriptions of the position of the body (mudra) and attitude of mind most conducive to proper and peaceful meditation.[33] The Buddhist iconography contains a wealth of other mudras for assistance in developing specific beneficial states of mind (Saunders, 1960).[34] Among the mudras given in this book, a number are derived directly from this iconography: the diamond, earth witness, ease, fearlessness, meditation, offering, reverence, and spiritual protection mudras.

As Zen monks, our experience with the anma arts has been primarily with their use in assisting ourselves to meditate more effectively and to harmonize body and mind by helping us to accept, understand, and relax away the physical and mental tensions of which people almost inevitably become aware once they seriously undertake the practice of meditation and religious training. Acupuncture is not well suited to this purpose because it involves the insertion of needles into the body. This is too invasive and violent a procedure to use with someone who does much meditation, for such a person's body becomes exquisitely sensitive and requires the utmost gentleness and respect. Acupuncture is also unsuited to these purposes because it requires considerable training in medicine in order to perform it safely and it is not easy to use on oneself. Moxibustion has many of the same drawbacks because it involves the burning of an herbal preparation on or near the body. I personally feel that these techniques can be of extraordinary value in the cure of serious physical and mental illness and that they should be learned by a significant number of professional workers in the health field. Most people, however, including most students of Zen, are not seriously ill most of the time, and do not require such gross and drastic types of assistance.

The various forms of anma massage or acupressure are safe, relatively gentle, and easy to do on oneself. There are two types of acupressure: the first is represented by shiatsu, G-Jo, and dō-in, in which single points are usually stimulated by pressure, rubbing, stroking, tapping, or vibration; the second is represented by Jin Shin Jyutsu and Jin Shin Dō, in which a pattern of points are gently held two at a time. The former class of methods is simpler and involves more direct stimulation and manipulation of the body. As such it seems to be preferable for helping oneself and others with illnesses which are well developed and when the body has become relatively insensitive, but it is still too coarse for use in dealing with the subtle tensions that are uncovered by meditation in normal individuals.

As currently formulated, Jin Shin Jyutsu and Jin Shin Dō are the most recent acupressure systems. They trace their direct ancestry to the work of Jiro Murai in Japan in the early part of this century. The basis of his approach, however, is the ancient system of anma and the mudras illustrated in the Buddhist iconography (Teeguarden, 1978, p. 28).[35] We were introduced to the systems of Jin Shin Jyutsu and Jin Shin Dō several years ago by students of them who kindly instructed us in the basics of their use and shared with us their notes on some of the patterns of points (called "releases") commonly used. In time, it became evident that even the Jin Shin releases were too coarse for use with people who meditate very frequently. Although Jin Shin Dō is recognized as being an inherently meditative art in the Taoist tradition (Teeguarden, 1978, pp. 28, 122 and 155), there seems to be something about it which is still very slightly invasive or manipulative. While it states that the recipient of the Jin Shin "treatment" is ultimately in control of what happens within him, there is an emphasis on the guiding role of the person giving the treatment: "The recipient is, in a sense, an instrument; the energy flows being played and tuned are like the strings of an instrument." (Teeguarden, 1978, p. 155).

Perhaps part of the reason for this approach lies in the Taoist cosmology and part in the nature of the Jin Shin releases themselves. The Taoist explanation for the phenomena of anma is basically one of a dynamic equilibrium of yin and yang energy which flows in the various meridians of the body and, in a perfectly healthy person, is in complete accord with the Tao or Way of Nature. The converse of this proposition is, of course, that the presence of any imbalance, block, tension, ailment, etc. is proof that a person is not in accord with the Tao. From this it is a short step to the view that it is the role of the person performing the Jin Shin releases to guide the other person back to the Way, and hence a subtle attitude of superiority and manipulation may arise.

The Buddhist approach, detailed more fully in the next chapters, is an open-ended one. Enlightenment in Zen is not a state; it is a *process* which continues and always deepens and expands. "Going on, going on, always going on, always *becoming* Buddha" says the Scripture of Great Wisdom;[36] "Always we must be disturbed by the Truth" says Dōgen Zenji. Thus the presence of tension is regarded as an opportunity to train oneself and experience the Truth more deeply. Therefore, when a person helps another by using a mudra of harmonization, there are simply two people seeking together the Life of Buddha.

To one who has done considerable Zen meditation, the releases of Jin Shin, regardless of the attitude of mind of the one who is doing them, inherently have a slightly coarse and manipulative feeling about them. It is as if the "energy flows"[37] are sometimes temporarily channeled backwards through the meridians or are run back and forth to "scour out" the blocks. Of course there are times when this is precisely what is needed; I have personally seen great good accomplished through the use of these releases. Some of them seem particularly suited to assisting a person in recalling memories of early traumatic experiences and even karmic memory traces of unresolved problems from previous lives. As such, I believe that they could be of considerable use in psychotherapy. Others seem particularly suited to certain physical problems. It was our feeling, however, that the harmonization of body and mind for the purpose of meditation could be approached in a still more subtle and gentle way. Thus this book is based upon the ancient charts of the meridians of anma, the *Taisodaisokyo*, the Buddhist iconography, the mudras practiced by the old monks of the Far East, and our own meditation.

CHAPTER II.

HOW TO USE A MUDRA.

The mudras of harmonization are given in Chapter VI. Each mudra is presented in a table which indicates where on your body to place your left and right hands and the sequence in which to move them. An example is:

RIGHT MUDRA

Step	Place your left hand on your:	Place your right hand on your:
1	right C2	right X1* *or* touch right middle finger to right F1
2	right C1	
3	right B1	
4		touch right middle finger to right F1

Most mudras affect one of a pair of bilateral meridians which are diagrammed on the page facing the mudra table. Should you wish to affect the meridian on your left side, you would use the mudra labelled "LEFT MUDRA" and conversely for the right side. Naturally there will be times when you wish to do both, and you will use both mudras, one after the other. You should also know that performing the mudra to relax one side of your body will, to some extent, also assist the meridian on the opposite side. Some mudras affect energy flows which are central, and these have just one mudra given in the table.

First find a suitable place in which to relax and concentrate on the mudra; a quiet, clean, fresh room with good ventilation and adequate warmth is best. A comfortable couch or bed or a reclining easy chair are the most suitable furniture on which to rest for most mudras. Have a quilt or blanket available in case you become cold (it sometimes happens that most of one's energy goes deep within one when a mudra is used, leaving the extremities unusually cool). If a friend is assisting you, make sure that he or she has something comfortable on which to sit or kneel and that he or she does not have to strain or bend over for a long period of time in order to reach the necessary points on your body. Take off your shoes, wristwatch and rings, and loosen your belt, necktie, collar or tight-fitting clothing. It is neither necessary nor advisable to remove other clothing. These mudras may be used by placing your hands in the proper locations on your fully-clothed body or even, if necessary when you are ill in bed, on a thick quilt or heavy bedclothes. Try to arrange for sufficient uninterrupted time for the unhurried use of the mudras, plus a quarter or half an hour of rest thereafter. Try to make provisions for someone else to answer your telephone during this time or resolve not to answer it (and bury it under a pile of blankets or in a drawer if need be to muffle its ring). The hour after a meal or after heavy exercise is not a conducive time for using most mudras. Except for your relaxed reclining position, the surroundings and circumstances should be those suggested for ordinary Zazen meditation,[38] as such meditation is essential to the use of these mudras.

Selecting, for example, the right mudra above, we find that it has four steps. In the first step you would place your left hand on the point designated as "C2" in the chart on page 108 on the right side of your body and with your right hand either touch the point labeled "X1" in the chart on page 116 on the right side of your body or place your right middle finger on the point labeled "F1" on your right thumb. An asterisk following a point indicates that it may be awkward to reach on oneself and that its use is optional depending upon your comfort. It is usually better to omit an awkward step than it is to twist oneself up into a position which is incompatible with relaxation and the release of tension. In general, the entire hand is not placed on a point, but only the tips of the fingers, often only the thumb or the index, middle, and ring fingers. Rest the remainder of your hand and your arm in a comfortable position. Where a mudra table says to connect two points with one hand, you would place part of your hand on one point and part on the other. Where it says to use one point *or* a second, as in the first step here, choose the one which seems best. If you are already familiar with another system of notation for the points on the body, there is no need to learn the system used in this book. The last table in Appendix A provides a means of converting our system into the traditional acupuncture notation as well as into the systems used by Jin Shin Dō and G-Jo.

Finding the correct location of the points can be very important and is not really difficult. Study the general point charts at the beginning of Chapter VI thoroughly as well as the meridian drawing facing the particular mudra table you are using. This drawing will illustrate all of the points necessary for use in that particular mudra, but because of limitations in the size of the drawings, the location of the points may not be as accurate as on the main charts.

Place your hand on the general area indicated and you will be able to sense the correct location of the point for you at this moment. I say "at this moment" because some of these points seem to move with time (points A4, J1, C1 and Z5 are notoriously variable, hence they are indicated as a general area rather than a specific point). You should be aware also that point locations may vary from person to person, and thus if you are using a mudra to assist a friend, he or she is the one to tell you whether or not your hand is on the correct point. This is true even if you have used a mudra many times and are certain of where the point is on yourself while your friend is using the mudra for the first time. Please note that some of these points are near the genitals or other sensitive areas. When I am assisting a friend by using a mudra which involves these points, I consider it polite to ask my friend to find the points and direct my hand to them; I do not poke around to find them myself. Mutual respect and simple courtesy are an integral part of this technique.

Aside from sensing intuitively where a point is located, there are other indicators that you can use if you are not sure that you are on the correct spot. The skin over the point may feel different from that adjoining it; it may be hard and stiff or especially soft; it may be warmer or cooler, or somehow just "different." These differences can usually be felt through the clothing. When a hand is placed on the correct location, the point itself may tell you that the hand is properly located. It may seem particularly sensitive, even painful, or it may seem numb; it may seem to vibrate, or muscular spasms or twitches may develop.

There is usually a subtle pulsation to be felt by your fingertips when they are on the correct location, which differs from that felt on the surrounding area. This pulsation requires some concentration to feel, but can usually be felt even through heavy clothing or a quilt. It may be useful to practice finding this pulsation on yourself at all of the various locations given on the points charts. If you have difficulty finding them, start with points Z1, I2, A1, and R3, which are the strongest in most people. If they still elude you, try placing the balls of your fingertips on some hard, flat, smooth, *inanimate* object such as a table top. Close your eyes and concentrate on the sensations in your fingertips until you can feel the pulsation generated by the flow of blood through your own fingertips. The pulsations you are trying to sense are similar in intensity to these, although you will quickly realize that they are not *simply* the pulsations in your own fingers, as they have a habit of changing in speed and amplitude when the fingers are placed on different points on the body. The pulsations that you feel in, say, your *right* fingertips may change considerably when you move your *left* hand from one point to another. I know of no one who cannot feel these pulsations; it is simply a matter of undisturbed concentration and knowing what you are trying to find. If you have difficulty in feeling them at first, do not worry. Simply place your fingers on the indicated points. The mudras will still be effective, and sooner or later your fingers will discover the pulses.

Once you have found the correct points to touch with both hands, simply hold them gently until the pulsations you feel in the tips of the fingers of both hands have become equal in speed, pattern, and strength. If you know that one hand is in the correct position yet you cannot feel any pulsation there, try gently rubbing the point with a clockwise circular motion for a minute; this will often cause the pulsation to be perceptible. If it does not, then it may be necessary to hold the point more firmly, or even press it rather hard for a bit, or it may be advisable to place your hand closer to the body, perhaps directly on the skin. Remember that if you are assisting a friend, he or she must decide what should be done at all times; this is *not a treatment* which you *do to* someone. Also please bear in mind that this is not a form of massage and does not generally require that you press, rub, or otherwise manipulate the body. It is a spiritual exercise for which it is usually quite sufficient to place the fingers lightly on the indicated point, even though they are separated from the body by clothing or several inches of blankets. The reasons for this are discussed in the next chapter.

When the pulsations are balanced in strength, speed, and pattern it *may* be time to move to the next step of the mudra; you (or the person you are assisting if you are doing the mudra on someone else) must decide this intuitively. In general, in mudras which have only a very few steps you will want to hold each step for a relatively long period of time (as much as ten or twenty minutes in some cases). Sometimes the pulses will simply refuse to come into balance; they should not be forced to do so. When this happens there will come a time when it seems right to go on to the next step, and you should do this even if the pulses are not balanced. The same thing holds true if you can find no pulsations whatsoever for a particular set of points; simply hold them until it seems best to go on and then do so.

In the case of the sample mudra given above, the second step for the right mudra is to move your left hand to the right point "C1," while leaving your right hand where it was on point "X1" or "F1" (this is indicated by the arrow in the column for the right hand, which indicates that it maintains the first position through steps two and three). You then hold these points as you did the first two and, when the time is right, proceed to step three. In this step you again move only your left hand, this time to point "B1" on the right side of the body. Hold these points as you have the others; then go to the fourth step. This time you leave the left hand where it is and move the right hand so as to bring the right middle finger to touch point "F1" on your right thumb (if you chose this option in step one instead of holding point "X1," then there is nothing further to do in this step; you have completed the mudra). Wait until these points have achieved balanced pulsations and you feel that the mudra is complete and then stop. You may wish to go on to another mudra or not, as you see fit. In any case, after the last mudra you will probably not wish to get up immediately. Allow some time to relax and let the effects of the mudra work on the meridian without distraction. When you wish to get up, do so gently and do not immediately rush about.

Remember that you are ultimately in charge of how a mudra should proceed on you. This is true whether you are doing it on yourself or whether a friend is assisting you. If at any time you feel strongly that a particular step should be omitted, altered, or an additional one added, please do so. This does not often happen, but occasionally it is necessary to modify the mudras in this way. Here the charts of the lines of flow of the associated meridians can be of great value. If an additional step is needed, it will usually involve a point which is on one of the branches of the meridian illustrated for that mudra. It is best to place a hand on it in such a way that the natural flow of energy in the meridian is enhanced, not impeded. To do this, note the direction of the arrows on the chart which indicate the normal direction of energy flow in the meridian. Place your hands so that your left hand is "upstream" of your right hand. In that way the additional channel formed by your hands and arms will help convey the energy from the point which your left hand is holding to the point held by your right hand.

The most common reason to need to modify a mudra is the presence of a scar along the lines of flow of the associated meridian. Whether the scar be the result of accident or surgery, it seems to remain as a weak point in the meridian, one where tensions are likely to accumulate and cause a blockage in the flow. For this reason, a scar often requires extra attention and the extra application of the touch of a loving hand. It seems almost as if each part of the body has a memory of its own, and a scar "remembers" the violence done to the body at that place. In the case of an injury, it will recall the cause and agent of the injury, and it is wise not only to transmit love to the wound but also to make sure that a similar cause and agent are not encountered by that part of your body again. This is true whether the wound is an old one or whether it be in the process of healing. In the latter case, of course, one does not remove the dressings and touch the wound, but rather places one's right hand (the right hand is usually best for this purpose) above or near the wound and wills love into it indirectly.

With a surgical incision, the same principles apply, but the wound will also "remember" the attitudes of the surgeon and his staff during the operation. A surgeon who finds this book useful might wish to consider the implications of this observation. If the surgeon is angry or upset during the operation or if his patient does not completely understand or agree with what he is doing, it may have an effect on the healing of the wound and upon the relative resistance of that part of the body to future illness. Such a surgeon might also wish to consider spending a moment after the surgery transferring love to the incision with his right hand and, as it were, explaining nonverbally to it that its injury was not caused callously or out of anger or greed but was truly necessary for the preservation of life and health. He might also transmit to the incision the regret of those who performed the surgery that it was necessary to cause the body this pain and injury.

Beneath the table of each mudra you will find a section on how to use it to assist a friend. Often this will simply tell you on which side of the person to sit so as to perform the mudra most comfortably, together with instructions to place your hands on his or her body in the same places which you would use on yourself. In some cases the mudra for assisting a friend will be different from the one for use on yourself; this is usually because a number of points on the mudra cannot be reached on oneself. The mudra for self use has therefore been modified.

Using our sample mudra as an illustration, since the first step for the right hand is awkward to do for oneself when it is listed as "right X1," the self mudra might have been written with that step as "touch right middle finger to right F1" and a separate mudra been written for use when assisting a friend which would have "right X1" as its first step. In our sample mudra both of these options were written into the mudra table, so no separate table was required. If there were many such steps, however, the table would have become confusing and separate tables would have been created for self use and use with a friend. The two mudras are usually equivalent, but if you feel that the mudra you have used on yourself hasn't done quite all it might, you could consider having a friend use the other form of it with you.

Do not, please, reverse your hands in order to get to a point on yourself or someone else which you could not otherwise reach. There is a general direction of energy flow from the point which your left hand touches, through that hand and your body down to your right hand, and thence to the point which it is touching. This flow of energy assists the normal flow of the meridian, which is from the former point to the latter. If you reverse your hands, the normal direction of flow is reversed, either in the meridian or between your two hands, and the result in either case is not what the mudra was designed to accomplish. If you cannot reach a point or it is awkward to hold so that you cannot do so in a relaxed position, simply go on to the following step. Above all, always bear in mind when assisting a friend that you are simply providing an extra pair of hands to do *his or her will.* Follow your friend's directions and do not impose upon your friend your ideas and opinions as to what should be done. If you are not a doctor you have no business trying to diagnose or treat any illness with this or any other method. Even using these mudras on a friend to "treat" or "correct" a nonmedical condition could constitute the practice of massage without a license. Therefore you must keep in mind at all times when assisting a friend that it is your friend who is in charge of what is going on and it is not your place to "treat," "correct," or otherwise manipulate anyone. You are there to help your friend by doing whatever mudra he or she may request and by placing your hands where he or she may direct them.

The next information given for each mudra is the time of day during which the energy flow in the associated meridian is most intense. Many of the energy pathways illustrated in this book are temporarily created by use of the associated mudra; others are in continuous flow. Some of the meridians, however, are known to be particularly active at specified hours of the day. Information on these meridians is derived from the traditional acupuncture literature on the meridians, and there is some disagreement as to the exact times (some sources list times one hour earlier than the ones given in this book).The hours given here are the ones which I have found to be most useful. Please note that they are in standard time; you must correct for daylight savings time or other changes. If you move rapidly across a number of time zones, expect a period of adjustment before the times given are applicable. This period is quite variable and may range from a day or two for a young person to several weeks or even months for an older one. The times of maximal energy flow in the meridians are times when the mudras may have the most beneficial effect. The next most useful time to work on a meridian which is time-dependent is the period twelve hours opposite from the given time. The time periods immediately prior and immediately following the hours of maximal energy flow are also particularly good. Any mudra may be performed at any time; these listings of hours need not restrict you. However, given a choice, you may wish to make use of this time information. This time data can, of course, be used in reverse, as part of the "self detective work" you may wish to do in the process of using the mudras to assist you with a particular tension or problem (this is described in detail later). If you have a tension which seems time-related, this may suggest using the mudras for the time at which it is strongest (or the mudras for the previous, following, or opposite hours).

The next section lists some of the common uses of the mudra. This is given primarily to help you decide which mudra would be most beneficial in your current situation. The physical conditions which the mudra may affect are listed first. They are given not in terms of medical diseases but rather simply as tension, pain, stiffness, muscular spasms, soreness, tenderness, or any other unusual sensation which may arise from tension in certain parts of the body. This is because I do not view the mudras of harmonization as a form of alternative medicine. If I am feeling ill, I meditate as deeply as possible and consult my body as to what is necessary and good for it. If it seems good to consult a physician, I do so without hesitation and, if it seems good, I take what he may prescribe. If I am not truly ill but am experiencing the effects of some tension which my meditation has uncovered, if I am ill and the doctor can do nothing to help, or if I feel that a mudra could assist in addition to his prescriptions, then I may use a mudra. If you believe that you may be genuinely ill, please *do not* use these mudras as "home remedies" or, worse yet, begin to play doctor with someone else's illness. I say this not because I am legally bound to do so, but because it is my firm belief. There is no inherent conflict between the use of these mudras and the seeking of traditional (or non-traditional) medical assistance. When each is used properly, the two complement each other. Of course, most of the time it is not a question of illness or possible illness; one simply becomes aware of a persistent tension or other sign of some disharmony of body and mind, and one proceeds to find out its causes and what to do about it. It is for this that these mudras are best suited. Even when using the mudras in this way, however, you must keep in mind that *there can be other causes for unusual physical sensations besides tension.* You have a right to your own body and a privilege to learn from it; that is what this book is about. With these rights and privileges comes the responsibility to care for it sensibly and to use good judgment in seeking professional advice when you might be ill.

The results of using a mudra on a tension which is perceived as a physical pain, stiffness, etc. may be several. Usually during and immediately after the mudra there is relaxation. Sometimes this in itself is sufficient to correct a minor problem in the associated meridian. Such problems are usually of recent origin and their causes may or may not become apparent. Thus, many trainees in the monastery at Mt. Shasta use some of these mudras at the end of a particularly hard or stressful day to free themselves of any accumulated tensions before sleep or before evening meditation. For us this is their most common use.

At other times, when a tension in a particular meridian is of more remote origin and/or there has been a chronic problem, the effects of the mudra may be rather different. The initial relaxing effect may wear off after a while, and the mudra may need to be done again and again. *There may also be a paradoxical effect of increased sensations of pain and tension* as the mudra begins to loosen a particularly tight area which has been rendered insensitive by the chronic tension. This can be quite unpleasant, but it is not a reason to become worried; as the tension relaxes further, the pain will subside. It can, of course, happen that the insensitivity produced by chronic tension has masked the symptom of an illness and relief of that tension will permit the symptom to be felt. Pain due to this source will probably not be transient, and if you ever have reason to believe that you are in this situation, please consult your physician.

As the tensions in a meridian begin to relax sufficiently, gradually (or suddenly) something in the meridian changes and a flood of energy may course through the meridian. This sometimes causes sensations of considerable heat or muscular spasms, twitches, or even thrashing movements of large sections of the body as it passes. These effects may not occur while the mudra is being used, and can come up to several days later. This can be rather a surprise to one who is not expecting it, and it is well to be aware of this possibility. It can be suppressed if necessary (e.g. if you are driving or performing some exacting or dangerous work) but it is best to allow such "throwing off" of tension to occur freely if possible. Often when such a major area of tension releases, the causes which produced it may come to mind, either immediately or during one's meditation, or even in dreams. This can be extraordinarily valuable information, both for making sure that the same thing does not happen again and for teaching one how to live in better accord with the Buddha's Precepts by not doing acts which would cause similar tensions to build up in other people. Sometimes a number of different mudras must be tried, their results kept in mind, clues as to what has caused the tension noted and followed up, and even substantial changes in one's living habits made before the tension will release. In such ways our bodies become the agency of the Buddhas in teaching us how to train ourselves more fully and how to harmonize our bodies and minds more completely with That Which Is.

The most common mental tensions assisted by any given mudra are listed next. These are not given in psychiatric diagnostic terms as I do not view the use of these mudras as a substitute for psychotherapy. It is clear, however, that they may exert a particularly beneficial influence on the mind and as such are potentially an excellent *adjunct* to psychological or psychiatric assistance. For most of us most of the time, however, this is not necessary, and we may use the mudras for help in dealing with ordinary mental tensions in much the same way as we do for those tensions which result in physical discomforts. Sometimes when a tension is rather large, its cause is a repressed emotion or a traumatic memory from childhood which has been lying dormant and which, due to the increasing depth of our meditation, is beginning to come into awareness. This situation is an excellent opportunity for increased mental health and deeper religious awareness, and it seems to happen to some degree at least once to most people who meditate seriously over a period of years. The only difficulty is that it is sometimes *very* uncomfortable. There is, of course, really nothing to do but go on, as it would not be coming into awareness unless we were prepared to face it and learn something constructive. This can, however, be a time when a talk with someone close to you or to your religious advisor or a professional counselor can be reassuring.

If this process of coming into awareness seems to become stuck in some way, or if for any other reason it seems wise to do something to relax you and make the process more acceptable, a mudra which affects that particular type of tension may be of use. If you choose to use a mudra under these conditions, I would suggest having a trusted friend nearby, as on occasion the added relaxation of the mudra will enable you to recall the dormant emotion or memory and someone to talk to or a shoulder to cry on can be very welcome. Again, as with the physical releases, such a mental release need not necessarily come while the mudra is being used; it can come any time in the succeeding few days, and this can be quite distressing if you are not prepared for the possibility. As with the physical manifestations of a tension releasing, the mental ones can be suppressed by an act of will, but it is far better to allow them to happen naturally if possible.

One is not always aware that a traumatic memory or emotional tension exists and is close to awareness. Thus, once in a while, a mudra done for a completely different reason can relax one sufficiently that such a memory or emotion comes to mind, apparently "out of the blue." It is therefore advisable to glance over the types of mental tensions which a mudra may affect before using it, so that you are not bewildered should a related memory or emotion take you by surprise. This is particularly true if you use the will-despair mudra, which can help with the acceptance of the very deepest of fears and despair.

As with the physical manifestations of a tension, the mental ones are not always assisted by one use of a mudra, and it may be necessary to repeat it, use several others, follow up clues of all sorts, meditate more deeply, and change what one is doing before the tension will dissolve.

The last of the listed effects for each mudra are those on tensions which have their origin in, or are manifested as, karmic memories from earlier in this lifetime or from times prior to this lifetime. Rōshi Jiyu-Kennett has discussed the Buddhist view of karma as it applies to physical and mental health in Book I. The doctrines of karma and of rebirth are perhaps the most radical of the Buddhist doctrines to the Western mind and, as the Buddha said of all of His teachings, you are not asked to believe them simply because we say that they are true (see the Kalama Sutra of the Anguttara-nikaya and the Vimamsaka-suttra of the Majjhima-nikaya).[39] I would ask solely that you entertain the possibility that there could be some valid basis for such beliefs and wait until your own experience provides confirmation or denial thereof. Regardless of the state of your belief on these subjects, it would be well to acquaint yourself with some of the phenomena which we attribute to them if you intend to meditate seriously over a period of time or use these mudras on any regular basis, as you may well encounter some form of these experiences.

Disturbances in the meridian flows which manifest as karmic memory traces usually are not uncovered until a person has been meditating for some time (there are, of course, exceptions to this). They tend to be more subtle than the tensions which have physical or mental manifestations and therefore usually occur only after the major blocks of these types have dissolved. Furthermore, as they often appear in order to provide an opportunity to cleanse the stream of karma of a past being which we have accidentally inherited, they usually do not come to awareness until one has done a reasonable job of learning how to live by the Precepts so as not to produce quantities of unfortunate karma in *this* lifetime (again, there are exceptions; see Chapter IV).

Memory traces of karmic origin may appear at first as recurrent dreams, waking or dozing visions, or vivid recollections of scenes from past times and places; they may appear as strong intuitions of a karmic origin to some current problem, or simply as recurrent physical or mental tensions, pains, etc. which, upon thorough investigation, have no discernible physiological or psychological explanation. An increased awareness of congenital birthmarks, injuries, or defects can also be an indication of the arising of a karmic memory. This is not the only possible cause of a changing awareness of these things, however; please do not hesitate to consult your physician if you believe that a physiological change in a congenital anomaly is taking place.

The mudras of harmonization may be of use in helping to relax you so that you may bring into awareness and clarify these karmic memories and so that you may better accept and assimilate such memories when they arise. The method of doing this is discussed in detail in Chapter IV. It will suffice here to say that such memories are usually of two types: memories of great suffering and memories of having caused great suffering. The former require acceptance, empathy, love, and compassion to cleanse and set to rest the disturbance in the stream of karma; the latter require the same and, in addition, the wisdom to understand the ways in which the potential for making the same mistake exists now. Whether the karma is something which you created earlier in this life or whether it is something created by some other being in ages past, there is always a definite and valuable teaching to be found about one's current life. Therefore tensions arising from karmic memories are another opportunity to learn the Teachings of the Buddhas through the aegis of our bodies and minds.

As with the physical and mental manifestations of meridian energy disturbances, karmic memories may not be affected by the mudras while those mudras are being used, nor is one always aware before doing a mudra that the real cause of the tension on which one is working is karmic. Thus you would do well to examine the possible types of karmic memories which could arise before using a mudra for any purpose. I should say that this is particularly true if you do *not* believe in rebirth, as the sudden and vivid reliving of what appear to be the events of ages past could be most disconcerting if you are not aware that this is a possibility.

The following section of information for some mudras is on the factors which can exert a particularly beneficial influence on the associated meridian. In Buddhism it is said that training and enlightenment are one[40] and the religious training of our daily life has the greatest influence upon the harmonization of body and mind. The real Buddhist follows the Buddhist Eightfold Path[41] and develops the paramitas (wisdoms arising from meditation), not to attain physical and mental health, but because they are the Way of the Buddhas and Patriarchs, the Way of the Wheel of the True Law, the Way, in other words, of the natural and harmonious flow of All That Is. This does not mean, however, that the practice of these good things is without effects on the body and mind, and hence it is of use to indicate which of them are especially beneficial for the well-being of those meridians that they influence most profoundly. Conversely, the breakage of the Buddhist Precepts, the tenfold attachments, and the three poisons of greed, anger, and delusion are not without their harmful influences upon oneself. These are listed in the next-to-last section under the mudras for which they are most relevant.

The principal use which I find for such information occurs when I discover a tension or disturbance in a particular meridian. By considering deeply the harmful and beneficial influences upon that meridian, I am often able to find the cause of the tension in something that I am doing (or failing to do) in my life. This information is therefore of great value in the "detective work" each of us must do on ourselves if we wish to continually deepen our training. Many times the cause is a subtle one (the more one meditates and trains oneself in a religious life, the subtler they seem to become), so do not regard the information given too casually. "Lying," for example, could be failing to tell the whole truth on a government form because there was no room to put it all down and the official in charge wasn't interested in hearing about it anyway. "Stealing" can be taking a nail from a box of nails your landlord has left rusting in the rain and using it to fix the house. There is not *always* something you should be doing differently, so do not obsess upon this information. Sometimes it is quite enough to relax and allow the cleansing flow of the energy through the meridian to melt the tension away.

The sections on beneficial and harmful influences sometimes contain additional information. Some meridians can be benefitted by the use of certain types of foods. When there is a definite disturbance in the lung meridian, for example, I often find that a hot bowl of onion soup in winter or a tomato and onion salad with vinegar in summer will be of real assistance. These foods are taken *in addition* to a balanced diet; they are supplements, not substitutes. My body has never required of me, nor have I ever suggested to anyone else, that I go on a diet of nothing but onions, tomatoes, garlic, and vinegar in order to "clean out" my lung meridian. Such excesses just do not seem to make sense to my body (nor to nutritional science), and I strongly recommend a reasonable approach to diet based both upon the middle way between extremes and upon meditating and listening to your own body and giving it what it tells you that it needs. In this regard, I have no doubt that the lists of beneficial food supplements given in this book are incomplete, and I would be interested in learning of additions which you may find.

This information can, of course, be used for self detective work as well. If you find yourself craving eggs, mayonnaise, and oily foods, for instance, you may well consider that there might be a disturbance either developing or coming to the surface in the liver or gall bladder meridians. Doing the relief-frustration and/or compassion-anger mudras could, in turn, help you find out that you are, let us say, continually irritated by the behavior of one of your co-workers. Careful examination of the specific events which make you angry and further meditation might, for example, reveal that he reminds you of yourself in some respects. Changing how you behave in these respects might not only decrease your frustrations but possibly change your dietary habits, relieve those intermittent headaches you didn't even suspect were connected to this situation, and bring you closer to understanding true compassion (the Heart of the Bodhisattva Kanzeon, which is the first major step in Zen training). All this might transpire because you diligently pursued a simple clue like a craving for eggs and oils.

Another piece of supplementary information is sometimes given: emotional states which have a harmful effect. It is obviously not possible to avoid all occurrences of worry, grief, anger, sadness, etc.; one would have to withdraw from human contact and become quietistic, and Zen is distinctly opposed to both. The Zen Master, although he or she may not often experience anger or worry, for example, because these emotions arise primarily from attachment, will still very definitely feel sadness and grief. The experience of enlightenment does not bring a perpetual state of happiness but rather an awareness of things as they really are, and "things as they really are" are often quite sad. Thus it is neither possible nor desirable to entirely avoid all of the emotions listed as having a harmful influence on the meridians. This does not change the fact that they have such an influence. Therefore it is often good to give extra attention and care to a meridian after having experienced an emotion which may damage it. This may involve the use of an appropriate mudra, a supplementary meal, meditation on acceptance, or sharing the burden with a willing and sympathetic friend. In this way it is possible to avoid hanging on to an unpleasant emotional state for longer than is necessary or, worse, repressing it and having it turn into a new tension in a meridian. This is one of the most common uses of the mudras in a monastery: after a trainee has suffered a necessarily upsetting experience, a friend will offer to do a mudra with him to assist him in accepting the situation, letting the upset pass on, and allowing the cleansing flow of the love of both the Buddhas and his fellow man to flood through his meridians.

The final piece of information given for each mudra is its origin. Many of the mudras given in this book are the product of the meditation of Rōshi Jiyu-Kennett, myself, or others at Shasta Abbey. Some have arisen entirely from our meditation, usually in response to a particular need which could not be met by a known mudra. These are indicated as being "derived intuitively from meditation." A large number were derived by meditating upon the ancient meridian diagrams (which often have considerably more information than is found in modern acupuncture charts) and the excellent and detailed modern diagrams found in Felix Mann's *The Meridians of Acupuncture* (London: Heinemann,

1964). Through such meditation and the use of the resulting mudras on ourselves, we have endeavored to arrive at a version of each which is relatively brief, gentle, and yet effective. Other mudras were taken directly or adapted slightly from the Buddhist iconography, the traditional practices of monks in the Far East, and the *Taisodaisokyo,* and are credited accordingly. Finally, a few of the mudras are our adaptations of some of the releases of Jin Shin Jyutsu or Jin Shin Dō, and these are noted as such.

The mudras included in this book are the ones I believe to be the most valuable for commonly encountered tensions in normal individuals. There are hundreds more mudras which we have not included, and there are other, specialized, uses for the mudras given in this book. Anyone wishing more information about them is welcome to contact us to inquire about further instruction. Seminars in this subject are held from time to time at Shasta Abbey, and we are particularly happy to share such information with members of the religious, health, and mental health professions. I am also interested in hearing from any readers of this book who may find uses and/or properties of these mudras which are not included here. Persons wishing information or instruction in the other anma arts might wish to contact some of the following:

Acupuncture: Academy of Eastern Medicine
1414 Maria Lane
Walnut Creek, CA 94596
(415) 937-3331

Jin Shin Dō: Acupressure Workshop
2309 Main Street
Santa Monica, CA 90405
(213) 392-3919

or

Acupressure Workshop
1533 Shattuck Avenue
Berkeley, CA 94709
(415) 845-1059

Jin Shin Jyutsu:	Jin Shin Jyutsu, Inc.
	2919 North 67th Place
	Scottsdale, AZ 85251
	(602) 945-8588
Shiatsu:	Shiatsu Education Center
	52 West 55th Street
	New York, NY 10019
	(212) 582-3424

or

North American Shiatsu Institute
P.O. Box 1139-A
Vancouver, BC, Canada
(604) 684-3717

This concludes the technical information on how to use the mudras of harmonization. These aspects, however, are the *least important* ones. What is absolutely vital is that they be done with the mind of meditation and with absolute respect and reverence. This is the subject of the next chapter.

CHAPTER III.

YOUR HANDS ARE THE HANDS OF GOD.

These mudras will be useless to you unless they are done with the mind of meditation: at best they will be simply a pleasant exercise in relaxation; at worst they may become a vehicle for manipulation; most probably there will be so little effect from them that you will soon conclude that they are worthless. It is the mind of meditation which gives them their efficacy and which gives you the intuitive understanding necessary to use them properly both upon yourself and with your family and friends.

There is much written on the mind of meditation in the literature of Zen. I am hardly qualified to give more than a most rudimentary explanation of it; for a more comprehensive one you might wish to consult Dōgen Zenji, "Gyakudo-yōjinshu," and "Shushōgi," Keizan Zenji, "Sankon-zazen-setsu" (in Kennett, *Zen Is Eternal Life* [Emeryville, CA: Dharma Publishing, 1976], pp. 123-38, 154-63, and 269-70), and Rōshi Kennett in Chapters 4-7 of the same book, and in her more recent *How to Grow a Lotus Blossom* (Mt. Shasta, CA: Shasta Abbey Press, 1977). Even with the best of references, however, the mind of meditation is something which can only be understood by experience. The best sources of practical instruction of which I know in how to do this in the Sōtō Zen tradition are to be found in the "Fukanzazengi" of Dōgen Zenji[42] and, among modern works, in the booklet *Zen Meditation*.[43] There are many other meditation practices besides the one used in Sōtō Zen, and if you are already practicing one of them, there may be no need to switch to our form of meditation in order to use these mudras beneficially. If, however, you try them and find the mudras to be ineffective, you may wish to consider adopting the Sōtō Zen form of meditation for a while in order to see if it develops a state of mind more conducive to their use.

Put briefly, I view Zen meditation as a state of mind of relaxed yet intense awareness and concentration. It is a receptive state in which awareness is expanded to include many subtle stimuli, both internal and external, which would ordinarily be unnoticed. It is at the same time a state of concentration and single-pointedness of mind, yet without the excluding or screening-out property which the word "concentration" usually implies. This simultaneous awareness and concentration occurs in a mind which is at ease and quiet, yet bright and alert rather than trance-like or hypnotic. In Zen training, this state of mind is first learned in formal seated Zazen practice and then gradually applied to all of daily life. It is not possible to learn meditation from reading a description such as this or even from reading the best of meditation instructions. It must be learned for oneself by the practice of formal Zazen and daily training over the course of time. Meditation is the state of mind in which these mudras should be done. Then you will be intuitively aware of the clues which your body and mind are giving you about why a meridian is having tension and what you can do about it.

Sometimes in order to learn such things it is necessary, while using a mudra, to concentrate in a slightly different way from that used in pure Zazen. In Zazen, one is told neither to try to think nor to try not to think. That is, neither actively follow a particular line of thought nor repress thoughts, but simply allow all thoughts, sensations, emotions, etc. to rise and fall naturally without any conscious direction. It will sometimes occur during a mudra that something comes to mind which is intuitively important to follow. In such a case it is sometimes good to do so and consciously devote your attention to entering into that train of thought, image, emotion, sensation, or whatever it may be, with all of your effort. I call this directed concentration rather than meditation.

It is through meditation that you will know whether you are using the correct mudra and whether it should be modified in some way for your particular situation. Sometimes one feels these things by sensing the flowing of energy;

sometimes one sees them; sometimes one simply knows them. Each person is different in this regard, and such differences are unimportant. It is not necessary, therefore, that you feel energy flowing along the pathways diagrammed for a given mudra, nor is it wise to try to visualize these pathways as a mudra is being done. What matters is that you enter into the use of these mudras in the mind of meditation and that you trust yourself and the Buddhas (or God or whatever name you use for That Which Is) to guide you to do what is best.

It is this faith in Something greater than oneself and the reverence which it brings that is the other vital aspect of using the mudras of harmonization. One of the priests at Shasta Abbey, after doing these mudras for some time, said to Rōshi Jiyu-Kennett that the only way in which he could do them was if he approached his body with utter respect, regarded his hands (which were doing it upon him) as literally the Hands of God, and gave himself into these Hands. This is precisely the way in which these mudras should be done, whether upon oneself or with a friend. There is no manipulation, either of oneself or another person; there is an absolute trust and reverence. You, personally, are not the Buddha, and yet there is absolutely nothing in you which is other than the Buddha. As Rōshi Jiyu-Kennett said to this priest, "You are *not* God and there is nothing in you which is not *of* God." It is only with this degree of reverence and faith that you, as doer of the mudra, can be sure of doing that which is good; it is only with this degree of reverence and faith that you, as receiver of the mudra, can trust to open yourself to it utterly and allow it to work deeply upon you.

Thus the use of these mudras is ultimately a religious act and an act of deep love. An understanding of the nature of the "energy" which passes through the meridians will give a better insight into this. When one undertakes Zazen properly, one of the effects thereof is to set up a subtle flow of energy up the spine, over the head, and down the torso.[44] To most people, most of the time, the existence of this flow is unnoticed during Zazen. At the time of a profound religious transformation or *kenshō*, however, this energy becomes as a great spiritual fountain, flooding through the entire body and mind, overwhelming, cleansing, and transforming it.[45] It is then that one realizes that this so-called "energy" is a direct and intimate part of Something far greater than one's egocentric self. It is also not confined to the meridians shown in books such as this, but rather it streams into and around each of us from a Source which is incomprehensible in Its Love and Wisdom. It radiates from each of us to all things around us as well as back to that Source, which is no different from all of those things around us and yet is not limited by them. In this view the use of mudras is not a matter, as it is in the Taoist approach, of tonifying the deficient energy pathways and sedating the excessive ones—of "tuning an instrument"—it is a matter of allowing that pure Love which is of the Buddha, and *is* the Buddha, to flow through oneself to oneself or to another being in absolute trust and with absolute reverence for That Which Is. It is, in other words, a sacramental act.

This "energy," being the Love of the Lord, is not bounded by the limits of physical anatomy. Therefore the points used in these mudras are not restricted to where the meridians come to the surface of the body as they are in shiatsu, acupuncture, and moxibustion. It is for this reason that the meridian charts included here contain extra branches and lines of flow which are not to be found on most modern acupuncture charts (although, interestingly enough, they are often illustrated in the ancient ones). This Love can flow into the meridians no matter how deeply they run within the body. It can also pass through the air or through thick coverings, hence one is not required to have one's hands in direct contact with the body. Occasionally, direct touching may be good when using these mudras, not because the energy cannot otherwise pass effectively, but because it is sometimes important to know that one is loved by man as well as by the Cosmic Buddha, and there is no more effective way of knowing this than to feel the warm touch of a loving hand on your body. Finally, it is not even necessary to use mudras at all; the energy can be directed and tensions in the meridians can be cleansed solely through the power of meditation or contemplative prayer. This, however, is usually possible only after one has meditated and lived the religious life for some time and is beyond the scope of this book.

Since the rightful use of the mudras of harmonization is as a sacramental act of love, it follows that their use cannot become a profession. How could one charge a fee for sharing with another person in the Love of the Lord? How could one set oneself up in the superior position of a professional person who has his "patients" whom he "treats" with his "expertise," when that "expertise" is the sole property of the Cosmic Buddha? A purely professional approach to these mudras is bound to create manipulation and interference in the flow of pure Love, and thus cannot succeed. There can only ever be the shared awe and wonder of two people searching together for the Truth, if the use of these mudras is to remain pure and effective. As Rōshi Jiyu-Kennett said,

> There is an absolute trusting of one's own hands to find the block, to place the hands on a certain place and listen: "Why is there tension here? If it is good, please let me hear." Your hands then act as the instruments that allow you to understand the cause of the tension and allow you to remove it—and allow it to be offered up to the Lord. That is their completely rightful use. But suppose you are very weak or for some other reason feel the need of help in doing this, then another person who approaches you with the attitude of "May I touch That which is of God?" and whom you look at and say, "Yes, I regard you as fully equal in the sight of God and your hands as the Hands of God," can work with you. This can only happen if such a degree of respect is there; it is more than just respect, it is almost worship. Each time you use one of these mudras you must ask, "Is this good? Does it feel good to you? Is it wise that I do this? May I do this?" Unless you can understand that this is the attitude of mind with which you go to do this, you might as well be holding a couple of pork chops, for you certainly will not be doing any good, and you can turn the entire effort into something very sleazy.

This is not to say that a professional health or mental health worker cannot use mudras to assist him in his work; that is an excellent thing to do. In fact, we offer seminars at Shasta Abbey on occasion to teach such professionals how to do precisely this. Even then we suggest that they not learn how to use the mudras by practicing on their patients but rather by using them on themselves and with their loved ones until they know first-hand the degree of love and mutual respect which is necessary. It would be extremely unwise to set oneself up as a professional mudra-doer or for a member of the helping professions to charge extra for the application of this "treatment." When someone comes to us to learn in more detail about the mudras, we do not charge them more than for their room and board and for the time which the officers of the temple have to take away from their normal duties in order to teach them. The assistance of these mudras *must* be freely given in love, mutual respect, and humility before the Buddhas.

We have developed a simple form of blessing which expresses this understanding for use at the beginning of any sequence of mudras when two friends are assisting one another. Both make the reverence mudra (see page 244) and spend a moment in meditation or prayer. Then the one who is about to do the mudra touches the other's forehead briefly at points A, right A1, and left A1. The other person then blesses the first person in the same way. This seems to help set the right frame of mind for the use of the succeeding mudras.

The fact that a powerful stream of love flows between two people when they seek together for the harmonization of body and mind can cause a very intimate and exquisite bond to form between them over the course of time. This bond can at times have aspects of sexual attraction, and there is nothing abnormal or improper in this. The act of assisting one another in harmonization can, for instance, be an act which has the secondary effect of bringing a married couple into closer communion with each other. In other circumstances, should sexual feelings arise towards a person with whom you use these mudras regularly, neither try to push these feelings away nor act upon them. Just regard them as you would anything else which arises while meditating: allow them to arise and to pass on naturally, neither clinging to them nor repressing them. Should sexual desires come about while using a mudra, they will in no way hinder or "defile" the flow of the mudra as long as the desires are simply accepted and not acted upon. Any act of love between two people will sometimes produce sexual arousal; please do not be worried by this and, above all, do not take advantage of this fact to satisfy your selfish desires.

Another occasional effect of the use of these mudras is that a person may become extraordinarily sensitive, rarified, and vulnerable for a while. This sensitivity results from any intensive period of meditation; it is one of the factors which *can* mark the beginnings of a profound religious experience. To the untrained observer, however, it can also look somewhat like an incipient mental breakdown. A person may become so aware of the condition of all the things around him and so empathically linked to them that he feels the pain when a flower is picked or suffers the strain placed on a spring. At such times one may require a temporary abeyance of the normal duties of job and family, an atmosphere of quiet simplicity, and a social life that is reduced to the companionship of one or two trusted friends. Unlike a mental illness, however, there is no confusion or disturbance of the thought processes; there is a bright stillness, even when there is considerable fear. Although this degree of sensitivity is rare and is usually part of a major breakthrough in religious understanding, it can occur to lesser degrees as a partial result of regular use of the harmonization mudras. It is not a cause for worry and should be allowed to take place unhindered. If there is any question about this, a competent teacher of meditation who is familiar with this process should be consulted. In time the ability to deal with everyday matters will return in full, and with it a greater strength, efficiency, and wisdom than one had previously known.

In the case of someone whose doctor has recommended the use of these mudras as an adjunct to the treatment of a serious illness, a variant of this process may take place in which all of the person's vital energy retreats inside him in order to heal the damage, leaving virtually nothing left for any external activity. It may appear that the person is getting considerably weaker and his condition is therefore deteriorating. In time, however, the energy returns to the surface and not only is the person able to resume his or her normal activities, but also the diseased areas may be greatly improved. It is not necessarily easy to distinguish between this phenomenon and a genuine deterioration due to the downward course of an illness. This is another reason why it is imperative to work together with your physician if you are doing these mudras while ill. If your energy is going deeply within you to heal you, the doctor's instruments will usually detect no significant deterioration in the fundamental condition which you are both working to improve. This retreat of the energy from the surface to deep within you can be a crucial step in the course of the illness, and the demands for rest, quiet, and peace which the body may make at such a time should be respected absolutely if further healing is to occur.

Finally, it is necessary to state the obvious fact that if two people are using the mudras of harmonization together, they must both put in the effort required to do the mudras in the mind of meditation and with absolute love and respect. The person on whom the mudra is done must receive it in this mind and be willing to direct his concentration to follow important clues which may arise. He or she must also be willing to face whatever may arise in his body and mind, accept it, and embrace it with love and with the faith that at the origin of every desire and act, no matter how bizarre or destructive, there is something pure and undefiled. Unless he or she is willing to do this, the other person doing the mudra with him or her may expend needlessly a tremendous amount of energy and become drained, exhausted, and possibly rendered more susceptible to illness and disharmony.[46] Remember, the flow of love does not come personally from the person doing these mudras with you nor is he or she healing you or otherwise doing anything *to* you. If you and he are not seeking together to find the Truth, helping each other as best each can in the situation in which you now find yourselves, then nothing will result from the use of the mudras except possibly the exhaustion of one or both of you. When you both are in the mind of meditation, it is the Cosmic Buddha Whose Love does whatever is to be done, and That is a Source which can *never* be drained.

CHAPTER IV.

KARMIC MEMORIES OF PAST LIVES.

When a person has been in religious training for some years and has begun to learn how to cease from producing further karma by conquering his cravings, attachments, and passions (for which the Sanskrit word is *klessa*), and when, through meditation, reflection, and the harmonizing of body and mind, he has understood and accepted the events of this lifetime which led to the building of his egotistical self, then there may arise certain delusive proclivities, desires, or other spiritual, mental, or physical tensions which seem to lack a basis in the events of this lifetime. Upon further meditation, and especially at or near the time of the experience of full kenshō which breaks through the old patterns of thought and perception, these remaining hindrances to training are seen to be the residual effects (impregnations, or "perfumes," for which the Sanskrit word is *vassana*) of the karma of past lives. When the time seems good for recognizing, accepting, and clearing away these residuals, the harmonizing mudras may again be used as adjuncts to Zazen.

This use of the mudras will result in more subtle, yet far-reaching, effects than those discussed previously and requires considerably greater experience in meditation on the part of those involved in the process. When the karmic traces, or *klessa vassana,* appear, it is usual to visit the temple or monastery of one's Master and seek his or her advice and assistance. *This is the best way and should be followed when-ever possible.* In this country of few priests and great distances, however, the sometimes sudden appearance of these karmic memories may require that a few trusted friends, with whom one has meditated and shared one's religious training, be called upon instead. In many cases, they can be of real assistance provided that they are pure of heart and approach the task as suggested below with both faith and love.

Appearance of the Vassana.

Except in unusual and particularly pressing cases, the vassana do not appear in a recognizable form until after several years of serious meditation or perhaps after the first kenshō. The person may then, either in dreams or while awake, begin to have intimations of a past life or lives through visual images, sounds, tastes, smells, bodily sensations, emotional states, or intuitive awareness. These occurrences differ from *makyo* (obstructing illusions which can arise in meditation as a result of incorrect posture, breathing, or other stress) in several ways. Makyo generally occur to the inexperienced meditator and are transitory and ephemeral phenomena which disappear as soon as the posture or breathing is returned to normal. The vassana usually appear to an experienced meditator and become more coherent and clear with time. Unlike makyo which disappear unless one clings to them, the vassana become stronger the more one meditates with non-attachment, and they tend to appear at other times than when one is engaged in formal Zazen. The most important difference is that makyo will create a false sense of importance or spiritual accomplishment in one who becomes attached to them, whereas the vassana can leave but one impression: there is much more to be done in one's training and there is something unquiet that urgently yearns to be set to rest.

At first there may be no apparent connection between the arising of the vassana and the state of religious training in which the person currently finds himself. The person at this point should continue in his Zazen until these perceptions fade away, having been cleansed by Zazen, or until he spontaneously starts to vividly reexperience some event in a past life and his own Heart (or religious intuition) says that the time is right to explore the crucial events of that life. At this point one should remember that the karma generated by events in the lives of previous beings can condition our own proclivities in this life. Thus the appearance of the vassana is an excellent opportunity to understand more clearly the Second Noble Truth of Buddhism: the cause of suffering is attachment. By seeing the attachment which long ago started a karmic stream that has remained unquiet to this day, one has not only the opportunity to set it to rest for oneself and all those previous beings which it affected, but also the chance to understand the attachment which caused it and which could therefore cause one to create similar karma in this life if one is not aware. Therefore, although the appearance of the vassana may be somewhat unpleasant or disturbing, bear in mind that this is an unexcelled opportunity for religious training.

There is no point in trying to force oneself to relive these experiences prematurely and there is an intuitive sense within oneself when they are ripe for being accepted. This state of ripeness is frequently characterized by the sensations being so insistent upon one's mind that they occupy one's consciousness almost continually. If the mind is not ready to understand and assimilate the vassana, it is not possible to learn from them fully nor to set the karma completely to rest. It is for this reason that I oppose hypnotic regression techniques and "past-life therapies" which bring these memories to consciousness before they appear naturally. Memories of past lives are too valuable to religious training to be wasted by forcing them upon a mind which is not absolutely ready to learn from them and to accept them with compassion. As only the person himself and the Buddhas can know when the mind is in this state, the decision as to when memories of past lives should occur is best left to them!

When the time is right, the harmonizing mudras can be used to relax the tensions arising from these karmic memories and thus enable the person to more fully reexperience the important aspects of the events, see through the delusions or pain which beclouded the understanding of the being which experienced them the first time, find compassion for all those involved, and see the pattern which originated in that event and continues into the present life. This is the seeing of suffering's cause: the source of the kōan. Although this reliving can be done alone and without the use of any harmonizing mudras, it is safer, quicker, and generally less painful to have assistance. One should have several well-trusted fellow trainees at hand, at least one of whom is capable of using the harmonizing mudras for this purpose.

Preparation.

The person should relax on a comfortable bed or sofa, loosen any restricting garments, remove eyeglasses, false teeth, and other objects which could cause harm if he or she were to thrash about in the course of experiencing the karmic memory. The room should be secluded so that the person need not fear should he feel the necessity to shout, moan, or even scream if a particularly painful experience is re-lived. Every effort should be made to assure that there will be no interruptions. Among the few trusted fellow trainees present, it is best to have at least one person who is experienced in doing harmonizing mudras, one person whose meditation is sufficiently developed that he or she may intuitively follow the events which the person may experience in order to help the person keep his perspective on what he sees and feels, one person to remain free to get any other person, piece of scripture, or object which may be requested and, most importantly, either the person's Master or some other highly trusted and spiritually mature individual who can help keep up the person's will and faith and who can otherwise minister to his or her spiritual needs. This is the ideal situation, but it is difficult to find outside a large religious training center. When necessary, any of the few trusted friends who are called upon to assist may be asked to fill these roles as best they can.

Prior to beginning the mudras, the person should remember that he must concentrate his mind entirely on experiencing completely any event or sensation of which he may become aware and which intuitively feels important. He must enter into it absolutely and not turn away, no matter how painful or difficult it may become. At this same time he should keep in mind throughout that the experience he sees, feels or knows is *not him; he* is not personally responsible for the events he experiences, rather he has been willing to take on this karmic vassana in order to cleanse it and thereby put it to rest. It is vital that the person do both of these things. If he turns away at a crucial moment he may lose this opportunity to deal with the karmic residue. Worse yet, the residue of the mental or physical pain which the original being felt may be so intense that, if it is not experienced and embraced by the person who, by his very existence in this life, agreed to love and accept it, it may, as it were, "reach out" to one or more of the other people present and cause them to experience it instead. This can be very exhausting to the other person, and is ultimately not a satisfactory solution. Conversely, if the person forgets that he is *not identical* with the being whose life he is reexperiencing, he may become so horrified by what this being did that he believes that *he* has no right to continue living in *this* life. For these reasons the person who is offering spiritual guidance during the re-living may need to quietly but firmly remind the person either to love, accept, and convert the karmic residue or to remember that, *"You are not him."* This person and the person doing the harmonizing mudras should *both* satisfy themselves that the person who wishes to clear the vassana understands these points, and agrees both to enter into the experiences as fully as he can and not to give up or die no matter what he finds out.

Selecting and Applying the Harmonizing Mudras.

The mudras to be used depend in part upon the crucial events which are being re-lived. Usually a past life leaves a strong karmic memory when either the former being created extensive negative karma by its wrong actions and/or when it died a violent, rejected, or otherwise disturbed death. It is usually these wrong actions and/or traumatic death which must be reexperienced. Sometimes the person or his religious friends will know ahead of time some aspects of the nature of the problem, and mudras may be selected from the appropriate table in Appendix A, understanding that these tables are applicable only in general, and the spiritual intuition of those involved should be respected absolutely. These tables may also be of use during the reexperiencing to select mudras to help keep the person relaxed once some details of the karmic memory appear.

It is of vital importance that the mind of each person concerned be one of absolute humility, respect, and love; this has been described in detail in the previous chapter. After each person is satisfied that it is good to proceed and the person using the mudras has agreed with his friend where to begin, the process may commence. The mudras generally should be done slowly and with utmost concentration in order to give maximum assistance. The person may or may not wish to discuss what he is experiencing and should not be pressured to do so. It is often helpful, however, both to himself and to those in assistance if he can let them know what is going on.

If the person reexperiences some aspect of either this life or a previous one, then, once the first mudra is completed, others may be used depending upon the intuition of the person who is being assisted. He or she may know exactly what is required next and his or her wishes should be absolutely respected. If the person is not certain what is required, he may at least be able to indicate a part of the body which is particularly salient to the experience or describe some aspect of that experience or his current reactions to it. These should give those in assistance indications as to how to proceed.

Should none of this be possible and yet the individual still feels that something further should be done, one of the friends who is experienced in meditation may pass his or her *left* hand slowly over the body of the person at a height of about four inches above the body surface. This friend should concentrate his attention on the temperature of the person's body as perceived by his left hand and place himself in the service of the Lord to notice any major areas of unusual heat or cold. If it is good, he may find such areas, usually of increased heat, and these may indicate areas where the flow of the person's energies is in some way disturbed. This may then suggest a mudra or sequence of mudras which could be helpful to relax this tension. Incidentally, it is usual, at least in young and middle-aged adults, to find such a warm area over the genitals. This does not necessarily indicate that this area is of particular significance in the cleaning of the klessa vassana. The fact that most adults have a noticeable temperature difference in this area may be used by an inexperienced assistant to learn to identify the type of temperature gradient for which he is searching.

Another approach, should this procedure reveal nothing of use, is to try the discovery mudras or one of the other mudras listed as having a discovery property in the tables in Appendix A. These are mudras which tend to relax the type of tensions which prevent us from becoming aware of things. The mudras themselves do not "discover" anything; they merely tend to reduce the tensions which keep one from meditating deeply enough to be aware of these things. Unless a person is willing to meditate with energy and courage, these mudras will do nothing. Should none of these mudras be of use in helping to continue the process, it may be best to cease the effort until the person has had more time to meditate and inwardly "ripen" himself.

If this course of action also seems somehow not right, then an experienced priest should be consulted by telephone. Above all, a person should not force himself to continue if it does not seem wise to do so or if he cannot seem to gain any further benefit from it. In the latter case he should simply continue his normal meditation and daily training in the faith that the vassana will be cleansed at whatever time and in whatever way is best. There must *never* be any attempt to force this process or induce it artificially through suggestion, hypnosis, drugs, or other manipulative means. Unless one forces oneself by such means, one can rely on the fact that nothing will arise which one cannot accept and learn from successfully. The harmonization mudras suggested here do *not* induce the process; they merely assist an already ongoing experience to be a little more comfortable and easier to accept by relaxing the body and mind.

Should it happen that during the first few mudras a person does not reexperience any aspect of his or her vassana or anything of significance from this lifetime, the procedures described in the previous paragraphs may be applied to assist him, provided the same warnings are heeded.

In Case of Difficulty.

As long as the cautions given above are kept in mind, there should be no major difficulties. Serious problems result only when not everyone present is a trusted friend, when someone ceases to maintain a meditative frame of mind (or, worse, tries to manipulate or force another person), when a person either forgets that what he experiences is *not him* or, conversely, refuses to accept and enter into the experience positively, or when someone forgets to listen with humility to the Lord within and follows his own ideas and opinions as to what to do. Should any of these events take place, they must be immediately corrected in the most gentle and loving manner possible or the process must be stopped. It is extremely unlikely that a person will adamantly refuse to believe that what he is experiencing is *not him*, but should someone become stuck with that idea, it is imperative that a qualified priest be consulted immediately because the person *can* make grave mistakes if he or she begins to act on that notion.

Barring these serious problems, the most usual difficulties are either that nothing much happens or that someone becomes fearful when the experience becomes all too real. Should the latter occur, it is necessary for everyone else to remain in meditation and urge the person to place complete faith in the Cosmic Buddha. He also should be reminded that his friends are with him and will under no circumstance abandon him or permit harm to come to him or to anyone else. If he is still fearful the process should be terminated as there is no value in continuing if fear is stronger than faith. It is also possible that the karmic memory of which the person is beginning to become aware would be too painful for him to face at the moment. There are some things which cannot be safely accepted and embraced until a person has very strong faith (or even a *certainty* derived from profound personal religious experience) and a priest of his religion with considerable experience in these matters is present. It is for this reason that priests in our Church are not permitted to assist anyone in cleansing the klessa vassana until they have had a number of years of experience and are fully qualified teachers of Buddhism in their own right. This is also the reason why no one who is *not* so qualified should ever attempt to persuade someone to continue with this process when his or her faith is weak or they become fearful. When the process of experiencing a past life is terminated for these reasons, a relaxing mudra may be done to help relieve the anxiety and a rest under a warm quilt and/or a warm shower can be useful. The person should then simply continue with his regular meditation and daily practice until he or she can consult a qualified priest.

Although difficulties are unlikely if everyone involved in the cleansing of the klessa vassana enters into it with a pure heart and with the willingness to embrace and love whatever is found and offer it up to the Source, the problems mentioned here are a possibility and this fact should be recognized. For this reason it is not advisable for someone who is mentally sensitive or unstable to undertake this process without the advice of a therapist. It is also highly recommended to have a fully qualified priest in attendance or, failing that, to contact one by telephone for consultation before commencing.

Learning from Karmic Memories.

Karmic memories, whether of past lives or of this life, arise when they are of use in our daily training. Therefore, there is always a clue to be found in any such experience which points to a way to deepen our present level of religious practice. To simply re-live past events without learning from them is to waste an invaluable lesson in the Dharma.

The fundamental purpose of the arising of karmic memories is to show us the cause of suffering and bring to life the Four Noble Truths of Buddhism. These Truths are the result of the Buddha's Enlightenment and are: the Truth of the existence of impermanence and suffering, the Truth of the cause of this suffering in attachment, the Truth of the cessation of suffering in Enlightenment through non-attachment, and the Truth of the Eightfold Path which leads to the cessation of suffering and shows us how to continue to cease from attachment and the production of karma after the experience of Enlightenment. These Truths are the Buddha's solution to His own kōan of the reason for the existence of birth, old age, disease, and death, and are That as to which He was Enlightened.

The experience of the night of His Enlightenment had three aspects according to Buddhist scriptures.[47] In the first hours of the night His meditation revealed His past lives, thus showing Him the cause of suffering in attachments. In the middle hours His meditation showed to Him the cycle of death and rebirth of all beings, thus enabling Him to understand the Truth of impermanence and suffering and the reasons for His kōan of birth, old age, disease, and death. In the final hours of the night He developed understanding of the cessation of suffering and the Way of attaining and maintaining it. At this point He attained to Full Enlightenment and saw all things as they really are. Thus the seeing of past lives was an integral part of the Buddha's own Enlightenment and is the opportunity *par excellence* to understand the nature of attachment and the cause of suffering. The seeing of past lives is not a prerequisite for having a kenshō or enlightenment experience. It is, however, the natural way in which the Buddhas teach the trainee the cause of suffering and how to avoid the clouding of his realization which would result from repeating the same mistakes that started the chain of suffering long ago. Therefore if you ask a Zen Master if it is necessary that you see your past lives, he will say "No," and he will probably tell you to stop thinking about such things and go back to your meditation, and he will be right. On the other hand, should such things arise *naturally*, do not automatically dismiss them as makyo; they might just be an incredible opportunity to deepen your understanding of the cause of suffering and the Way to Enlightenment.

The second fundamental purpose of the karmic memories is to allow us to deepen our compassion and empathy by embracing and putting to rest an unquiet residue of past karma. I believe that each of us who is born human brings with us some such residue out of our inherent compassion.

To convert it and embrace it, whether through training in daily life, through pure Zazen, or by actively reexperiencing it and setting it to rest, is thus to fulfill one of our purposes for living and is a Bodhisattva act. I believe that one of the basic religious purposes for our lives is the purification of such residues, which brings peace not only to ourselves but to the world.

A karmic residue which is with us at birth conditions our personality (it is sometimes even remembered directly by young children in whom the memory trace is relatively strong compared to the environmental factors which will later shape the personality). As such, it produces the tendency discussed above for us to in some way repeat the mistake someone else made years before our birth or, in attempting to avoid it, to make an equal and opposite error. When we have converted this proclivity and transcended it in this life, the task is largely completed and, if necessary, the karmic residue comes into direct conscious awareness so that the last trace of it can be embraced and laid to rest. When this is fully accomplished, one of the principal purposes of our lives has come to an end. One then finds oneself at a spiritual crossroads, and a new purpose for living must emerge. This purpose is ours alone, and there is often a feeling of lightness and newness, as if a burden had been set down or an old skin shed and a newborn creature emerged. At this time it is well to remember the four vows of the Bodhisattva,[48] for if the purpose for living is not a worthy one, the weight of karma will soon accumulate again. One must also remain ever vigilant lest one slip back into old patterns of behavior which will tend to produce suffering. Although these patterns have been broken and the cause of suffering seen, you cannot be in this lifetime as if they had never existed, and they can still act upon you. In this regard, pay particular attention to the past life you have experienced which is most remote in time from the present. In the traces of that existence you will find the cause of suffering in its most subtle and yet powerful form. It is that attachment which you are most likely to repeat in this lifetime unless you keep up your meditation and training. The pattern I have outlined thus far is the usual one when karmic memories appear shortly after an experience of enlightenment and it is their highest purpose. Karmic memories can also come forth before we have converted their associated tendencies in this lifetime. Then they serve to help us to convert them by pointing out some aspect of those tendencies of which we were previously unaware. Thus it is important to look carefully for the connection between what we have re-lived and the state of our present life. This is especially true if more than one past life is experienced within a few months. The karma of the past is shown to us by the mercy of the Buddhas and Bodhisattvas to help us in our training so as not to make the same (or opposite) mistake again. Look carefully for the common elements in such a sequence of past lives, and compare them to this life. Somewhere a connection is to be found, and once it has been discovered and taken to heart, a major step forward in religious training has been taken and it is likely that no further karmic memories will arise for a while. This is one of the most direct and profound ways in which the Buddhas and Bodhisattvas teach us how to draw closer to the Truth, and it is an opportunity not to be discarded.

There can be other reasons for the arising of karmic memories, but they occur less frequently. I have occasionally seen such memories arise in someone for whom the karmic residues are extraordinarily strong and are causing a great deal of suffering in terms of physical illness or mental torment. In this case the reexperiencing of the usually traumatic past events and their acceptance both by the person himself, by a priest (who can assure him that the Cosmic Buddha does not turn away from him in this), and by a friend (who represents mankind which also must be seen to love and not to turn away) can bring a great measure of peace to the person and sometimes have profound effects upon his or her physical and mental condition. Having the burden thus eased, the person can then go about the business of Zazen and daily life and eventually convert the tendencies which that karmic residue has imparted in his or her personal constitution. Situations of this kind can be dangerous to approach without the assistance of a qualified priest in conjunction with medical and/or psychological treatment. In cases such as this it is imperative to remember that the presently living person is *not responsible* for the acts of the previous beings whose residue he or she has acquired. I have nothing but the deepest respect and gratitude for such a person; after all, when entering this life he or she had the compassion and courage to attempt to deal with a heavier karmic burden than most of us were willing to shoulder.

It follows from the purposes for which karmic memories arise that they are not to be taken lightly or frivolously. Memories of a past life (at least in the case of adults) rarely reveal the name of the previous person or any highly identifying features of the previous life because they are simply not relevant to the spiritual purpose for which the memory comes forth. To become fascinated with such trivia, especially with the attitude of, "Guess who *I* was in a previous incarnation!" is worse than useless. It can soon deteriorate into identification with the past life and deliberate attempts to repeat the patterns of the past. People have gone so far as to believe it to be their destiny to "take up where I left off last time." This entire approach is a complete misunderstanding of the nature of karma, rebirth, the self, and religious training. It opens the door to belief in all manner of fantasies produced in the service of the selfish self and to histrionics, self-aggrandizement, and delusion. It is a perversion of Buddhism and inevitably leads to selfishness, pain, and confusion. *DO NOT DO IT!*

CHAPTER V.

CHOOSING A MUDRA.

There is no formula which can be given for deciding which mudra to use; it is inherently an intuitive process and one which can only be learned by meditation and practice. This chapter is therefore simply a rough guideline to use in learning how to sense which might be the best mudra for you in a given situation.

I usually begin choosing a mudra by gathering information. I start with the main tension for which I desire the assistance of a mudra. I then find the mudras which are known to be of potential value for this tension. I examine what else is going on at the same time. What unusual conditions are there in my body? What is my mental and emotional condition? What is the state of my religious training, its current weaknesses and strengths? Are there intimations of karmic memories of any sort? At what hour is this tension most salient? Do I have a craving or aversion for particular foods? Each of these questions may point to several possible mudras, and there will usually be one or two mudras which are suggested by the answers to a number of these questions. Considering these mudras to be most likely, I then sit quietly for a moment in meditation and let the question "Is it good to use a mudra now?" reside in my mind. I do not try to rationally arrive at an answer to this; an answer comes spontaneously after a while simply by allowing the question to be present in the mind of meditation. If the answer is yes, I then ask in the same manner if one of the mudras I have selected is indeed the best one to do. Again I simply meditate after having asked the question in my mind, and in time an answer comes from deep within. I then do the mudra, or mudras, which have come to mind as most likely to be beneficial.

In order to help with the initial part of this process I have prepared the series of tables to be found in Appendix A. Each lists commonly encountered tension areas or other useful information and suggests some of the mudras which might be applicable. Once a set of mudras has been selected on the basis of these tables, I would suggest looking at the meridian chart and descriptive information for each of them in order to get a more complete understanding of the different actions of each. Then I would settle down in meditation to find out which seem to really be best.

Should there be a problem arriving at an answer by the above process, or should you wish additional information, there are two other tools at your disposal. The first is heat sensing. As described earlier, you may pass your *left* hand over your body (or that of a friend) at a height of several inches above the body surface and attempt to feel places which are unusually warm (or, occasionally, unusually cold). Since most adults have a warmer region above the genitals you can use this to calibrate the sensitivity of your hand. The presence of a hot spot (other than over the genitals) usually denotes tension and a blocked or impeded meridian. Look up the location of the place or places of temperature change in the physical information table and see what mudras may be suggested.

The second procedure is one well known to acupuncture and acupressure practitioners: pulse reading. A thorough discussion of this can be found in many sources[49] and therefore need not be repeated here. Suffice it to say that there are twelve pulses, similar to the ones you can feel at all of the mudra points, located on the inside of the wrist which provide information about the state of the twelve main organ meridians. There are three pulse positions on each wrist and each position provides information in two ways. These positions are illustrated on the following diagram:

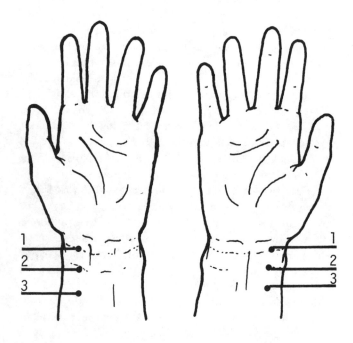

To feel the pulses on your right wrist place your left index, middle, and ring fingers respectively on points one, two, and three on the diagram. First feel the pulses under light pressure, such as you would use when holding any mudra point. Then bear down hard with your fingers and feel the pulses again, this time under heavy pressure. A similar set of three points can be felt in your left wrist by using the index, middle, and ring fingers of your right hand. Again, feel the pulses under both light and heavy pressure. You can find these pulses on a friend in the same way; just place the fingers of your right hand on the pulse positions of his or her left wrist and then the fingers of your left hand on the pulse positions of his or her right wrist. The pulses correspond to the twelve main organ meridians according to the following chart:

Point	LEFT WRIST		RIGHT WRIST	
	Light Pressure	Heavy Pressure	Light Pressure	Heavy Pressure
1	Sm. Intestine	Heart	Lrg. Intestine	Lung
2	Gall Bladder	Liver	Stomach	Spleen
3	Bladder	Kidney	Triple Warmer	Pericardium

Where one of the pulses feels different from the others (weaker, stronger, faster, slower, irregular, etc.) it indicates that the corresponding meridian is in some way tense. Should you find that all of the pulses in one wrist are unusual, it may mean that this side of the body is under more tension than is the other side. In this case it may be useful to perform whatever mudra you select on that side. It occasionally happens that a mudra used on one side of the body will actually have its effect on the opposite side. Thus if the mudra you select does not have much effect you might try using the same mudra on the opposite side of the body.

Pulse reading can be quite valuable but it takes time and practice to learn. If you wish to do this I would suggest either attending a seminar where this skill is taught or practicing pulse reading with a group of friends. When you and your friends all agree as to which pulses are unusual on a given person at a given time, you have probably learned to read them accurately. I have found that people can reach such agreement but, when you ask them to say in what way a pulse is different from the other pulses, one person will tell you that it felt faster, another will say that it was slower, and a third will report that it was stronger than the others. This is not a problem; as long as you can agree on which ones are unusual you have probably found the right pulses. This concludes all of the information which I can impart on how to choose a mudra. The rest can only be done by practice.

Once you have chosen a mudra or mudras and put them to use you should note carefully the results. Sometimes one application of one mudra will be sufficient assistance for a tension, but often it is not. In this case it is necessary to use the additional information you gain from having done the previous mudra in order to choose the succeeding ones. There is no rush in this; it is sometimes wise to wait for several days before doing the next mudra or set of mudras. This depends entirely on your intuition of what would be helpful. When you are ready to use another mudra, assess the situation again as suggested in this chapter and decide on the next mudra. This process may need to be repeated several times over the course of weeks or months as a continuing piece of self detective work. An example of this was given in Chapter II. It can be very valuable in doing this work to keep a private notebook in which you write down any "clue" that you can find, whether it be dreams, instances when you've lost your temper (and what brought it about), the weather, cravings for food, stray aches and pains, when the tension you are working on becomes worse or better, what Precepts you are having trouble with—anything which could possibly be of use. Keep this notebook completely private and look at it from time to time to see what patterns you can discern.

Above all keep going, continue your meditation, and train yourself every minute of the day. In this way you will come to find the ever-deepening freedom of Zen and know the harmonization of body and mind.

CHAPTER VI.

THE MUDRAS OF HARMONIZATION.

The effects of the use of any mudra will depend upon many variables including the state of health, frame of mind, past history, state of meditation, and way of life of the person using it. Therefore the lists of uses and possible effects given for mudras in this chapter, which are derived both from our own experience and from the classic literature of the anma arts, cannot be exhaustive or all-inclusive. It is possible that you will experience effects which are not listed for a given mudra or paradoxical effects which are opposite to the ones set forth here (this was discussed in Chapter II).

These mudras are designed for use by healthy and mentally mature individuals who wish to enhance their religious development through the harmonization of body and mind. They are not intended as medical or psychological treatments and should not be used as such unless recommended as adjuncts to therapy by a physician or psychologist. Professionals making such a recommendation should consider the adjunct use of these mudras as experimental, since neither controlled studies of their efficacy nor physiological research into their modes of action have been conducted (work in these areas is currently being done). The tables of physical and mental uses given for each mudra are not suitable for diagnosing physical or mental illness and should not be used for such a purpose. Remember also that there may be other causes for pain, stiffness, or unusual sensations of body or mind besides tension. In view of this, the reader is advised to consult a physician before using mudras during illness or pregnancy.

Please bear the above considerations in mind before deciding to use a mudra. If you do not misuse them, these mudras can make a significant contribution to your spiritual life.

MUDRA POINTS

Before presenting the mudras themselves it is necessary to indicate the precise locations of the mudra points. The following ten pages of point charts should enable you to find all of the points used in the mudras given in this chapter. Please study them carefully and refer to them whenever there is a question as to the location of a particular point.

Most points can be located either in relation to the skeletal structure or the configuration of the body surface. Some points, however, must be located solely by their position relative to the skeleton, and these are indicated by parentheses around their label on the point charts. The point designated as "(C5)" is an exception; it is located at the nipple on most men, but must be found by its relation to the rib cage on women.

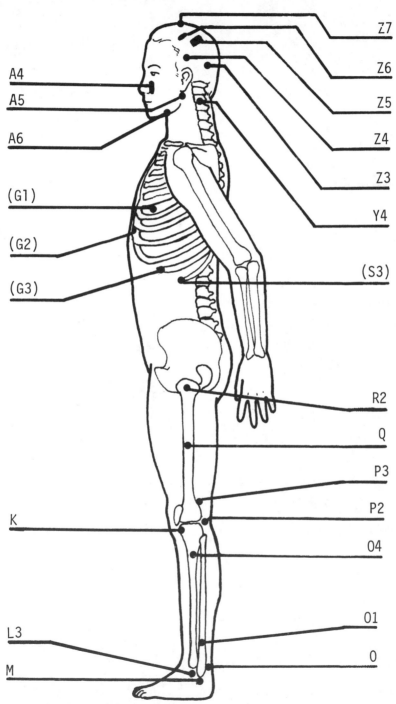

Z7

Z6

A4

A5

Z5

A6

Z4

Z3

(G1)

Y4

(G2)

(G3)

(S3)

R2

Q

P3

P2

K

O4

O1

L3

O

M

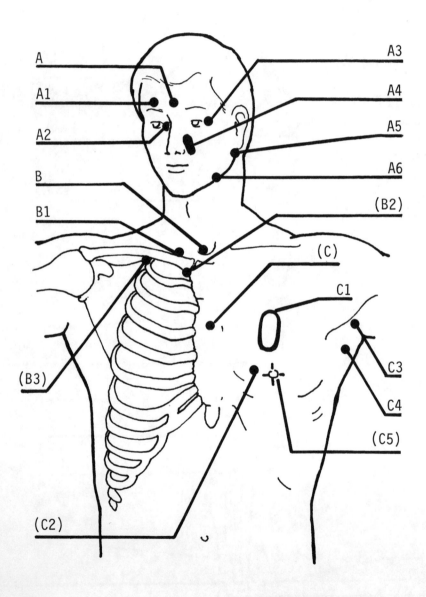

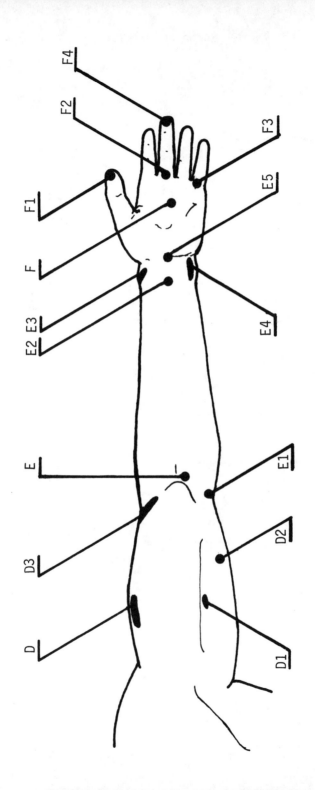

MUDRA POINTS D-F

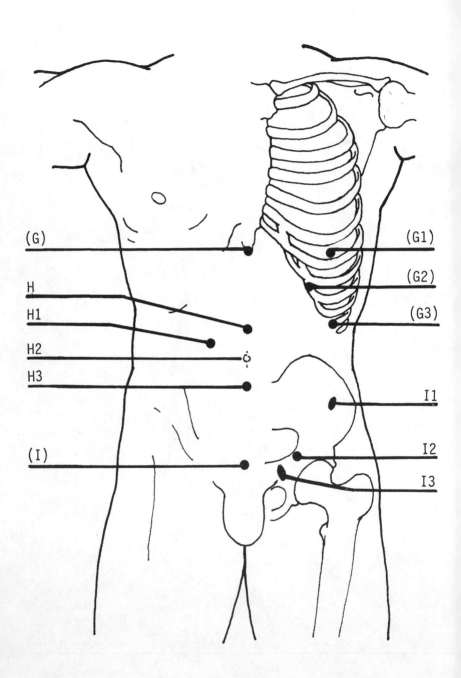

(G)   (G1)

H   (G2)

H1   (G3)

H2

H3   I1

(I)   I2

                I3

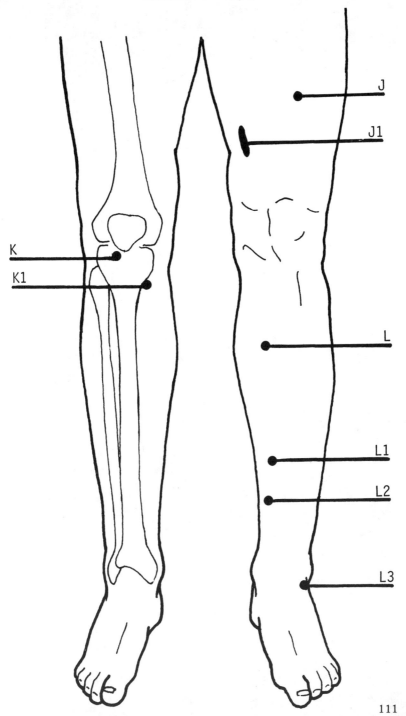

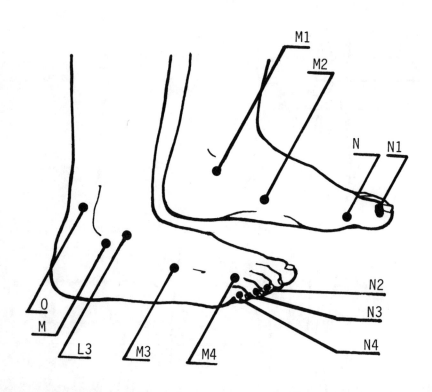

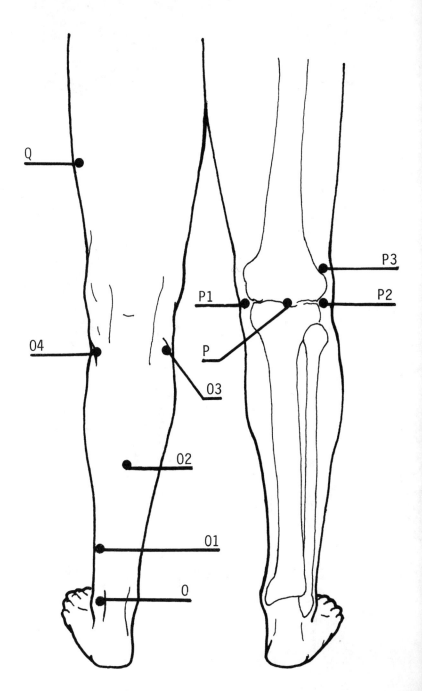

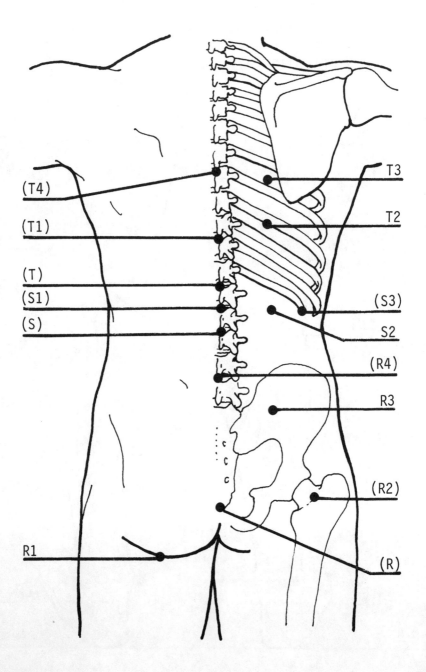

(T4)
(T1)
(T)
(S1)
(S)
R1

T3
T2
(S3)
S2
(R4)
R3
(R2)
(R)

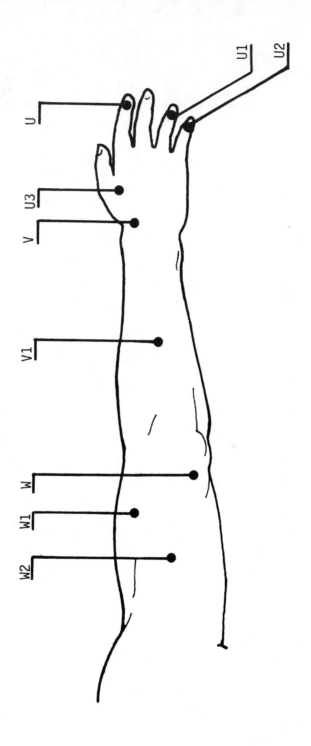

MUDRA POINTS U-W

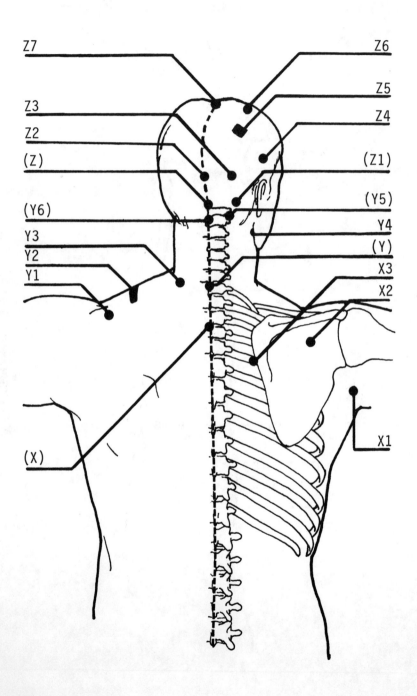

ABDOMINAL TENSION MUDRA

LEFT MUDRA

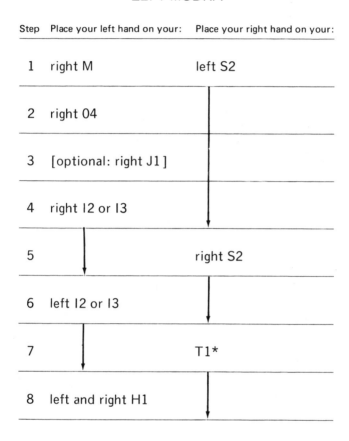

Step	Place your left hand on your:	Place your right hand on your:
1	right M	left S2
2	right 04	
3	[optional: right J1]	
4	right I2 or I3	
5		right S2
6	left I2 or I3	
7		T1*
8	left and right H1	

RIGHT MUDRA

Step	Place your left hand on your:	Place your right hand on your:
1	left M	right S2
2	left 04	
3	[optional: left J1]	
4	left I2 or I3	
5		left S2
6	right I2 or I3	
7		T1*
8	left and right H1	

TO ASSIST A FRIEND

Sit on her or his left side and place your hands as you would on yourself.

TIME

The flow of energy illustrated for this mudra is temporarily produced by its use.

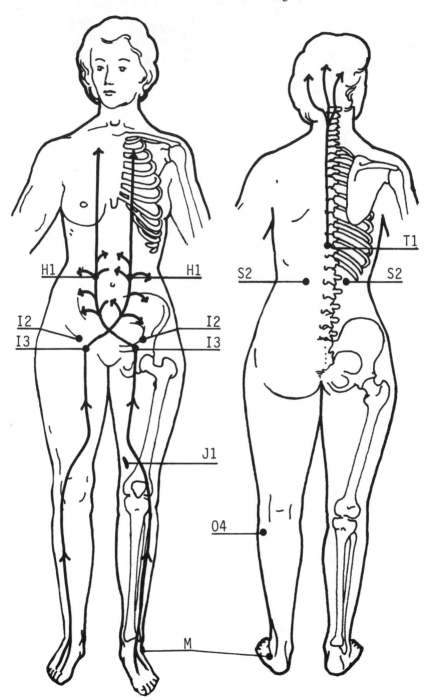

USES

The abdominal tension mudra was created to assist with tension centered in the abdominal and pubic areas, and this is its primary function. It appears to be connected with the stomach, liver, spleen and kidney meridians and may be of use when tensions exist in those meridians, especially near their intersections in the pubic and abdominal areas. The mudra may also be of use for tension in the forms of:

Physical: tension, pain, stiffness, etc. in the areas through which the flow of energy of this mudra passes; tension in the digestive system.

Karmic: karmic memories of having suffered or caused harm, in this or a previous life, by means of wounds along the pathway illustrated for this mudra, especially in the abdominal and pubic areas.

MUDRA ORIGIN

This mudra was adapted from a release of Jin Shin Dō.

BALANCING MUDRA

MUDRA

Rest your right arm in a comfortable position and touch your right thumb to the tip of your right middle finger. Place your left thumb on your right D (or between D and D1), with the other fingers of the left hand beneath your right arm. It sometimes may be necessary to use firm pressure with your left thumb in using this mudra. A variant of this mudra is done by placing the left hand on the right shoulder with the fingers touching points right Y1 and/or Y2 and pressing the right thumb on the left D (or between D and D1), with the remaining right fingers under the left arm.

TO ASSIST A FRIEND

You may place your left hand on her or his right D (or between D and D1) while she or he brings the right thumb and index finger together. This is particularly helpful if pressure seems needed on the D point and a person finds it difficult to maintain this pressure herself. Alternatively, you may sit on the person's right side and hold her or his right thumb and index finger with your right hand as well as touching the right D with your left hand.

TIME

The pattern of energy flow illustrated for this mudra is induced temporarily by its use.

USES

Of the mudras which have a primarily physical and mental rather than a spiritual use, this is the one most frequently seen to be used by Zen monks. It is easy to use while seated as well as lying down, simple to remember, and effective for a wide range of uses. Its primary property is one of relaxation, and it appears to act via the heart, liver, lung, large intestine, and pericardium meridians. Specifically, it may be of help in accepting, relaxing, cleansing away and/or discovering the causes of tensions which arise in meditation or daily life in the forms of:

Physical: tension, pain, stiffness, etc. along the lines of energy flow illustrated for this mudra; general physical tension; tensions in digestion, breathing, or circulation.

Mental: insomnia; tension or worry following demanding or stressful situations.

Karmic: karmic memories of suffering or causing harm, in this or a previous life, by means of wounds along the lines of flow of this mudra or in the heart, lungs, or intestines.

MUDRA ORIGIN

The mudra is routinely used by Zen monks in the Orient.

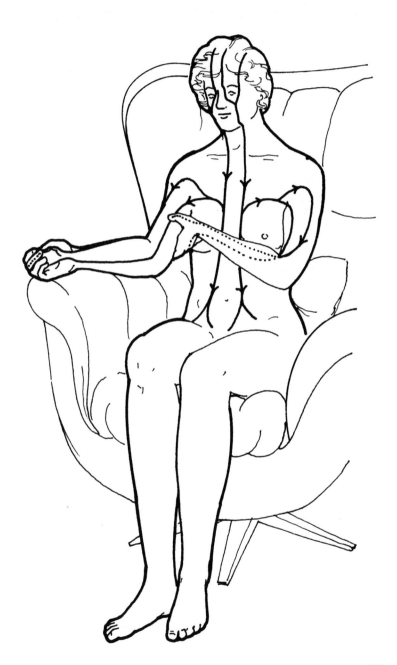

CLEANSING-STAGNATION MUDRA

Affects the Large Intestine Meridian

LEFT MUDRA

Step	Place your left hand on your:	Place your right hand on your:
1	touch left thumb to left U	left X1
2		left Y1
3	left X1*	
4		Y
5		Y6
6		left A6
7		right A4
8		right A1 and A3
9		[optional: left H1]

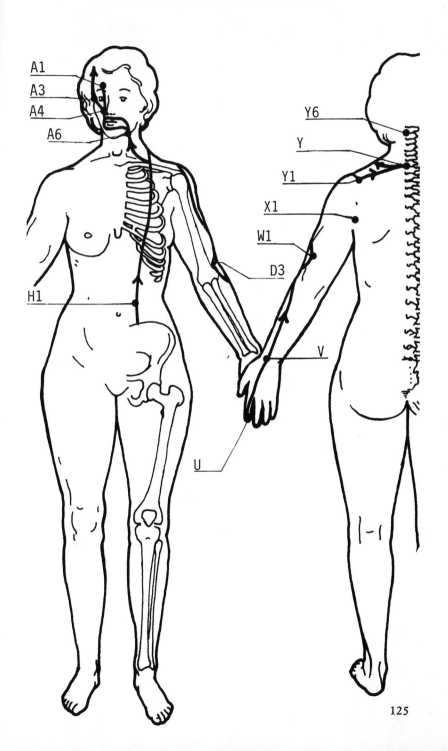

RIGHT MUDRA

Step	Place your left hand on your:	Place your right hand on your:
1	right U	right X1* *or* Y1
2	right V	
3	right D3	
4		right Y1
5	right W1	
6	right X1	
7		Y
8		Y6
9		right A6
10		left A4
11		left A1 and A3
12		[optional: right H1]

TO ASSIST A FRIEND

For the left mudra, sit on her or his left side and use the chart below; for the right mudra, sit on her or his right side and place your hands as you would on yourself.

LEFT MUDRA

Step	Place your left hand on her:	Place your right hand on her:
1	left U	left X1
2	left V	
3	left D3	
4		left Y1
5	left W1	
6	left X1	
7		Y
8		Y6
9		left A6
10		right A4

(continued)

Step	Place your left hand on her:	Place your right hand on her:
11		right A1 and A3
12		[optional: left H1]

TIME

The large intestine meridian has maximum energy flow from 6 A.M. to 8 A.M., standard time.

USES

The cleansing-stagnation mudra may assist you in accepting, relaxing, cleansing away, and/or discovering the causes of tensions encountered in meditation and daily life in the forms of:

Physical: tension, pain, stiffness, etc. along the path of the large intestine meridian; tension, pain, etc. in the area of the anatomical large intestine; tension in digestion and elimination.

Mental: depression, lassitude, inertia.

Karmic: karmic memories of having suffered or caused harm, in this or a previous life, by means of wounds in the large intestine area or along the lines of the meridian, illness in the large intestine area, sexual abuse, or by reason of jealousy.

BENEFICIAL INFLUENCES

The large intestine meridian may be benefitted by the exercise of Right Concentration on the Eightfold Path, by the practice of the paramita of the Precepts, and by developing a bright, alert, and positive attitude of mind. On the physical level, it may be aided by supplementing your balanced diet with extra tomatoes, onions, garlic, and vinegar.

HARMFUL INFLUENCES

This meridian may be harmed by attachment to avoiding old age and decay, by the poison of greed, and through breaking the Precepts against coveting and indulgent sexuality. Feelings of jealousy, depression, stagnation, and laziness are also damaging.

MUDRA ORIGIN

The cleansing-stagnation mudra was derived from the meridian through meditation.

COMPASSION-ANGER MUDRA

Affects the Liver Meridian

LEFT MUDRA

Step	Place your left hand on your:	Place your right hand on your:
1	left N1	I
2	left L1	
3	left L & 03	
4	left J1 & P1	
5		H2
6	left & right I3	
7		H
8		G or left G2
9		left G1

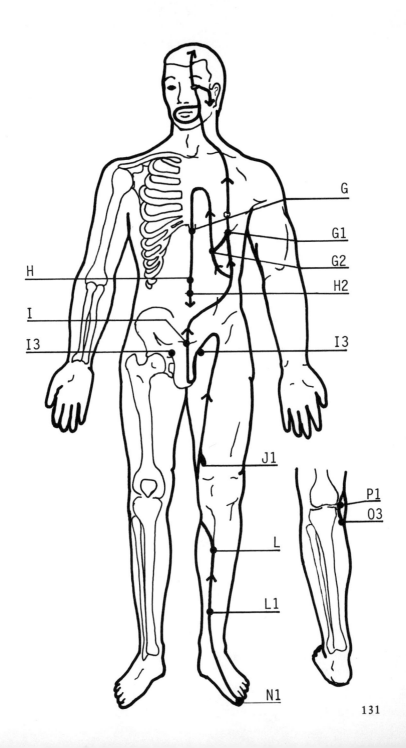

RIGHT MUDRA

Place your left hand on your:	Place your right hand on your:
1 right N1	I
2 right L1	
3 right L & 03	
4 right J1 & P1	
5	H2
6 right & left I3	
7	H
8	G *or* right G2
9	right G1

TO ASSIST A FRIEND

For both left and right mudras sit on his or her left side and place your hands as you would on yourself.

TIME

The liver meridian has maximum energy from 2 A.M. to 4 A.M., standard time.

The compassion-anger mudra may assist you in accepting, relaxing, cleansing away, and/or discovering the causes of tensions encountered in meditation and daily life in the forms of:

Physical: tension, pain, stiffness, etc. along the lines of the meridian; tension, pain, etc. in the area of the anatomical liver; tensions related to the appetite and digestion.

Mental: anger, frustration, depression, insomnia, and lust for power.

Karmic: karmic memories of having suffered or caused harm, in this or a previous life, by means of wounds in the liver area or along the liver meridian, illness in the liver area, poisoning, or by reasons of anger or hatred.

BENEFICIAL INFLUENCES

The liver meridian may be benefitted by the exercise of Right Mindfulness on the Eightfold Path, by the practice of the paramita of patience, and by the development of compassion and empathy. On the physical level it may be assisted by supplementing your balanced diet with extra eggs and oils, especially in combination such as in mayonnaise or Hollandaise sauce.

HARMFUL INFLUENCES

The liver meridian may be harmed by attachment to dislike of other people, by the poison of anger or hatred, and by breaking the Precept against being angry. Abuse of power is also a source of damage, as is any act of violence.

MUDRA ORIGIN

The compassion-anger mudra was derived from the liver meridian through meditation.

DIAMOND MUDRA

MUDRA

Whatever the position of the rest of your body, wrap the
fingers of the left hand around the thumb to make a fist
and place it against your right chest, then do the same with
your right hand and cross it over the left arm to rest on the
left chest.

TO ASSIST A FRIEND

This mudra of protection is for self use only.

TIME

The mudra renders all of the meridians in the chest and arms
inaccessible to external influences during the time it is used.

USES

This is the stronger of the two protection mudras. As in the
spiritual defense mudra, the closed left hand is a statement of
resolve not to allow any negative influences to disrupt one's
training. In the diamond mudra, however, both fists are
closed, and the active right hand is locked over the receptive
left hand in a gesture of complete defense. Called the diamond mudra (or *sankaisaishō-in*) because it is found in the
Buddhist iconography chiefly on statues of Vajrasattva,[50]
the Diamond One, symbolic of the immovability and in-
destructibility of the Buddha Nature,[51] it partakes of both
the advantages and disadvantages of its namesake. It is a
gesture of absolute resolve, completely sealing off all possibility of being influenced by evil or disruptive forces from
without; thus it has the hardness of diamond. However it
is also an inflexible and purely defensive posture which has
no room for positive action. It protects the heart absolutely,
but leaves unprotected the stomach and spleen areas, which

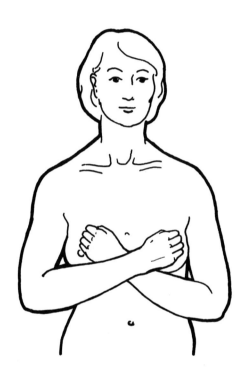

can be quite vulnerable to tension created by external conditions. In this way it shares the brittle nature of diamond. It is unsurpassed for absolute protection, but may be too rigid and exclusive for the experienced meditator or for one who has a strong measure of faith.

MUDRA ORIGIN

The mudra is found in the Buddhist iconography.

DISCOVERY MUDRA

LEFT MUDRA

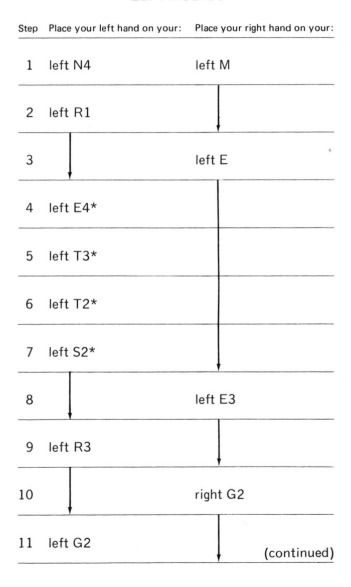

Step	Place your left hand on your:	Place your right hand on your:
1	left N4	left M
2	left R1	
3		left E
4	left E4*	
5	left T3*	
6	left T2*	
7	left S2*	
8		left E3
9	left R3	
10		right G2
11	left G2	(continued)

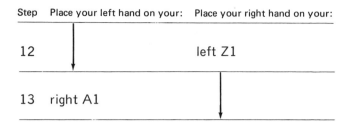

Step	Place your left hand on your:	Place your right hand on your:
12		left Z1
13	right A1	

RIGHT MUDRA

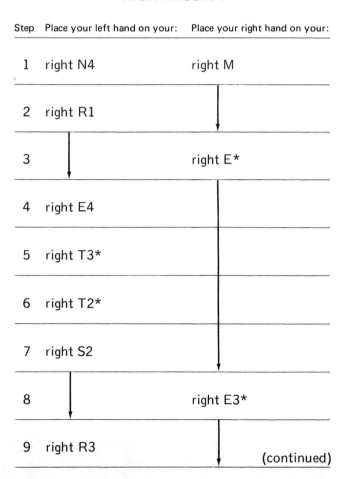

Step	Place your left hand on your:	Place your right hand on your:
1	right N4	right M
2	right R1	
3		right E*
4	right E4	
5	right T3*	
6	right T2*	
7	right S2	
8		right E3*
9	right R3	

(continued)

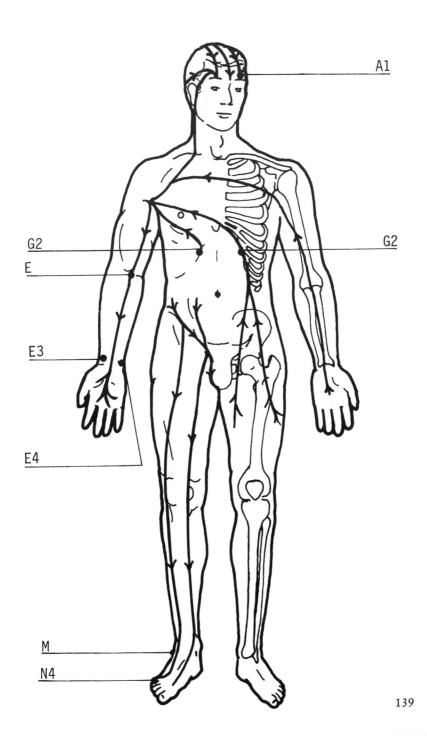

A1

G2

G2

E

E3

E4

M

N4

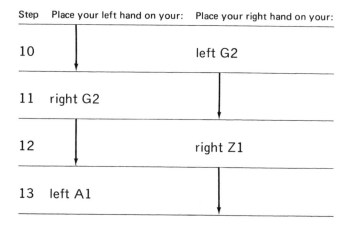

Step	Place your left hand on your:	Place your right hand on your:
10		left G2
11	right G2	
12		right Z1
13	left A1	

TO ASSIST A FRIEND

For the left mudra sit on his or her left side; for the right mudra sit on his or her right side. Place your hands as you would on yourself.

TIME

The pattern of flow diagrammed for this mudra is created temporarily by its use.

USES

The mudra of discovery was formulated to assist people in discovering the nature and/or causes of tensions about which insufficient information has been obtained during use of the usual mudras. While all mudras tend to some extent to produce both general relaxation and the type of mental relaxation and acceptance which are necessary for the discovery of new information, this mudra has far more of the latter property than of the former. It will not be likely, therefore, to bring much in the way of general rest and refreshment and its result may at times be frankly upsetting, painful or disquieting, sometimes for several days after its use.

DISCOVERY MUDRA (right-back)

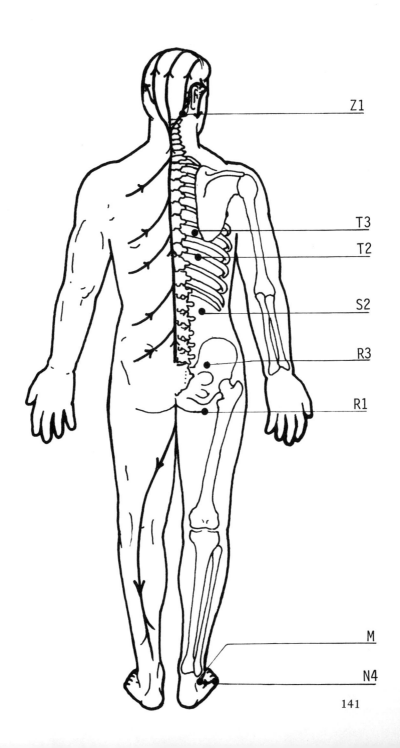

Z1

T3

T2

S2

R3

R1

M

N4

It can be valuable on occasion when you wish to bring up
forgotten memories of important events both from this
lifetime and before. It should *never* be used in an attempt to
force oneself or, worse yet, someone else to rediscover such
events. It may be useful, however, when you feel that there is
something important just beyond the reach of your awareness which, with a little help, will come forth and help relieve your tension. Remember that the discovery mudra, like
all mudras, does not do anything by itself; you must be in
meditation for it to have any effect. Remember, also, that
some people meditate naturally without any formal meditation practice and without realizing that they are doing so.
Therefore please heed the warning given above whether you
think you know how to meditate or not.

The mudra of discovery is usually used in conjunction
with another mudra or mudras which seem to be relevant to
the tension on which you are working or which are suggested
by the results of using the discovery mudra. If nothing is
uncovered by this means, *do not force yourself;* wait and
continue your daily training and meditation in the faith that
the information will ripen and become accessible to you
later if it is good for you to know it. Remember also that
the mudra of discovery sometimes has a long "fuse" and its
effects are not always apparent for a day or two. Finally,
because one frequently feels uneasy or uncomfortable after
having used this mudra, it is probably wise when using it to
conclude the sequence of mudras with one which has primarily relaxing properties.

The mudra of discovery has other secondary uses, but
given its primary property of discovery, it is probably *not* the
mudra of first choice for assisting you with any of the following tensions:

Physical: tension, pain, stiffness, etc. along the pathway
illustrated for this mudra; tensions related to the appetite;

feelings of cold or overfullness in the abdomen; tension in the shoulders or muscles of the rib cage, perhaps with resulting breathing difficulty; pain and stiffness in the lower back; general weakness; tensions associated with headaches, especially around the eyes, and with general itching and discomfort.

Mental: anxiety, fears, lightheadedness, depression, excessive talkativeness.

Karmic: karmic memories of having suffered or caused harm, in this or a previous life, by means of wounds along the line of the energy pathway induced by this mudra, especially in the chest and abdomen.

MUDRA ORIGIN

The mudra of discovery was derived and adapted from the releases of Jin Shin Dō and Jin Shin Jyutsu.

DORSAL LINKING MUDRA

Affects the Dorsal Linking Meridian

LEFT MUDRA

Step	Place your left hand on your:	Place your right hand on your:
1	left L3 & M	left O4
2		left P3
3		left Q
4		left S3
5		left G2
6	left S3	
7	left S3 & G2	left X1*
8		left X2*
9		left Y5
10		left Z1

(continued)

DORSAL LINKING MUDRA (left)

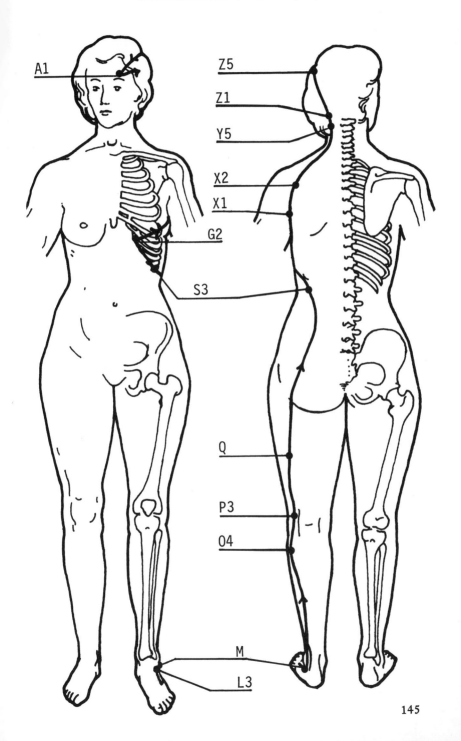

A1

Z5

Z1

Y5

X2

X1

G2

S3

Q

P3

O4

M

L3

Step	Place your left hand on your:	Place your right hand on your:
11		left Z5
12		left A1

RIGHT MUDRA

Step	Place your left hand on your:	Place your right hand on your:
1	right L3 & M	right O4
2		right P3
3		right Q
4		right S3
5		right G2
6	right S3	
7	right S3 & G2	right X1*
8		right X2*
9		right Y5

(continued)

Step	Place your left hand on your:	Place your right hand on your:
10		right Z1
11		right Z5
12		right A1

TO ASSIST A FRIEND

Sit on her or his left side and place your hands as you would on yourself.

TIME

The dorsal linking meridian has energy passing through it intermittently as needed.

USES

This meridian ascends the body, linking and affecting the interaction between the following organ meridians: stomach, large intestine, small intestine, triple warmer, bladder, and gall bladder. Its most profound effects are upon the latter two meridians. In consequence the dorsal linking mudra may affect tensions encountered in meditation and daily life which manifest themselves as any of the conditions listed under those six organ meridians and, in addition, it has uses peculiar to itself for tension in the forms of:

Physical: tension, pain, stiffness, etc. along the lines of flow of the meridian, tensions accompanying problems of general weakness, weight regulation (especially underweight), and temperature regulation (especially excessive cold).

Mental: general tension and insomnia.

Karmic: karmic memories of having suffered or caused harm, in this or a previous life, by means of wounds along the lines of the meridian, cold, starvation, or abandonment.

MUDRA ORIGIN

The dorsal linking mudra was derived from the meridian through meditation.

DYNAMO MUDRA

MUDRA

Step	Place your left hand on your:	Place your right hand on your:
1	right O4	left O4
2	G	T4*
3	left D1*	
4		left T3*

Hold the first step for a relatively long time. It may be difficult to do any of the other steps on yourself, in which case the first step may be used alone.

TO ASSIST A FRIEND

Sit on his or her left side and place your hands as you would on yourself.

TIME

The pattern of energy flow shown on the facing page is induced temporarily by use of the mudra.

USES

The dynamo mudra has both relaxing and invigorating properties and is therefore excellent for fatigue due to overwork and the insomnia which can result from being "too tired to

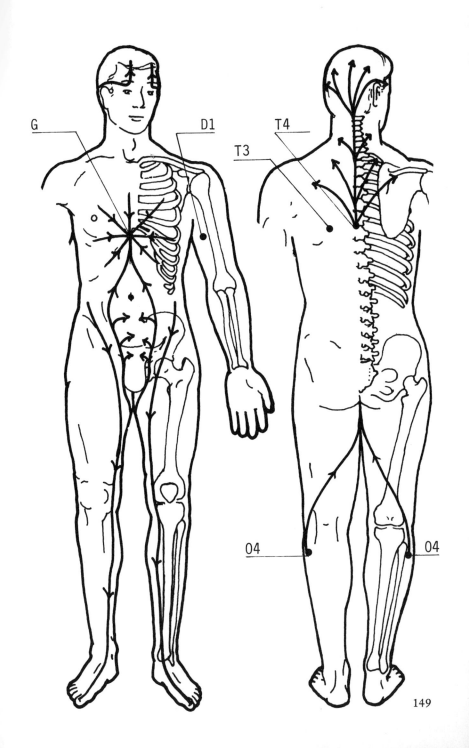

sleep." Its primary function, however, is spiritual: as a means of invigorating the will and of promoting awareness and stillness under difficult circumstances. Its effects are somewhat peculiar and hard to describe. It is not recommended for use by those who do not meditate regularly. It may also be of assistance when tensions arise in meditation and daily life which take the forms of:

Physical: tension, pain, stiffness, etc. along the energy pathway illustrated for the mudra; tension in the joints, especially those of the shoulder, hip, pelvis, and leg; general pelvic tension.

Mental: general tension, fatigue, or insomnia.

Karmic: karmic memories of having suffered or caused harm, in this or a previous life, by means of wounds along the path of energy flow induced by this mudra, or by suffocation.

MUDRA ORIGIN

The dynamo mudra was derived and adapted from several of the releases of Jin Shin Jyutsu.

EARTH WITNESS MUDRA

Sit or kneel in a meditation position.[52] Place your left hand in your lap, palm up, and your right hand in front of you on your right side with the fingers or entire hand touching the ground, as indicated below. In an emergency it is sufficient to touch the ground with the palm of your right hand regardless of the position of the rest of your body.

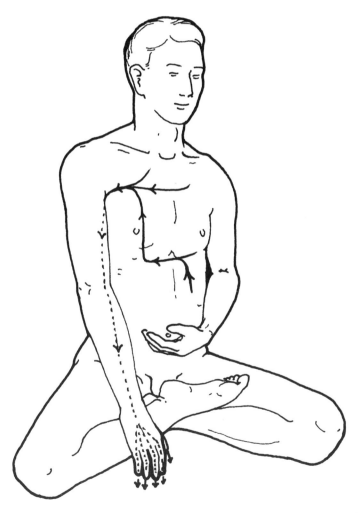

TO ASSIST A FRIEND

This mudra is designed for self use. If extra assistance is needed when you are doing it, you may have a friend kneel behind you, place his or her left palm over your points left G1 or left T3, and place his or her right hand on the ground.

TIME

The flow of energy depicted for this mudra is temporarily produced by its use.

USES

The earth witness mudra (or *sokuchi-in*) is one of the most useful of the traditional Buddhist mudras. It is said to have originated at the time of the Buddha's Enlightenment when, alone and beset by all of the forces of Darkness, He touched the earth which gave witness to His right to sit steadfastly in meditation until His complete Enlightenment.[53] Thus this mudra assists one to be steadfast when confusion, doubt, distractions, and dangers of all kinds abound. It is somewhat like putting down a "ground" wire to an electric circuit: when there is a short circuit and sparks are flying in all directions, the ground wire safely conducts the unchannelled electric power back into the all-accepting earth. This mudra can assist you to do the same with doubts, fears, anger, anxiety, or other sensations that may tend to overwhelm you, whether they arise from within you or externally. With the left hand closed in a fist for protection (see the diamond and spiritual defense mudras), the earth witness mudra may help you maintain resolve and equanimity amidst trying or chaotic external conditions.

For someone who has been meditating for some time there are two further uses. If karmic memories arise so strongly that it is difficult to accept them and learn from them, use of the earth witness mudra may release some of their excessive intensity and make the use of other mudras more fruitful. This may be done even while another mudra is being used, simply by reaching out the right hand to touch the ground. Also, there may be times in advanced meditation when the Fountain of the Cosmic Buddha floods you with such intense ecstasy that it is difficult to maintain consciousness. In this circumstance, momentary use of the earth witness mudra will offer a little of this Gift to the earth and all its creatures and so enable you to continue in meditation.

This mudra is most effective if you can actually touch the rock or soil of the earth itself. It is least effective when touching the floor of a building, especially several stories up. In this latter situation I find that it seems to help to touch a water pipe or other object which is directly connected to the ground and which would, in fact, "ground" an electrical charge. This is not to imply that electricity has anything to do with the "energy" which flows through the meridian channels of the body; it is simply an observation.

The earth witness mudra is closely related to the offering mudra. In the latter case one offers things up to That Which Is and is completely open to receive all things. The earth witness mudra also offers things back to the Source, but it does so in a way which asks for steadfastness and protection from being overwhelmed.

MUDRA ORIGIN

The earth witness mudra is found in the Buddhist iconography.

EASE MUDRA

MUDRA

Seated on a chair or sofa, allow your right leg to hang comfortably over the edge of the seat, while placing your left foot against your right knee touching points K1 and/or L. Rest your back comfortably against a pillow so that it remains erect in its natural curvature and place your left hand over your right shoulder so that the fingers rest on points Y1 and/or Y2. Rest your right hand, palm upward, on your right thigh and bring together the thumb and middle or ring fingers.

TO ASSIST A FRIEND

This mudra is designed for self use only. If a friend wishes assistance in general relaxation, use the relaxation mudra or one of the other mudras listed under the heading of "general tension" in the table of mudras organized by mental tensions in Appendix A.

TIME

The lines of energy flow illustrated on the accompanying diagram are established during use of the mudra.

USES

This is a mudra of general relaxation and ease. It is particularly helpful when tension centers in the neck, shoulders, chest, and stomach, or blocks the lung, pericardium, or triple warmer meridians. Since it is done in a seated position, the ease mudra can be used when it is undesirable or impractical to lie down. It combines the hand mudra of unity (*an-i-in*) with the seated mudra of ease (*lalitāsana*), and is frequently found in statues of the Bodhisattva of Compassion (Kanzeon).[54] The positions of the fingers of the right hand connect the lung and either the pericardium or

triple warmer meridians, depending upon whether the middle or ring fingers are used. The position of the left hand tends to release tension in the neck, as it is placed over the intersections of the bladder, dorsal linking, gall bladder, large intestine, small intestine, stomach, and triple warmer meridians.

MUDRA ORIGIN

The ease mudra is found in the Buddhist iconography.

FAITH-DOUBT MUDRA

Affects the Bladder Meridian

LEFT MUDRA

Step	Place your left hand on your:	Place your right hand on your:
1	right Z5	left R3
2	left Y5	
3	left T3*	
4		left Q
5	left S2	
6		left P & P2
7		left O1
8		left M3
9	R	
10		left N4

RIGHT MUDRA

Step	Place your left hand on your:	Place your right hand on your:
1	left Z5	right R3
2	right Y5	
3	right T3*	
4		right Q
5	right S2	
6		right P & P2
7		right O1
8		right M3
9	R	
10		right N4

TO ASSIST A FRIEND

Sit on his or her right side and place your hands as you would on yourself.

TIME

The bladder meridian has maximum energy flow from 4 P.M. to 6 P.M., standard time.

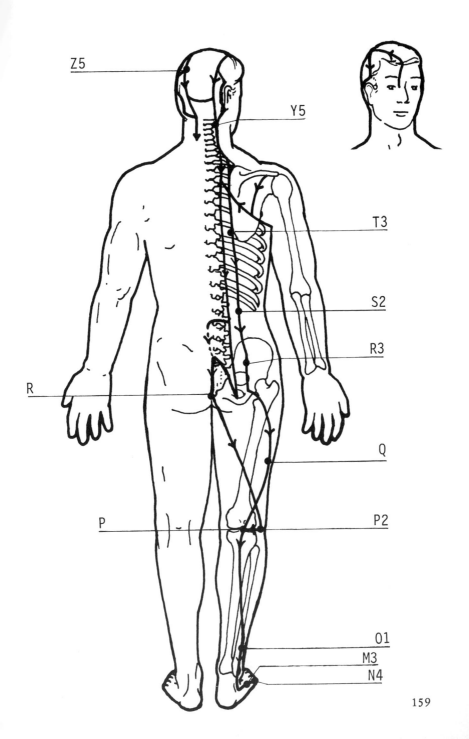

Z5
Y5
T3
S2
R3
R
Q
P
P2
O1
M3
N4

USES

The faith-doubt mudra may assist you in accepting, relaxing, cleansing away, and/or discovering the causes of tensions encountered in meditation and daily life in the forms of:

Physical: tension, pain, stiffness, etc. along the path of the meridian; tension, pain, etc. in the area of the anatomical bladder or around point G1; tension related to difficulty in holding or expelling water.

Mental: doubts, subtle fears, feelings of inferiority, inadequacy, pride, complacency, anger or grief.

Karmic: karmic memories of having suffered or caused harm, in this or a previous life, by means of wounds in the bladder area or along the path of the meridian, illness in the bladder area, mental illness, sexual abuse, doubt, loss of faith, inadequacy, or by deception or magic.

BENEFICIAL INFLUENCES

The bladder meridian may be benefitted by the exercise of Right Thought or Right Intention on the Eightfold Path, by the practice of the paramita of commitment, and by the development and exercise of faith. On the physical level, it may be assisted by supplementing your balanced diet with extra celery, carrots, fresh (not dry) peas and beans, sage, and thyme.

HARMFUL INFLUENCES

The bladder meridian may be harmed by attachment to false notions of self or of existence, by the poison of delusion, by breaking the Precepts against defaming the Three Treasures of Buddha, Dharma, and Sangha, and against being proud of oneself and devaluing others. The mental states of doubt, fear, inferiority, and pride are also damaging.

MUDRA ORIGIN

The faith-doubt mudra was derived from the bladder meridian through meditation.

FEARLESSNESS MUDRA

MUDRA

The right hand is open and raised to the level of the shoulder with the palm outward. The left hand is open, resting on the lap if one is seated or at the level of the navel if one is standing.

TO ASSIST A FRIEND

This mudra is for self use only.

TIME

The line of flow illustrated here is present while the mudra is in use.

USES

The mudra of fearlessness (*semui-in*) is said to have been used by the Buddha to subdue a mad elephant which a disgruntled disciple had loosed in order to try to kill Him.[55] It expresses fearlessness, inner peace, and a willingness to accept whatever happens in complete oneness with the Dharmakaya. It is a statement of willingness to endure all things without fear in order to become one with the Lord of the House. Thus its primary use is when frightening events occur internally or externally. It assists one in one's resolve to go forward in spite of all obstacles, with one's only real protections being faith in the Buddhas and Bodhisattvas and the merit of one's own acts.

This mudra, like the earth witness and offering mudras, is an act of offering. In this case it is an offering upward of one's faith and steadfast purpose both to the Buddhas and to all creatures. It can have the effect, therefore, of transferring peace of mind and security to others who are in fear. For this reason in some Buddhist countries it is a mudra used when giving teaching.

When used during meditation it helps to gather the Waters of the Spiritual Fountain at the base of the spine, and may create the sensation of particles of some non-material substance collecting there. As these "particles" gather and rise, meditation deepens, the will is strengthened, and one becomes more resolute and steadfast. This mudra is associated with the "Litany of the Great Compassionate One,"[56] a few lines of which are:

> Om, to the One who leaps beyond all fear!
> Do, do the work within my heart.
> O great Victor, I hold on, hold on!
> Of daring ones the most joyous, hail!

MUDRA ORIGIN

The fearlessness mudra is found in the Buddhist iconography.

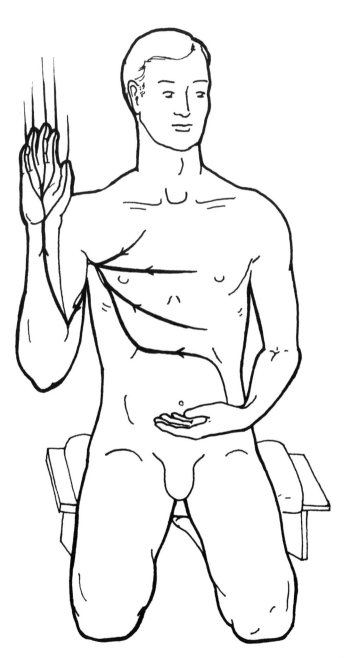

FOUNTAIN MUDRA

Affects the Heel Vessel Meridians

LEFT MUDRA

Step	Place your left hand on your:	Place your right hand on your:
1	left M & O1	left R3
2	left P2	
3		left Z3
4	left R3	
5	left thumb to left U1	
6		left Z6
7		left A1
8		left G2
9	left C2	
10		left J1
11		left N1

FOUNTAIN MUDRA (left-front)

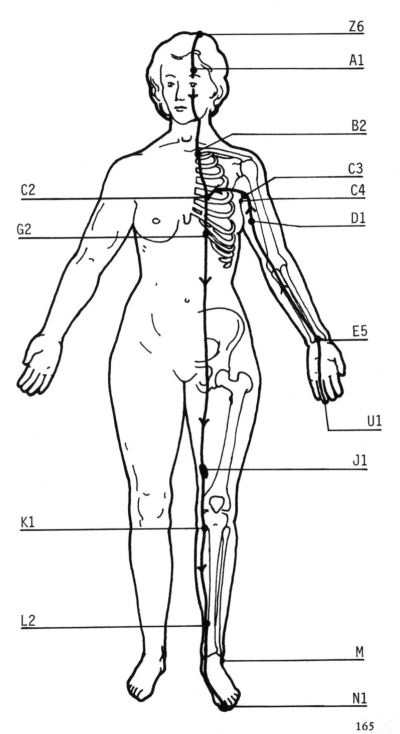

Z6

A1

B2

C3

C2

C4

D1

G2

E5

U1

J1

K1

L2

M

N1

RIGHT MUDRA

Step	Place your left hand on your:	Place your right hand on your:
1	right M & O1	right R3
2	right P2	
3		right Z3
4	right R3	
5	right E5	
6		right Z6
7		right A1
8		right G2
9	right C2	
10		right J1
11		right N1

TO ASSIST A FRIEND

Sit on her or his right side and either place your hands as you would on yourself or, for a more complete mudra, place them as follows:

LEFT MUDRA

Step	Place your left hand on her:	Place your right hand on her:
1	left M & O1	left R3
2	left P2	
3		left X3
4	left R3	
5		left Z3
6	left X3	
7	left C3	
8	left D1	
9	left E5	
10	left U1	(continued)

167

Step	Place your left hand on her:	Place your right hand on her:
11		left Z6
12	left V	
13	left W2	
14	left C4	
15		left A1
16		left B2
17		left C2
18		left G2
19	left C2	
20		left J1
21		left K1
22		left L2
23		left N1

FOUNTAIN MUDRA (left-back)

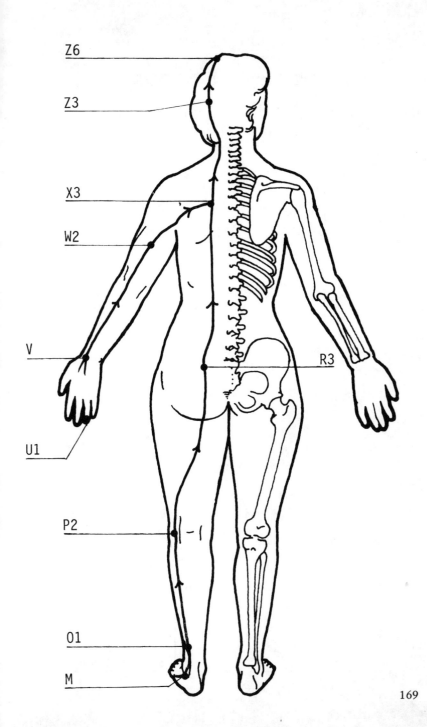

Z6

Z3

X3

W2

V

R3

U1

P2

O1

M

RIGHT MUDRA

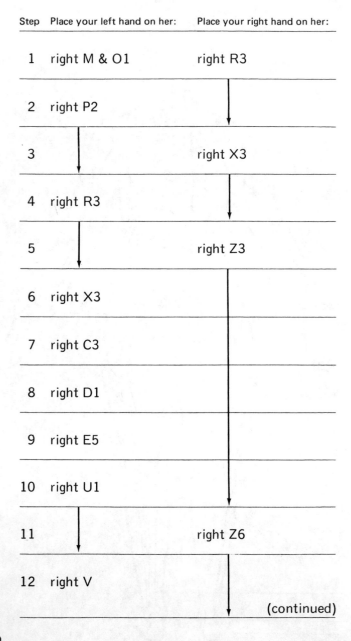

Step	Place your left hand on her:	Place your right hand on her:
1	right M & O1	right R3
2	right P2	
3		right X3
4	right R3	
5		right Z3
6	right X3	
7	right C3	
8	right D1	
9	right E5	
10	right U1	
11		right Z6
12	right V	

(continued)

Step	Place your left hand on her:	Place your right hand on her:
13	right W2	
14	right C4	
15		right A1
16		right B2
17		right C2
18		right G2
19	right C2	
20		right J1
21		right K1
22		right L2
23		right N1

TIME

The meridian through which energy passes when the fountain mudra is used runs parallel to the governing and conception vessel meridians, with the addition of a branch to the arm. This meridian does not seem to be widely used in the anma arts other than in Jin Shin Jyutsu and Jin Shin Dō, both of which discuss it extensively. They state that it has a regulatory function on all of the organ meridians and that in consequence energy flow within it is irregular, as adjustments are needed.

USES

Our use for this mudra is primarily a spiritual one and is based less upon its function of regulating the other meridians than upon its property of stimulating indirectly the flow of energy in the governing and conception vessel meridians and hence facilitating the free flow of the Spiritual Fountain.[57] In addition to this spiritual use it may be of assistance in accepting, relaxing, cleansing away, and/or discovering the causes of tensions which arise in meditation and daily life in the forms of:

Physical: tension, pain, stiffness, etc. along the meridian, especially in the head during headaches and congestion.

Mental: for relaxation after stressful situations.

Karmic: karmic memories of having suffered or caused harm, in this or a previous life, by means of wounds along the lines of the meridian.

MUDRA ORIGIN

Derived and adapted from releases of Jin Shin Jyutsu and Jin Shin Dō, which are based upon the heel vessel meridians.

FOUNTAIN RIM MUDRA

Affects the Lower Belt Meridian

MUDRA

Step	Place your left hand on your:	Place your right hand on your:
1	S1	left S2
2		left S3
3		left G3
4		left H1
5		left I2
6		left I3
7		I
8		right I3
9		right I2
10		right H1

(continued)

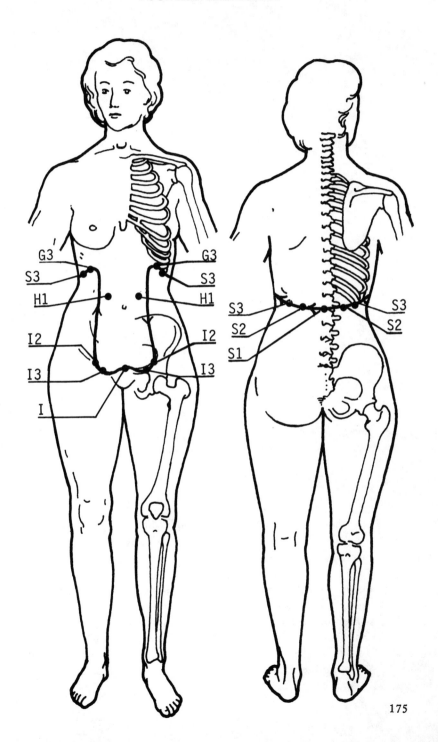

Step	Place your left hand on your:	Place your right hand on your:
11		right G3
12		right S3
13		right S2
14		left S2

TO ASSIST A FRIEND

Sit on her or his right side and place your hands as you would on yourself. This mudra is done in only one direction; please do not reverse it.

TIME

Energy in the lower belt meridian flows continuously in a clockwise direction and increases or decreases as needed.

USES

The lower belt meridian binds together all of the organ meridians and those other meridians which pass through the lower back or abdomen. It unifies and harmonizes their functioning and thus permits the Water of the Spiritual Fountain to circulate without dissipation. It joins together the meridians at the region of the pelvis and assists the energy to pass freely between the upper torso and the lower portion of the body. It is a delicate and important meridian and, like the other belt meridians which follow, it is sensitive to disturbances in any of the meridians which it unites. Therefore the fountain rim mudra may be of assistance as an adjunct to other mudras whenever a block or disturbance is encountered in any of those meridians. A feeling of separation or disharmony between the rest of the body and the portion below this meridian is a characteristic indication of a problem with the meridian. There are a number of other uses characteristic of the fountain rim mudra, including assisting one in accepting, relaxing, cleansing away, and/or discovering the causes of tensions encountered in meditation and daily life in the forms of:

Physical: tension, pain, stiffness, etc. along the meridian or in the shoulder, arm, hand, leg, knee, ankle, or foot; general weakness or lack of energy; tensions associated with disturbances of weight regulation (especially underweight), digestion, bowel function, menstruation, or temperature regulation (especially excessive cold).

Mental: fatigue, weakness, fainting, insomnia.

Karmic: karmic memories of having suffered or caused harm, in this or a previous life, by means of wounds along the lines of the lower belt meridian or in the forms of bodily disintegration (especially breaking of the body around the level of the meridian), sexual abuse, difficulties of childbirth, starvation, abandonment, cold, or lack of love.

MUDRA ORIGIN

The fountain rim mudra was derived from the lower belt meridian through meditation.

FOUNTAIN SCREEN MUDRA

Affects the Middle Belt Meridian

MUDRA

Step	Place your left hand on your:	Place your right hand on your:
1	T4* [or left C3]	left T3*
2		left C3
3		left C1 or C2
4		right C1 or C2
5		right C3
6		right T3*
7		left T3*

TO ASSIST A FRIEND

Sit on his or her right side and place your hands as you would on yourself. This mudra is done only in one direction; please do not reverse it.

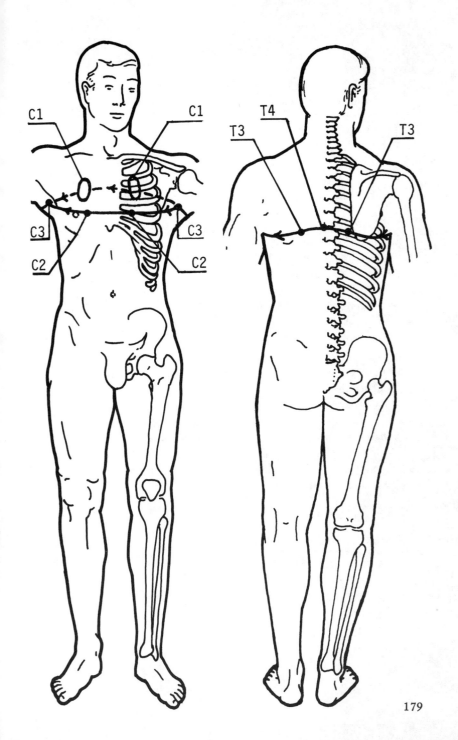

TIME

Like the other belt meridians, energy flows through this meridian continuously in a clockwise direction, changing in strength as needed to assist the other meridians.

USES

The middle belt meridian binds together all of the organ meridians and those other meridians which pass through the upper back and chest. It assists the passage of energy through this area and thus helps to prevent the Water of the Spirit from being dissipated at this level. The fountain screen mudra may be used as an adjunct to mudras affecting any meridian which seems to be disturbed in the upper back or chest. Other uses include assisting one in accepting, relaxing, cleansing away, and/or discovering the causes of tensions encountered in meditation and daily life in the forms of:

Physical: tension, pain, stiffness, etc. along the lines of the meridian; tensions associated with chest congestion and difficulties in breathing.

Mental: fatigue, grief, sadness, weakness.

Karmic: karmic memories of having suffered or caused harm, in this or a previous life, by means of wounds along the middle belt meridian or in the forms of bodily disintegration (especially breaking of the body at the level of the meridian) or suffocation.

MUDRA ORIGIN

The mudra was derived from the middle belt meridian through meditation. The middle belt meridian appears to be largely unknown in the other anma arts.

FOUNTAIN SPRAY MUDRA

Affects the Upper Belt Meridian

MUDRA

Step	Place your left hand on your:	Place your right hand on your:
1	Z2	left Z5 *or* Z3
2		left Z4
3		left A1
4		A
5		right A1
6		right Z4
7		right Z5 *or* Z3
8		left Z5 *or* Z3

TO ASSIST A FRIEND

Sit at his or her head (at the center or on either side as may be most comfortable for you) and place your hands as you would on yourself. This mudra is done in one direction only; please do not reverse it.

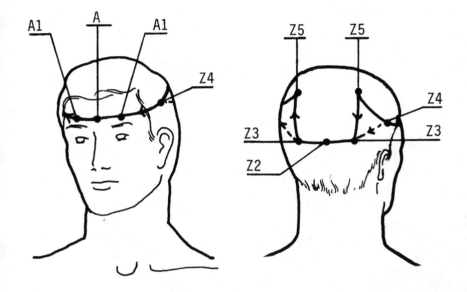

Energy flow in this meridian is continuous in a clockwise direction around the head. It fluctuates in strength as needed to assist other meridians.

USES

The upper belt meridian assists and influences the relationship of all other meridians passing through the head. This includes all of the organ meridians except those for the pericardium, spleen, and lung. It assists the Water of the Spirit to flow through this area and pass over the head from back to front to form the Spiritual Fountain.[58] The mudra may be of benefit in any condition in which a meridian is blocked in the head, and the upper belt meridian is sensitive to being disrupted by such blocks. It has the additional function of assisting with tensions in the forms of:

Physical: tension, pain, stiffness, etc. along the pathway of the meridian, especially tension involved in headaches.

Mental: fatigue (especially mental and spiritual), overstimulation, oversensitivity, general tension.

Karmic: karmic memories of having suffered or caused harm, in this or a previous life, by means of wounds along the meridian or in the form of bodily disintegration, especially decapitation or breaking of the head.

MUDRA ORIGIN

The mudra was derived from the meridian through meditation. The upper belt meridian appears to be largely unknown to the other anma arts.

GOOD DIGESTION MUDRA

Affects the Penetrating Vessel Meridian

LEFT MUDRA — ASCENDING

Step	Place your left hand on your:	Place your right hand on your:
1	left J1	left G1 *or* C2
2	left I3	
3	H3	
4	left H1	
5		left C1
6	left G1 *or* C2	
7		B *or* left B2

LEFT MUDRA — DESCENDING

Step	Place your left hand on your:	Place your right hand on your:
1	B *or* left B2	left G1 *or* C2

(continued)

Step	Place your left hand on your:	Place your right hand on your:
2	left C1	
3		left H1
4	left G1 *or* C2	
5		H3
6		left I3
7		left J1

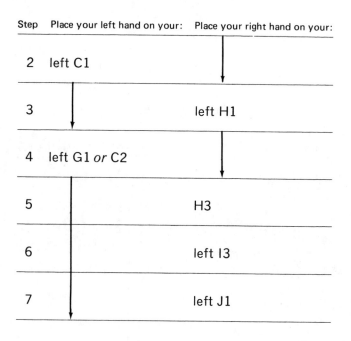

RIGHT MUDRA — ASCENDING

Step	Place your left hand on your:	Place your right hand on your:
1	right J1	right G1 *or* C2
2	right I3	
3	H3	
4	right H1	
5		right C1

(continued)

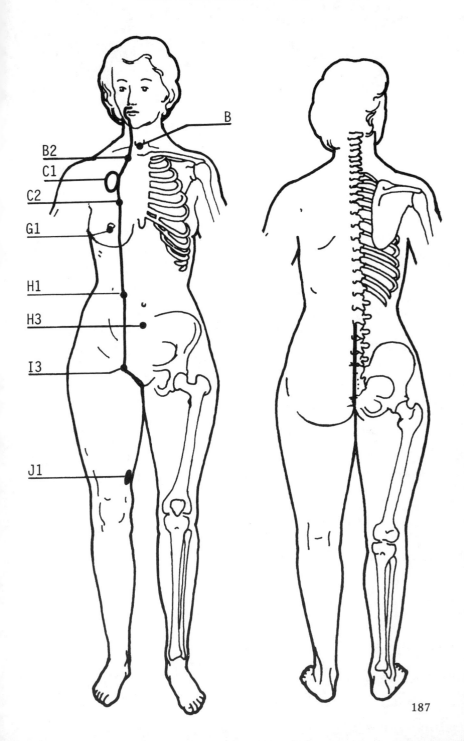

B
B2
C1
C2
G1
H1
H3
I3
J1

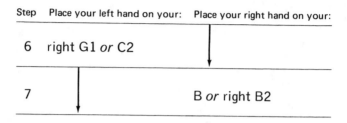

Step	Place your left hand on your:	Place your right hand on your:
6	right G1 *or* C2	
7		B *or* right B2

RIGHT MUDRA — DESCENDING

Step	Place your left hand on your:	Place your right hand on your:
1	B *or* right B2	right G1 *or* C2
2	right C1	
3		right H1
4	right G1 *or* C2	
5		H3
6		right I3
7		right J1

TO ASSIST A FRIEND

For the ascending mudras sit on your friend's left side; for the descending mudras sit on her or his right side. Place your hands as you would on yourself.

TIME

The penetrating vessel meridian has energy flow through it intermittently as may be needed.

USES

The penetrating vessel meridian affects all twelve organ meridians and helps to balance the quantity of energy which flows through them. In the ascending direction it affects primarily the stomach, small intestine, large intestine, triple warmer, bladder, and gall bladder meridians; in the descending direction it influences the lung, heart, pericardium, spleen, kidney, and liver meridians. Therefore it may have uses related to all of these twelve meridians and their functions. Additional uses characteristic of this meridian are for tensions found in the forms of:

Physical: tension, pain, stiffness, etc. along the lines of the meridian and especially in the genitals, heart (*see cautionary statements given under the life-death mudra before using it when tensions exist that are related to the heart*), abdomen, or an interaction thereof; tensions which affect the regulation of menstruation or of appetite, digestion, and/or bowel function.

Mental: the mudra has a generally calming and refreshing effect upon body, mind, and spirit.

Karmic: karmic memories of having suffered or caused harm, in this or a previous life, by means of wounds along the lines of the meridian or by means of starvation, terror, sexual abuse, or difficulties of childbirth.

MUDRA ORIGIN

The mudra was derived from the penetrating vessel meridian through meditation.

JOY-SADNESS MUDRA

Affects the Pericardium Meridian
LEFT MUDRA

Step	Place your left hand on your:	Place your right hand on your:
1	G & H2	left C5
2		left X1
3		left D1
4		left E
5		left E2 & E5
6		left F
7		left F2
8		left F4

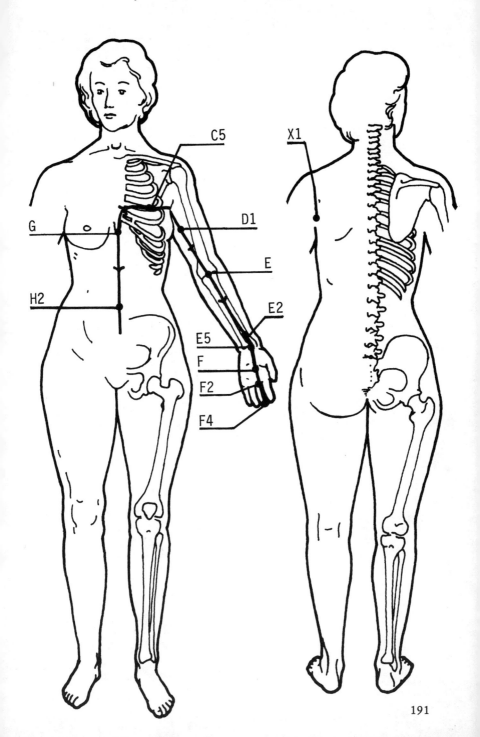

C5

X1

G

D1

E

H2

E2

E5

F

F2

F4

RIGHT MUDRA

Step	Place your left hand on your:	Place your right hand on your:
1	G & H2	right C5
2		right X1*
3		touch right thumb to right F2
4		touch right thumb to right F4

TO ASSIST A FRIEND

For the left mudra, sit on her or his left side and place your hands as you would on yourself. For the right mudra, sit on her or his right side and place your hands as follows:

RIGHT MUDRA

Step	Place your left hand on her:	Place your right hand on her:
1	G & H2	right C5
2		right X1
3		right D1
4		right E
5		right E2 & E5
6		right F
7		right F2
8		right F4

TIME

The pericardium meridian has maximum energy flow from 8 P.M. to 10 P.M., standard time.

USES

The joy-sadness mudra may assist you in accepting, relaxing, cleansing away, and/or discovering the causes of tensions encountered in meditation and daily life in the forms of:

Physical: tension, pain, stiffness, etc. along the pathway of the meridian; tension, pain, etc. in the area of the anatomical pericardium (*see cautionary statements under the life-death mudra before using it under these circumstances*); tension associated with disturbances of the circulation or of sexual function.

Mental: chronic mild sadness, alienation, loneliness, weakness, general malaise, and lack of energy; occasionally, tendency to uncontrollable laughter, especially when due to pent-up sadness or worry.

Karmic: karmic memories of having suffered or caused harm, in this or a previous life, by means of wounds in the pericardium area or along the meridian, illness in the pericardium area, severe bleeding or other circulatory trauma, electrocution, poisoning, systemic infection, sexual abuse, general terror, deceit, magic, lack of love, abandonment, or refusal of assistance.

BENEFICIAL INFLUENCES

The pericardium meridian may be benefitted by the exercise of Right Action on the Eightfold Path, by the practice of the paramita of strength, and by finding and sharing joy and selfless love.

HARMFUL INFLUENCES

The pericardium meridian may be harmed by attachments to a false notion of self and existence, to avoiding old age, and to always being with loved ones. It is further harmed by the poison of greed and through breaking the Precepts against coveting and indulgent sexuality. Feelings of sadness and alienation are also damaging.

MUDRA ORIGIN

The joy-sadness mudra was derived from the meridian through meditation.

JUNCTION MUDRA Z1

LEFT MUDRA

Step	Place your left hand on your:	Place your right hand on your:
1	left Z1	left Z5
2		left & right A1
3		right Z1
4		left X1*
5		left G2
6		right S2
7		R
8		I
9		[optional: right L3]
10		[optional: left L3]

RIGHT MUDRA

Step	Place your left hand on your:	Place your right hand on your:
1	right Z1	right Z5
2		left & right A1
3		left Z1
4		right X1*
5		right G2
6		left S2
7		R
8		I
9		[optional: left L3]
10		[optional: right L3]

TO ASSIST A FRIEND

Sit on his or her right side and place your hands as you would on yourself.

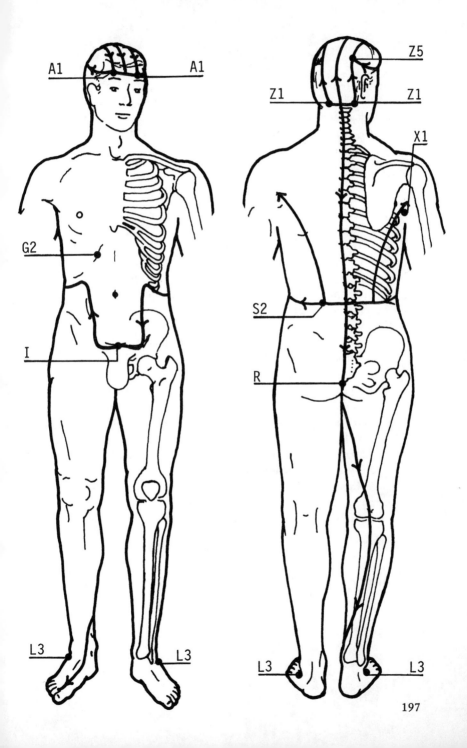

TIME

Junction Mudra Z1 uses in part the governing vessel, conception vessel, and upper and lower belt meridians, through which energy is in constant flow. The other branches illustrated for this mudra are temporarily activated by use of the mudra.

USES

As the flow of the Spiritual Fountain[59] rises up the spine, one of the last places in which it is often blocked by tension is the back of the head around points Z1. This mudra was designed to assist the flow of the Fountain past this point so that it might cascade over the head and transform the temporal outlook to the spiritual one. Since the bladder, dorsal linking, gall bladder, and upper belt meridians also intersect at point Z1, blocks in these meridians in this area also may be assisted by this mudra. It may be of further use when tension arises in the following forms:

Physical: tension, pain, stiffness, etc. along the flow lines illustrated for this mudra, especially in the head (when related to tension headaches), neck, legs, and knees; tensions associated with problems of head congestion and difficulties of circulation.

Mental: the mudra is good for general relaxation, especially after frustration.

Karmic: karmic memories of having suffered or caused harm, in this or a previous life, by means of wounds along the energy pathway illustrated for this mudra.

MUDRA ORIGIN

Junction Mudra Z1 was derived intuitively from meditation.

KARMA MUDRA

Affects the Triple Warmer Meridian

LEFT MUDRA

Step	Place your left hand on your:	Place your right hand on your:
1	touch left thumb to left U1	left X1
2		left Y2
3	left X1*	
4		left B3
5		C
6		G
7		H3

KARMA MUDRA (left)

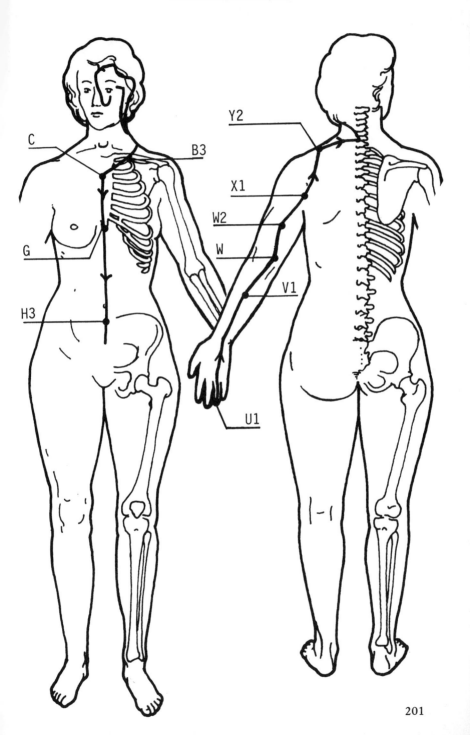

RIGHT MUDRA

Step	Place your left hand on your:	Place your right hand on your:
1	right U1	right X1* *or* Y3
2	right V1	
3	right W	
4	right W2	
5		right Y2
6	right W2 & X1*	
7		right B3
8		C
9		G
10		H3

TO ASSIST A FRIEND

For the left mudra, sit on her or his left side and use the mudra table which follows. For the right mudra, sit on her or his right side and place your hands as you would on yourself.

LEFT MUDRA

Step	Place your left hand on her:	Place your right hand on her:
1	left U1	left X1
2	left V1	
3	left W	
4	left W2	
5		left Y2
6	left W2 & X1	
7		left B3
8		C
9		G
10		H3

TIME

The triple warmer meridian has maximum energy flow from 10 P.M. to midnight, standard time.

USES

The karma mudra may assist you in accepting, relaxing, cleansing away, and/or discovering the causes of tensions encountered in meditation and daily life in the forms of:

Physical: tension, pain, stiffness, etc. along the path of the triple warmer meridian or, indirectly, along that of the conception vessel meridian; tension which affects appetite disturbances, imbalances of body temperature, or sensations of excessive heat or cold.

Mental: insecurity, restlessness (especially during the time of the maximum energy flow), lassitude, weakness, flaccidity, dullness or confusion of the intellect, inability to enjoy real pleasure or distinguish between pleasure and pain, sexual frustration or tension.

Karmic: karmic memories of having suffered or caused harm, in this or a previous life, by means of wounds along the meridian, injury due to heat or (especially) cold, severe bleeding, sexual abuse, problems of childbirth, magic, or sadistic behavior.

BENEFICIAL INFLUENCES

The triple warmer meridian may be benefitted by the exercise of Right Action on the Eightfold Path, by the practice of the paramita of the Precepts, and by the performance of acts which have good consequences for self and other.

HARMFUL INFLUENCES

This meridian may be harmed by attachment to getting what one wants, by the poison of greed, and by breaking the Precepts against coveting and indulgent sexuality. It is also harmed whenever one acts in such a way as to produce suffering or harm of any type for oneself or other beings.

MUDRA ORIGIN

The karma mudra was derived from the meridian through meditation.

KARMIC ASSISTANCE MUDRA

LEFT MUDRA

Step	Place your left hand on your:	Place your right hand on your:
1	left M2	right A1 & A4
2	right G1 *or* G2	
3	left C3	
4	left T3*	
5	touch left thumb to left U	

RIGHT MUDRA

Step	Place your left hand on your:	Place your right hand on your:
1	right M2	left A1 & A4
2	left G1 *or* G2	
3	right C3	
4	right T3*	
5	right U	

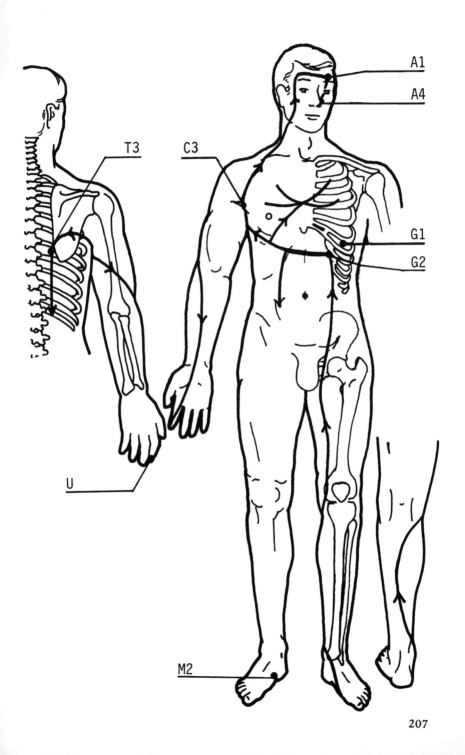

TO ASSIST A FRIEND

Sit on his or her left side and place your hands as you would on yourself. For the left mudra, step five, the point "U" may be held in the normal manner instead of using the thumb.

TIME

The energy flow illustrated for this mudra is temporarily created by its use.

USES

The primary use of this mudra is to assist you in the discovery and acceptance of karmic memories by relaxing the mind so that such memories produce less anxiety. It is not generally recommended as the first mudra to be used in a sequence, but rather as an intermediate mudra to be employed when the results of other mudras have begun to suggest the presence of a karmic memory which you cannot quite bring into full awareness. Steps number two, three, and four are especially valuable for this purpose and may be held for a relatively long time. The mudra has a general discovery property and you may find that not only karmic memories but other physical or mental sensations which were just beyond the reach of consciousness become more accessible. *The effects of this mudra may therefore be somewhat unpredictable, and it should be used with this possibility in mind.* Remember, however, that it is not the use of this or any other mudra which brings things into your awareness. Meditation alone does that; the mudras just relax you and thus make it easier to be aware of things which may tend to be tension-producing. In addition to these uses, the karmic assistance mudra may be of value in helping to accept, relax, cleanse away and/or discover the causes of tension encountered in meditation and daily life in the forms of:

Physical: tension, pain, stiffness, etc. along the lines of the energy pathway illustrated for this mudra, particularly under the arm, in the front of the head, around the eyes, and in the abdomen; tension related to tightness or feelings of constriction in the chest; blocks in other meridians which occur in the chest area.

Mental: the mudra may be used for general purposes of discovery.

Karmic: karmic memories of having suffered or caused harm, in this or a previous life, by means of wounds along the lines of the energy flow established by the mudra, especially stretching or crushing of the chest and suffocation.

MUDRA ORIGIN

This mudra was derived and adapted from a release of Jin Shin Jyutsu.

LIFE-DEATH MUDRA

Affects the Heart Meridian

LEFT MUDRA

Step	Place your left hand on your:	Place your right hand on your:
1	left C3*, T2*, X1*, X3*, or touch thumb to left U2	left Z5
2		left H1
3		right S2
4		left W2
5		left D2
6		left E1
7		left E4
8		left F3
9		left U2

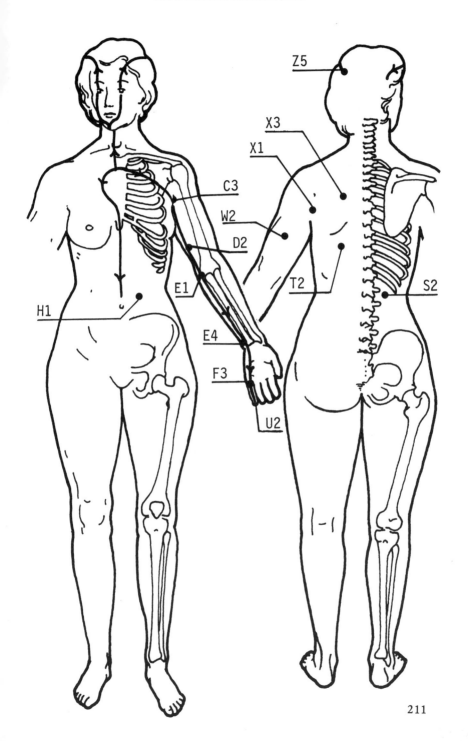

RIGHT MUDRA

Step	Place your left hand on your:	Place your right hand on your:
1	right C3, T2*, X1, *or* X3*	right Z5
2		right H1
3		left S2
4		touch right thumb to right F3
5		touch right thumb to right U2

TO ASSIST A FRIEND

For the left mudra, sit on her or his left side and place your hands as you would on yourself. For the right mudra, sit on her or his right side and place your hands as follows:

RIGHT MUDRA

Step	Place your left hand on her:	Place your right hand on her:
1	right C3, T2, X1, *or* X3	right Z5
2		right H1

(continued)

Step	Place your left hand on her:	Place your right hand on her:
3		left S2
4		right W2
5		right D2
6		right E1
7		right E4
8		right F3
9		right U2

WARNING

The life-death mudra can have effects upon the anatomical heart and can bring up issues of death and fears of dying. It should be used carefully and not too often. Do not exert pressure on the points of this mudra or otherwise attempt to force, rush, or intensify the flow of energy in the meridian. In cases of heart disease, consult your physician before using it. Although no mudra is effective without meditation, some people meditate to some extent without realizing that they do so. Therefore, please heed this warning whether or not you believe that you can meditate.

TIME

The heart meridian has maximum energy flow from noon to 2 P.M., standard time.

USES

The life-death mudra may assist you in accepting, relaxing, cleansing away, and/or discovering the causes of tensions encountered in meditation and daily life in the forms of:

Physical: tension, pain, stiffness, etc. along the pathway of the meridian; tension, pain, etc. in the area of the anatomical heart (*see warning and caution*).

CAUTION

Pain along that part of the meridian which traverses the chest and/or left arm can be a symptom of serious heart disease. Use of this mudra to attempt to relieve such pain should be done only on the advice of a physician.

Mental: anxiety in its various forms (for fear, point X1 is best in the first step of the mudra; for worry, try point T2; for tension, point X3), sadness, and states of physical, mental, or spiritual exhaustion (for these, point C3 may be best in the first step).

Karmic: karmic memories of having suffered or caused harm, in this or a previous life, by means of wounds in the heart area or along the heart meridian, illness in the heart area, suffocation, severe bleeding, electric shock, terror, magic, sadism, neglect, or lack of love; the mudra is also beneficial for karmic memories of having taken life in any form by any means.

OTHER MUDRAS

Other mudras may be used to exert an indirect influence on the heart meridian. Such an influence will tend to be milder and may be more appropriate for use in delicate situations. These mudras include the spiritual bathing, fountain, lightness-heaviness of spirit, security-vulnerability, compassion-anger, and balancing mudras.

BENEFICIAL INFLUENCES

The heart meridian may be benefitted by the exercise of Right Livelihood on the Eightfold Path, by the practice of the paramitas of giving, commitment, and strength, and the development and sharing of selfless love. On the physical level it may be aided by supplementing your balanced diet with extra green leafy vegetables.

HARMFUL INFLUENCES

The heart meridian may be harmed by attachment to avoiding the cycle of birth and death and to avoiding separation from loved ones, by the poison of greed, and by breaking the Precepts against killing, being mean in giving of one's wealth, oneself, or the Truth, and against defaming the Three Treasures of Buddha, Dharma, and Sangha. Inability to give love, threat of death, emotional states of terror or anxiety, and spiritual, mental, or physical exhaustion are particularly damaging.

MUDRA ORIGIN

The life-death mudra was derived from the heart meridian through meditation.

LIGHTNESS-HEAVINESS OF SPIRIT MUDRA

Affects the Small Intestine Meridian

LEFT MUDRA

Step	Place your left hand on your:	Place your right hand on your:
1	touch left thumb to left U2	left X1
2		left C1 & C4
3		left Y1 & Y3
4	left C1 & C4	
5		left Y4
6		left A4 & A5
7		left C1 & C2
8		left C2 & G2
9		left G2 & H1
10		right I2

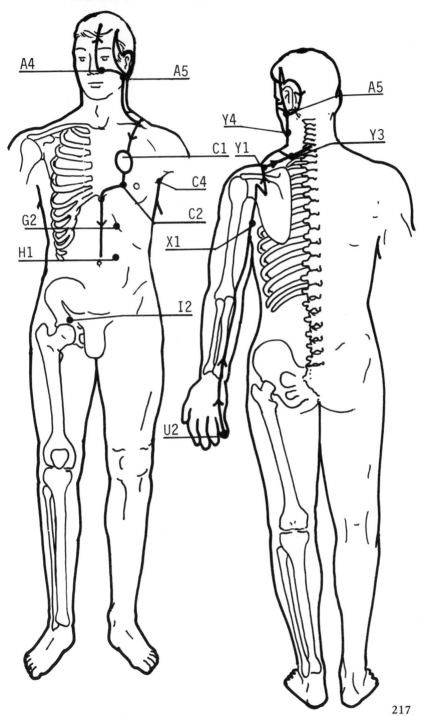

RIGHT MUDRA

Step	Place your left hand on your:	Place your right hand on your:
1	right U2	right X1* *or* right C1 & C4
2	right A4	
3		right C1 & C4
4	right X1	
5		right Y1 & Y3
6		right Y4
7		right A4 & A5
8		right C1 & C2
9		right C2 & G2
10		right G2 & H1
11		left I2

TO ASSIST A FRIEND

For the left mudra sit on his or her left side and use the mudra below. For the right mudra sit on his or her right side and place your hands as you would on yourself.

LEFT MUDRA

Step	Place your left hand on his:	Place your right hand on his:
1	left U2	left X1
2	left A4	
3		left C1 & C4
4	left X1	
5		left Y1 & Y3
6		left Y4
7		left A4 & A5
8		left C1 & C2
9		left C2 & G2
10		left G2 & H1
11		right I2

TIME

The small intestine meridian has maximum energy flow from 2 P.M. to 4 P.M., standard time.

USES

The lightness-heaviness of spirit mudra may assist you in accepting, relaxing, cleansing away, and/or discovering the causes of tensions encountered in meditation and daily life in the forms of:

Physical: tension, pain, stiffness, etc. along the pathway of the meridian; tension, pain, etc. in the area of the anatomical small intestine; tension related to problems of appetite, digestion, and bowel function.

Mental: generalized weakness, lassitude, and lack of coordination; specific and limited fears; distrust and jealousy.

Karmic: karmic memories of having suffered or caused harm, in this or a previous life, by means of wounds in the small intestine area or along the lines of the meridian, illness in the small intestine, sexual abuse, starvation, poisoning, abandonment, or the taking of life in any form.

BENEFICIAL INFLUENCES

The small intestine meridian may be benefitted by the exercise of Right Livelihood on the Eightfold Path, by the practice of the paramita of charity or giving, and by the development of a bright and positive attitude of mind. On the physical level it may be aided by supplementing your balanced diet with extra green leafy vegetables.

HARMFUL INFLUENCES

This meridian may be harmed by attachment to avoiding the cycle of birth and death and to avoiding separation from loved ones, by the poison of greed, and through breaking the Precepts against killing (especially as a means of livelihood), coveting, and meanness in giving of one's wealth, oneself, or the Truth. Fear, jealousy, and all lethargic and negative states of mind are detrimental.

MUDRA ORIGIN

The mudra was derived from the small intestine meridian through meditation.

MEDITATION MUDRA

MUDRA

The position of the body is important in practicing meditation successfully. It has been discussed in detail in "Zen Meditation" (*Journal of Shasta Abbey*, 1976, 7, nos. 9 & 10), to which the reader is referred. There are several positions of the legs which are conducive to good meditation, the one illustrated here, the full lotus position,[60] being the one which the Buddha used in His own meditation. An erect but relaxed spine and slightly lowered, but not closed, eyes are important in maintaining awareness and a bright mind. The hands rest open in the lap at the level of the navel (a pad may be placed in the lap and the hands rested on it, if necessary, to make them rest at navel height) with the non-dominant hand resting over the dominant one, thumbs touching together lightly and forming a circle with the index fingers. This position of the hands is known as the mudra of concentration (*jo-in*)[60] and is both symbolic of, and conducive to, the experience of profound meditation (*samadhi*). This position of the hands is also attributed to the Buddha Himself as He sat under the Bodhi Tree and was Enlightened some 2,500 years ago. The entire mudra is the traditional one for promoting meditation and awareness, and it has been used by Buddhists from the time of the Buddha to the present day. It is the mudra used for formal meditation in Zen temples.

TO ASSIST A FRIEND

Meditation, training, and enlightenment can be done only for oneself, therefore this mudra is inherently for self use. If you and a friend both desire to meditate, there can be some benefit from doing so at the same place and time. In this way you can assist each other, although each of you must do his or her own meditation. If you find it difficult to meditate, you should contact a competent meditation teacher.

USES

This mudra is for use in promoting proper meditation which will, among other things, set the Fountain of the Pure Love of the Buddhas in motion. This is experienced by different people in different ways, but has been described by Rōshi Jiyu-Kennett as follows:

> There is a feeling of particles collecting at the coccyx on inhalation. As these "particles" collect, they seem to coalesce into a unity, which is identified with the gathering together of the will to train oneself. As further inhalations occur, the particles ascend the spine and change in consistency as they do so. At the coccyx they are solid; in the lower lumbar area they are half solid—half liquid. At the waist they are like a heavy liquid such as mercury. By the time they have reached the heart level, the liquid is light and boiling into steam; at the back of the neck the feeling is one of a vapour. This passes over the head and descends the front of the body on exhalation. At the forehead the sensation is again of the collection of particles, small and golden. These become a golden light or liquid as they rush downward into the hara,[61] which is slapped by flattened warmth. Thereafter the body is infused with the joy of oneness with the Cosmic Buddha and the restatement of the certainty of His existence. This cycle of the Spiritual Fountain may be experienced only a few times in any given period even by an experienced meditator. It is the gathering of the will and the dispersing of the Rain of the Dharma.[62]

The ecstasy of meditation for an experienced meditator is actually indescribable. The reader should be aware that the fundamental purpose of meditation is union with the Source, the Cosmic Buddha, the Great Dharmakaya. Should you experience this ecstasy and then cling to it, it will immediately slip from your grasp. Meditation and daily training *are* Enlightenment; therefore in meditation there is no separation of means and ends.

MUDRA ORIGIN

The meditation mudra is found in the Buddhist iconography and is practiced daily in many schools of Buddhism.

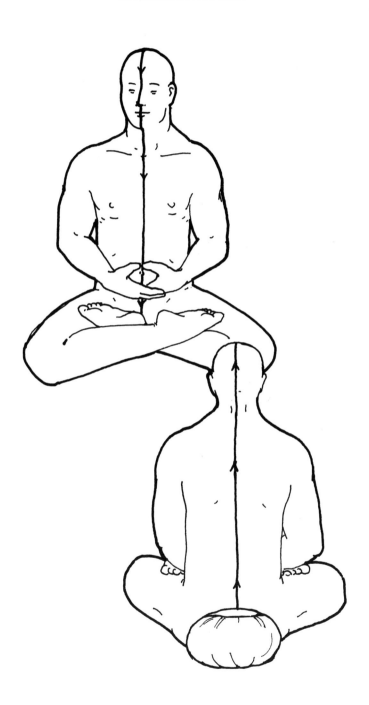

OFFERING MUDRA

MUDRA

Lie flat on a comfortable surface with your arms at your sides, hands open and palms upward. Be willing for all that is of the Lord to pass in through your left hand and enter your heart by the route shown on the facing page. Be willing to offer up to the Lord all within you from your heart across your chest and out your right hand. It is necessary to *want* to do this with your whole being in order for the mudra to have an effect. To use this mudra on yourself you need not touch the two points shown on the chart (they are for use when assisting someone else); just keep both palms upward, put your mind in meditation, and be willing. Whenever your hands try to close, make a point of keeping them open. A variant of this mudra may be used during seated meditation by opening both hands and resting them palms upward on the thighs. When this is done the flow of energy up the center of the back and down the front, which is characteristic of seated meditation, may interact with, and be predominant over, the energy pathway illustrated for this mudra.

TO ASSIST A FRIEND

She or he should follow the directions given above. You may sit on her right side and place your entire left hand on her chest with the heel of the hand on and a bit below point G and the fingers extending over point left G1. If urgent help is requested, it seems to be most effective to place your hand directly on your friend's chest under her or his clothing. This should be done only at your friend's request and, if your friend is female, please take care to respect her privacy as point G1 tends to be on or near the breast (it is located by its position relative to the ribs; the illustrated position relative to the breast may or may not hold true for a given person). Do not touch any points with your right hand; rather, open it fully and hold it palm upward. Allow anything which

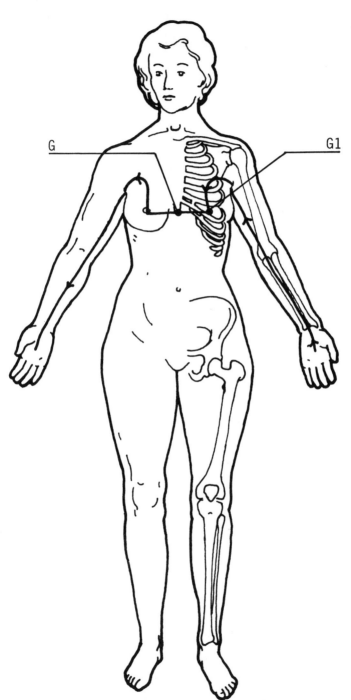

G

G1

enters from your friend through your left hand to pass through you along a path similar to the one illustrated here and be offered up out of your right hand. In this way you can assist your friend in offering up what is in her or his heart to That Which Is.

TIME

This pathway operates only when one is willing to give to, and receive from, all things without reservation.

USES

The mudra of offering is primarily a spiritual mudra. It is helpful when there is so much love in a person and so few opportunities to express it fully that it builds up and causes pain around point G1. It is also particularly good when sadness builds up around this point as a result of realizing that there is a great deal of suffering in the world and very little that one can do to ease it. Its greatest use is when one wishes to open oneself completely to the Buddhas and make a gesture of willingness to both accept and receive Them and all things and to give of oneself without reservation according to the vow of the Bodhisattva:

> However innumerable beings may be, I vow to save them all.
> However inexhaustible the passions are, I vow to transform them all.
> However limitless the Dharma is, I vow to understand it completely.
> However infinite the Buddha's Truth is, I vow to attain it.

There are also secondary uses when tension is encountered in the forms of:

Physical: tension, pain, stiffness, etc. along the lines of the pathway (*see caution given under the life-death mudra when heart pain is present*); tension associated with difficulties of breathing.

Mental: exhaustion, especially spiritual and mental; sadness or grief.

Karmic: karmic memories of having suffered or caused harm, in this or a previous life, by means of wounds along the path of energy flow or by means of abandonment; karmic memories of having taken life in any form and especially due to lack of love or by means of refusal of assistance.

WARNING

This is a mudra of absolute openness and receptivity. It may be unwise to use it when disturbing or harmful influences are present. Should you sense the proximity of any such negativity, you may close your left hand and switch to the diamond, earth witness, fearlessness, or spiritual defense mudra.

MUDRA ORIGIN

The mudra of offering was derived from the Buddhist iconography.

PEACE UPON THE PILLOW MUDRA

MUDRA

Step	Place your left hand on your:	Place your right hand on your:
1	left Z3	right Z3
2	left A1 & A	right A1 & A
3	right C1	left C1
4	right I2	left I2

In step two the fingertips of both hands meet at point A.

TO ASSIST A FRIEND

Sit on her or his left side and use either the mudra above or the one which follows:

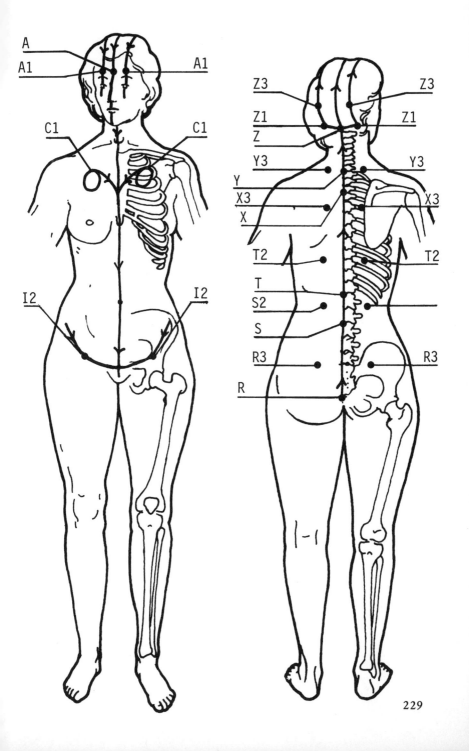

229

MUDRA

Step	Place your left hand on her:	Place your right hand on her:
1	Y	Z
2	X	
3	T	
4	S	
5	R	
6	left R3	right R3
7	left S2	right S2
8	left T2	right T2
9	left X3	right X3
10	left Y3	right Y3
11	left Z1	right Z1

TIME

The energy flow illustrated for these mudras is temporarily induced by the use of either of the mudras. These mudras affect the flow of the governing and conception vessel meridians and act to sedate and calm all of the other principal meridians.

USES

These mudras are used to promote a peaceful and relaxed sleep. You might also wish to consider taking the Three Refuges (I take refuge in the Buddha; I take refuge in the Dharma; I take refuge in the Sangha) before going to sleep and reciting the following mantra:

Peace Upon the Pillow
Makura Om
Makura Om
Makura Om

MUDRA ORIGIN

The mudra for self use was derived intuitively through meditation; the one for use with a friend was adapted from a release of Jin Shin Jyutsu.

PEACE-WORRY MUDRA

Affects the Stomach Meridian

LEFT MUDRA

Step	Place your left hand on your:	Place your right hand on your:
1	left Z5	left A4
2		left B2
3		left S2
4	left A4	
5		left G2 & H1
6		left I2 *or* I3
7		right J
8		right K & P1
9		right L2
10		right N1 & N2

PEACE-WORRY MUDRA (left)

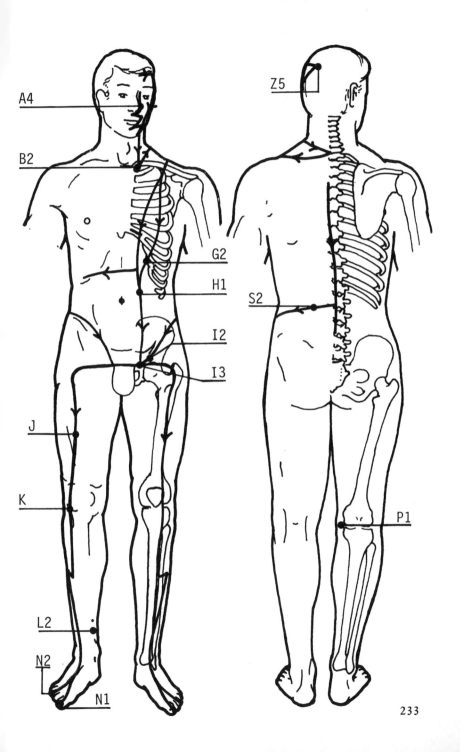

RIGHT MUDRA

Step	Place your left hand on your:	Place your right hand on your:
1	right Z5	right A4
2		right B2
3		right S2
4	right A4	
5		right G2 & H1
6		right I2 or I3
7		left J
8		left K & P1
9		left L2
10		left N1 & N2

TO ASSIST A FRIEND

Sit on his or her right side and place your hands as you would on yourself.

TIME

The stomach meridian has maximum energy flow from 8 A.M. to 10 A.M., standard time.

USES

The peace-worry mudra may assist you in accepting, relaxing, cleansing away, and/or discovering the causes of tensions encountered in meditation and daily life in the forms of:

Physical: tension, pain, stiffness, etc. along the pathway of the meridian; tension, pain, etc. in the area of the anatomical stomach; tension related to disturbances of appetite, digestion, or bowel function.

Mental: insomnia, anxiety, chronic worry, depression, oversensitivity, and distrust.

Karmic: karmic memories of having suffered or caused harm, in this or a previous life, by means of wounds in the stomach area or along the path of the meridian, illness in the stomach area, starvation, mental illness, stealing, deception, or slander.

BENEFICIAL INFLUENCES

The stomach meridian may be benefitted by the exercise of Right Understanding on the Eightfold Path, by the practice of the paramitas of knowledge and understanding, and by the development of all-acceptance and equanimity. On the physical level, it may be aided by supplementing your balanced diet with extra sweet ripe fruit, honey, mint, parsley, and asparagus.

HARMFUL INFLUENCES

The stomach meridian may be harmed by attachment to getting what one wants and to avoiding decay, by the poison of greed, and by breaking the Precepts against stealing, selling the wine of delusion, meanness in giving, and being proud of oneself and devaluing others. Emotional states of worry, anxiety, depression, and distrust have a detrimental effect, as does the taking of unnecessary physical or spiritual risks.

MUDRA ORIGIN

The peace-worry mudra was derived from the meridian through meditation.

RELAXATION MUDRA

MUDRA

Step	Place your left hand on your:	Place your right hand on your:
1	C	R
2		S
3		T*
4		T4*
5		Y
6		Z7
7	H	
8	I	A

TO ASSIST A FRIEND

Sit on his or her left side and place your hands as you would on yourself. You may make the mudra even more effective by placing your entire left hand over points C, H, and I instead of using just the fingers.

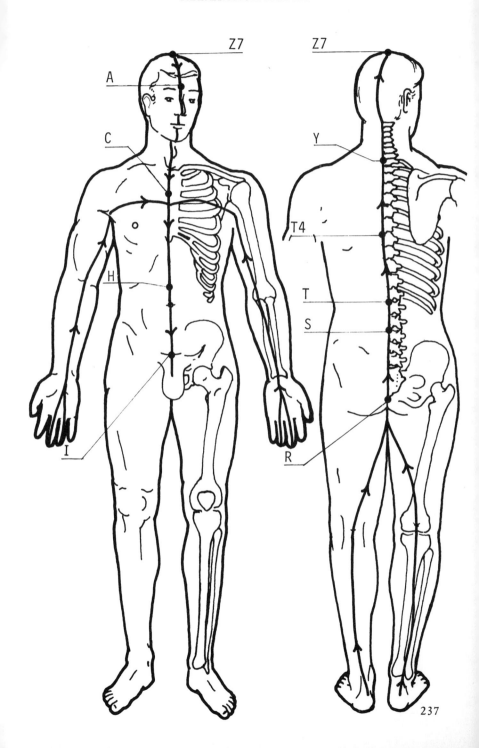

TIME

This mudra affects the governing and conception vessel meridians which have a continuous flow of energy through them. The arm and leg branches illustrated for this mudra are induced temporarily by its use.

USES

This is a variant of the spiritual bathing mudra and uses primarily the same meridians. It may be substituted for that mudra when a more physical and less spiritual effect is desired. Its primary use is as a powerful and deep relaxing mudra to counteract tension, overwork, and physical, mental, and spiritual exhaustion. Other uses include assistance with tension in the forms of:

Physical: tension, pain, stiffness, etc. along the lines of the pathway illustrated for this mudra; tension involved in tightness or congestion of the chest, or in the regulation of the appetite; the mudra is useful for simple general relaxation.

Mental: overstimulation, anxiety, general tension, vulnerability, fatigue, weakness, insomnia.

Karmic: karmic memories of having suffered or caused harm, in this or a previous life, by means of wounds along the path of the flow of this mudra (especially in the chest) or by exhaustion. This mudra is excellent for promoting relaxation after the reliving of a traumatic karmic memory.

MUDRA ORIGIN

This mudra was adapted from a release of Jin Shin Jyutsu.

RELIEF-FRUSTRATION MUDRA

Affects the Gall Bladder Meridian

LEFT MUDRA

Step	Place your left hand on your:	Place your right hand on your:
1	left A1 & A3	Y & left Y2
2	left Z5	
3	left Z3	
4		left C3 & X1*
5	Y & left Y2	
6		left G2 & S3
7		left I1 & R2
8		left P & P3
9	[optional: left C3 & X1*]	left L3 & O
10		left M4 & N3

RIGHT MUDRA

Step	Place your left hand on your:	Place your right hand on your:
1	right A1 & A3	Y & right Y2
2	right Z5	
3	right Z3	
4		right C3 & X1*
5	Y & right Y2	
6		right G2 & S3
7		right I1 & R2
8		right P & P3
9	[optional: right C3 & X1]	right L3 & O
10		right M4 & N3

TO ASSIST A FRIEND

Sit on her or his right side and place your hands as you would on yourself.

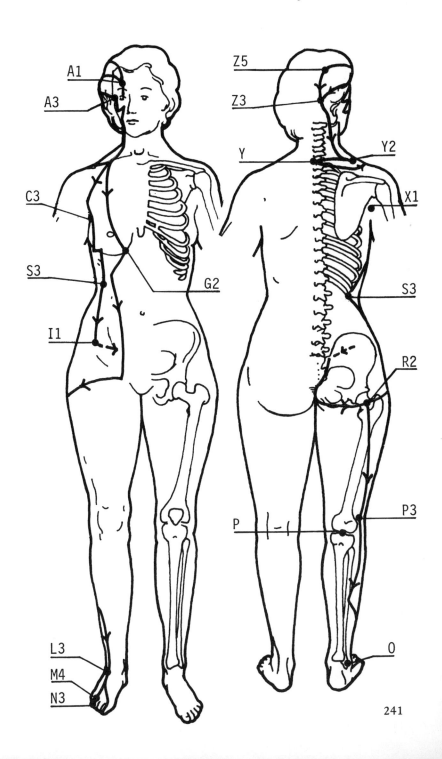

TIME

The gall bladder meridian has maximum energy during the hours of midnight to 2 A.M., standard time.

USES

The relief-frustration mudra may assist you in accepting, relaxing, cleansing away, and/or discovering the causes of tensions encountered in meditation and daily life in the forms of:

Physical: tension, pain, stiffness, etc. along the pathway of the meridian; tension, pain, etc. in the area of the anatomical gall bladder; tension which affects disturbances of digestion or temperature regulation.

Mental: frustration, anger (especially suppressed anger), depression, insomnia, restlessness, timidity.

Karmic: karmic memories of having suffered or caused harm, in this or a previous life, by means of wounds in the gall bladder area or along the lines of the meridian, illness in the gall bladder area, or by reason of anger.

BENEFICIAL INFLUENCES

The gall bladder meridian may be benefitted by the exercise of Right Mindfulness on the Eightfold Path, by the practice of the paramita of patience, and by the development of compassion both for others and for oneself. On the physical level, it may be assisted by supplementing your balanced diet with extra eggs, oils, and tart fruits, especially in combination with each other, as in Hollandaise sauce.

HARMFUL INFLUENCES

The gall bladder meridian may be harmed by attachment to dislike of other people, by the poison of anger, and by breaking the Precept against being angry. Among the mental states, frustration and chronic anger are most detrimental. Any act that produces tension or harm to any other organ or meridian in one's own body or that of another person will cause sympathetic tension in the gall bladder meridian.

MUDRA ORIGIN

The relief-frustration mudra was derived from the meridian through meditation.

REVERENCE MUDRA OR GASSHŌ

MUDRA

Regardless of the position of the rest of the body, open both hands and bring them together so that the palms and fingers of both are touching firmly. There should be no space between the hands or between the fingers of each hand. Bring the hands to your body so that the thumbs touch the chest and the arms are level.

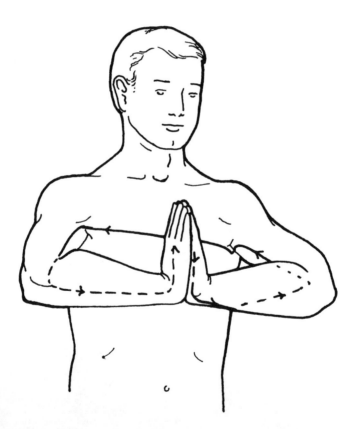

TO ASSIST A FRIEND

This mudra is for self use only.

TIME

The effects of this mudra are present during its use.

USES

The *gasshō* is the most commonly used of all Buddhist mudras. It is a mudra of reverence and sincerity, and it is the mudra with which the Buddha was greeted by His followers. It is used as a greeting between Buddhists, who recognize the inherent Buddhahood of their fellow men. It also helps to unify the body and mind and promotes right concentration on the Way of training. Thus it should not be done nonchalantly. The fingers and palms must not spread apart, for their union symbolizes, and is a direct expression of, the unity of all opposites. It is through use of the gasshō that we transcend the duality of heaven and hell and come to the realization of the harmony of body and mind. The gasshō is excellent to help unify and calm the body and mind when one has become scattered or distracted. The use of this mudra, even for an instant, can break the hold of seemingly frantic circumstances and give one a fresh perspective. Thus in a Zen temple you will see people making the mudra of gasshō not only to each other and to the Buddha statue and the Scriptures, but also to their work, their food, the mistakes they have just made, and in any situation where it is good to collect oneself in a state of single-mindedness and reverence.

MUDRA ORIGIN

This mudra is found in the Buddhist iconography, is used widely throughout Buddhism, and is explained in detail in the papers given to senior priests of the Sōtō Zen Church.

SECURITY-VULNERABILITY MUDRA

Affects the Spleen Meridian

LEFT MUDRA

Step	Place your left hand on your:	Place your right hand on your:
1	right N & N1	right M1
2		right K1
3		right P1
4		right J1
5	right P1	
6		I
7	right I2	
8		left H1
9	I	
10		left G2

(continued)

SECURITY-VULNERABILITY MUDRA (left)

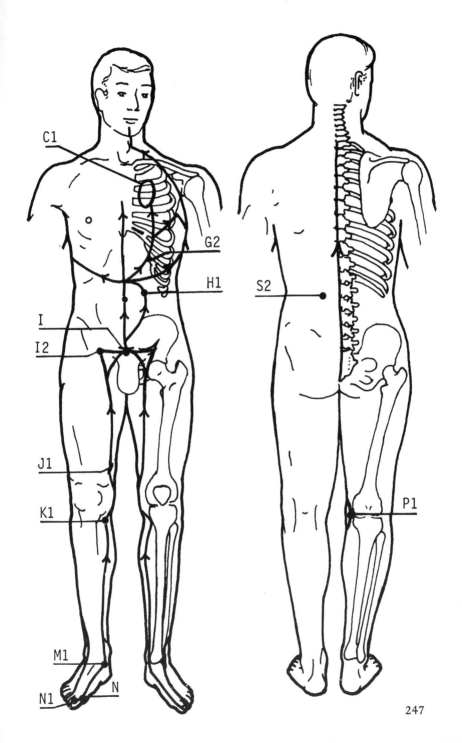

247

Step	Place your left hand on your:	Place your right hand on your:
11		left S2
12		left C1

RIGHT MUDRA

Step	Place your left hand on your:	Place your right hand on your:
1	left N & N1	left M1
2		left K1
3		left P1
4		left J1
5	left P1	
6		I
7	left I2	
8		right H1
9	I	

(continued)

Step	Place your left hand on your:	Place your right hand on your:
10		right G2
11		right S2
12		right C1

TO ASSIST A FRIEND

Sit on his or her left side and place your hands as you would on yourself.

TIME

The spleen meridian has maximum energy flow from 10 A.M. to noon, standard time.

USES

This mudra may assist you in accepting, relaxing, cleansing away, and/or discovering the causes of tensions encountered in meditation and daily life in the forms of:

Physical: tension, pain, stiffness, etc. along the path of the meridian; tension, pain, etc. in the areas of the anatomical spleen and pancreas; tensions related to disturbances of digestion and metabolism. Note: to affect the spleen, the left mudra is more effective; to affect the pancreas, the right mudra is preferable.

Mental: generalized anxiety, feelings of vulnerability and insecurity, insomnia, deep fatigue or exhaustion, obsession, oversensitivity, and excessive concentration.

Karmic: karmic memories of having suffered or caused harm, in this or a previous life, by means of wounds in the spleen or pancreas areas or along the lines of the meridian, illness of the spleen or pancreas, sexual abuse, or situations of extreme vulnerability.

BENEFICIAL INFLUENCES

The spleen meridian may be benefitted by the exercise of Right Understanding on the Eightfold Path, by the practice of the paramitas of knowledge and understanding, and by the development and exercise of all-acceptance. On the physical level it may be aided by supplementing your balanced diet with extra sweet ripe fruit, honey (especially Tupelo blossom honey), asparagus, parsley, and mint. A secure and protected environment for sleep is also highly beneficial.

HARMFUL INFLUENCES

The spleen meridian may be harmed particularly by attachment to avoiding disease and decay, by the poison of greed, and by breaking the Precepts against stealing and selling the wine of delusion. Suffering (or causing) insulting behavior, insecurity, or vulnerability have a deleterious effect, as does taking unnecessary physical or spiritual risks.

MUDRA ORIGIN

The security-vulnerability mudra was derived from the meridian through meditation.

SEXUAL PEACE MUDRA

LEFT MUDRA

Step	Place your left hand on your:	Place your right hand on your:
1	I	left R3
2		right X2*
3		left Z1
4	left G2	
5		left C1
6		left S2
7		R
8		right J1
9	left S2	
10		right L3
11		right N1

RIGHT MUDRA

Step	Place your left hand on your:	Place your right hand on your:
1	I	right R3
2		left X2*
3		right Z1
4	right G2	
5		right C1
6		right S2
7		R
8		left J1
9	right S2	
10		left L3
11		left N1

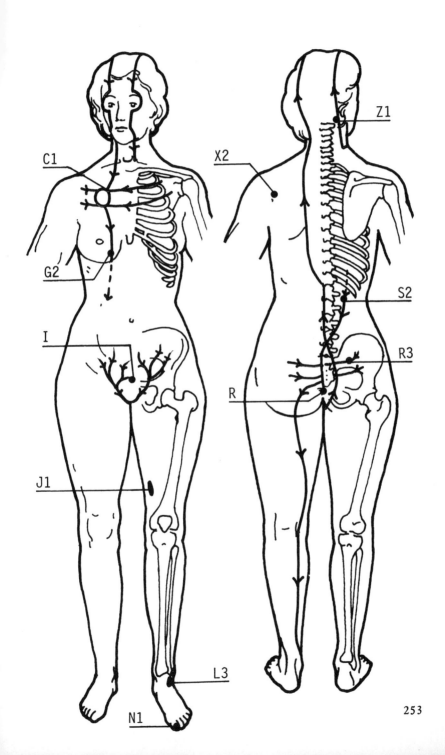

TO ASSIST A FRIEND

Sit on her or his right side and place your hands as you would on yourself.

TIME

Energy flows temporarily through the path illustrated for this mudra as a result of doing the mudra.

USES

The sexual peace mudra may be of assistance in accepting, relaxing, cleansing away, and/or discovering the causes of tensions encountered in meditation and daily life in the forms of:

Physical: tension, pain, stiffness, etc. along the lines of energy flow produced by this mudra; tension or pain in the sexual organs or pubic region generally; tension affecting sexual dysfunction or menstrual discomfort.

Mental: sexually-related tension, anxiety, or fear.

Karmic: karmic memories of having suffered or caused harm, in this or a previous life, by means of wounds along the lines of energy flow established by this mudra (and especially in the genitals), sexual abuse, or difficulties of childbirth.

MUDRA ORIGIN

The first three steps of this mudra were adapted from a release of Jin Shin Dō; the remainder were derived intuitively through meditation.

SPIRITUAL BATHING MUDRA

Affects the Governing Vessel and Conception Vessel Meridians

MUDRA

Step	Place your left hand on your:	Place your right hand on your:
1	Y6	Z
2	Z2	
3	Z7	
4	A	
5	B	Y
6	C	X*
7	G	T4*
8	H2	S or T
9	I	R

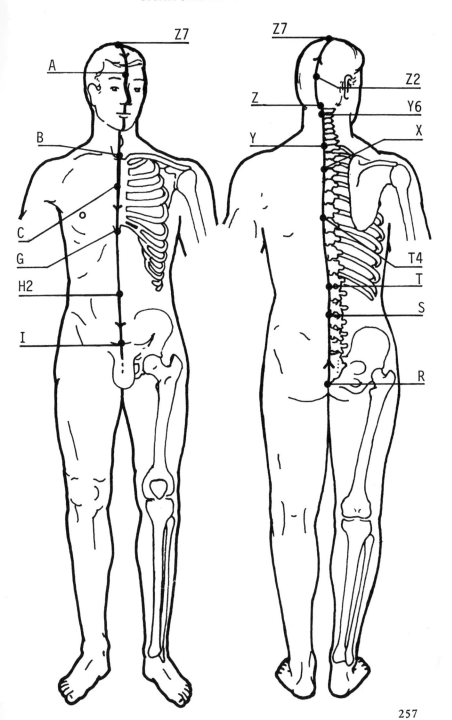

TO ASSIST A FRIEND

Sit on his or her left side and place your hands as you would on yourself. It is extraordinarily important that the movement of energy stimulated by this mudra run up the back, over the head, and down the front. Please do not reverse your hands or do anything which could cause it to move in the opposite direction.

TIME

The meridians of the governing and conception vessels have a continuous energy circulation up the back and down the front. This is the largest and most fundamental energy pathway of the body. It may fluctuate in strength from time to time as situations require.

USES

These two meridians are really one continuous loop and are thus considered as one meridian for the purposes of this book. This central meridian is the most important of all for the physical and mental balance of the body and for spiritual development. It is through this pathway that the energy rushes in religious awakenings such as the rising of the Kundalini in yoga[63] or the kenshō of Zen.[64] It is also the normal channel for energy flow during Zen meditation.[64] When this energy can be felt running through the body it is experienced as an exquisite bathing in a Fountain of Pure Love. The spiritual bathing mudra will not produce religious awakenings; there is no shortcut to the life of religious training and pure meditation. It can, however, be used to help remove tensions in the meridian which may cause fear or pain to be felt when the spiritual energy flows strongly. This is one of the primary uses of this mudra.

Since the central channel is also the largest and most powerful meridian, it exerts a strong influence on body and mind as well as spirit. Thus the spiritual bathing mudra may also be used to promote general balance and well-being. In fact, any condition which can be assisted through the use of any other mudra can also be assisted by the use of this one, although it may require a longer time or a more frequent use of the mudra. In addition to these functions the mudra also has uses when tension is found in the forms of:

Physical: tension, pain, stiffness, etc. along the pathway of the meridian (especially in the back), tension related to problems of appetite or temperature regulation (especially cold extremities), or to sexual dysfunction, general weakness, chest congestion and breathing difficulties, stiffness of the back, general rigidity of the body, and poor posture.

Mental: mental and/or spiritual unrest of all types, especially instability, tension, anxiety, vulnerability, and overstimulation; it may also benefit exhaustion and fatigue.

Karmic: karmic memories of having suffered or caused harm, in this or a previous life, by means of wounds along the path of the meridian, cold, starvation, abandonment, bodily disintegration, or electrocution.

MUDRA ORIGIN

The spiritual bathing mudra was derived from the meridian through meditation. Analogous releases are found in both Jin Shin Jyutsu and Jin Shin Dō.

SPIRITUAL CLEANSING MUDRA

Affects the Intersection of Meridians
at Junction Points I2 or I3

LEFT MUDRA

Step	Place your left hand on your:	Place your right hand on your:
1	left I2 *or* I3	right H1
2		left S2
3		left & right J1
4		right G2
5		left T3*
6		left & right P1
7		right X3*
8		all left toes
9		all right toes
10		left & right A1

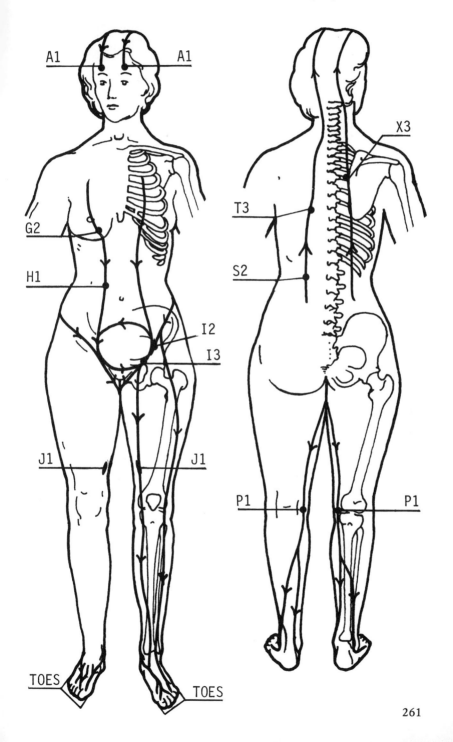

A1 · A1

X3

G2

T3

H1

S2

I2

I3

J1 · J1

P1 · P1

TOES

TOES

RIGHT MUDRA

Step	Place your left hand on your:	Place your right hand on your:
1	right I2 *or* I3	left H1
2		right S2
3		left & right J1
4		left G2
5		right T3*
6		left & right P1
7		left X3*
8		all right toes
9		all left toes
10		left & right A1

TO ASSIST A FRIEND

Sit on her or his left side and place your hands as you would on yourself.

TIME

The lines of energy flow illustrated for this mudra are temporarily brought into being by its use.

USES

Many people find tension in the pelvic area, and this tension is often of a type which makes it difficult for a person to become peaceful within himself and thus gain access to the spiritual life. This mudra was created to assist with such tension, which is often associated with one of the meridians which intersect at points 12 or 13: the gall bladder, kidney, liver, lower belt, penetrating vessel, spleen, stomach, and ventral linking meridians. It is particularly useful as the first in a series of mudras since it has a generally cleansing and relaxing effect. It may also assist when tension is encountered in the forms of:

Physical: tension, pain, stiffness, etc. along the energy pathway illustrated for this mudra, especially in the pelvis, abdomen, back and head; tension involved in disturbances of circulation, digestion, and bowel function; it is useful for general body relaxation.

Mental: sexual tension.

Karmic: karmic memories of having suffered or caused harm, in this or a previous life, by means of wounds along the lines of flow illustrated for this mudra or by sexual abuse.

MUDRA ORIGIN

The spiritual cleansing mudra was derived intuitively from meditation.

SPIRITUAL DEFENSE MUDRA

MUDRA

Regardless of the position of the rest of the body, make a fist of the left hand, fingers closed around the thumb, and hold it against the side of the abdomen on or near point left H1. If possible, bring the rest of your left forearm into contact with your abdomen and side. The right hand is free to do whatever may be necessary. In the ceremonial uses of this mudra, the right hand is often placed in the mudra of *kaiko* (illustrated here), a gesture of blessing in which the index and middle fingers are extended while the thumb covers the curled ring and little fingers.

TO ASSIST A FRIEND

This mudra is for self use only.

TIME

During its use, the mudra renders the meridians in the abdominal area inaccessible to external influences.

USES

This, like the diamond mudra, is a mudra of protection against influence by evil or disturbing external events. The spiritual defense mudra protects especially the stomach and spleen meridians, which are most likely to become tense in such situations. It protects one against feeling insecure, worried, or vulnerable and against being drained of spiritual energy by the demands, anger, or unreasonable behavior of others. Unlike the diamond mudra it does not protect the heart and so may not offer sufficient protection in extreme circumstances or for those whose faith and training are young. It does, however, offer the possibility of positive action with the right hand and is thus more adaptable and

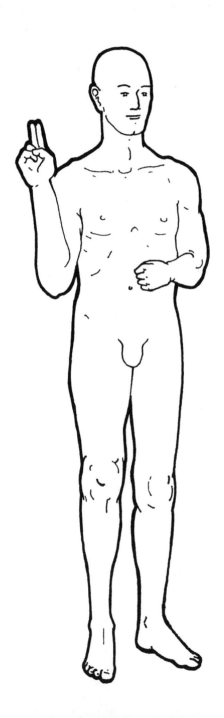

constructive than the purely defensive diamond mudra. It also has an advantage in that closing one hand and placing it at the waist can be done relatively unobtrusively and thus it can be used to help keep one's equilibrium in a social situation where the diamond mudra would look highly inappropriate. The simple closing of the left hand, even if not placed at the waist, gives some measure of protection from disturbing influences, as it seals the most receptive part of the body. The closed left hand can be used with other mudras (such as the earth witness mudra) to add an element of protection when advisable.

MUDRA ORIGIN

The spiritual defense mudra is seen in the Buddhist iconography and is found in the papers given to senior priests of the Sōtō Zen Church.

SPIRITUAL JUNCTION MUDRA

Affects the Intersection of Meridians
at the Junction of the Neck

MUDRA

Step	Place your left hand on your:	Place your right hand on your:
1	left &/or right Z1 or Y4 or Y5	Z7
2		B
3		left & right C1
4		G
5		left & right H1
6		I
7		left & right J1
8		left & right P1
9		left & right M1
10		left & right N1

(continued)

Step	Place your left hand on your:	Place your right hand on your:
11		R
12		left &/or right R3
13		S1 & T
14		[optional: T4*]

TO ASSIST A FRIEND

Sit on his or her right side and place your hands as you would on yourself.

TIME

This mudra makes use of the governing and conception vessel meridians which are in continuous flow up the center of the back and down the center of the front of the body. The branches illustrated on the accompanying diagram are temporarily created by use of the mudra.

USES

The neck is an area in which many people feel tension. This mudra was created to help alleviate such tension and understand its causes. It may be of assistance when a meridian which passes through the neck is blocked there. Since all of the main meridians except the pericardium and belt meridians have at least a branch in the neck area, this mudra can be very useful. Use whichever of points Z1, Y4, or Y5 is closest to the location of the tension or, if none of these seem right, place your left hand directly on the tense area.

SPIRITUAL JUNCTION MUDRA (front)

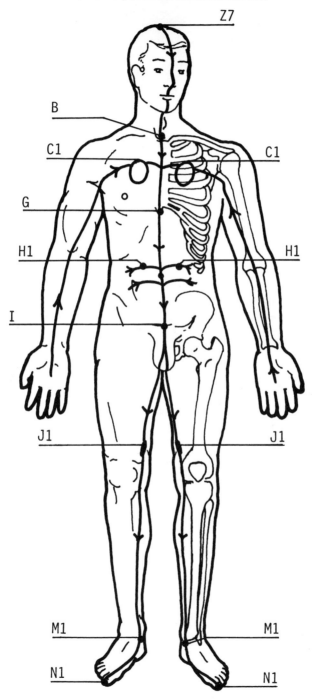

Z7

B

C1   C1

G

H1   H1

I

J1   J1

M1   M1

N1   N1

When the tension centers around points Z1, the use of junction mudra Z1 should also be considered. In addition to these uses, the spiritual junction mudra may also be of help for tension in the following forms:

Physical: tension, pain, stiffness, etc. along the pathway diagrammed for this mudra, especially in the form of general body tension or back tension.

Mental: general mental tension.

Karmic: karmic memories of having suffered or caused harm, in this or a previous life, by means of wounds along the pathway illustrated for this mudra, especially in the neck area.

MUDRA ORIGIN

The spiritual junction mudra was derived intuitively through meditation.

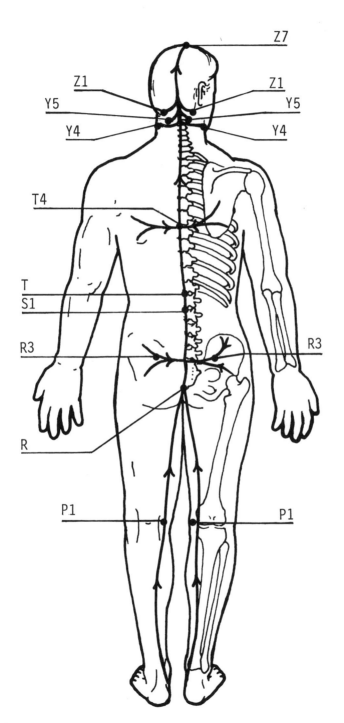

SPIRITUAL UNREST MUDRA

Affects the Intersection of Meridians
at Junction Point C1

LEFT MUDRA

Step	Place your left hand on your:	Place your right hand on your:
1	left C1	left T3*
2		C
3		Y
4		right D1*
5		left D1
6		G
7		touch thumb to right U2
8		touch thumb to right U
9		left U2
10		left U

(continued)

272

SPIRITUAL UNREST MUDRA (left-front)

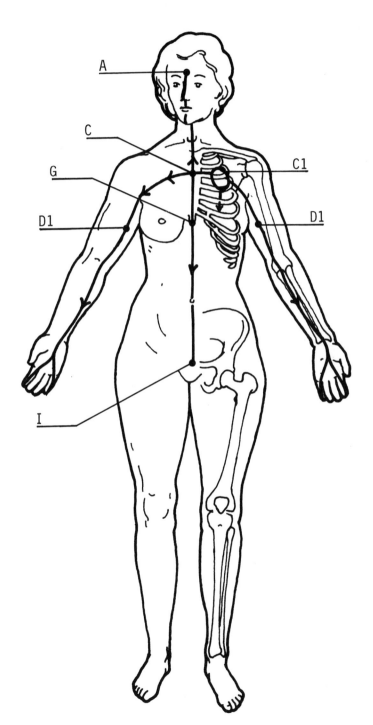

Step	Place your left hand on your:	Place your right hand on your:
11		I
12		T4*
13		T
14	A	R4

RIGHT MUDRA

Step	Place your left hand on your:	Place your right hand on your:
1	right C1	right T3*
2		C
3		Y
4		left D1
5		right D1*
6		G
7		left U2

(continued)

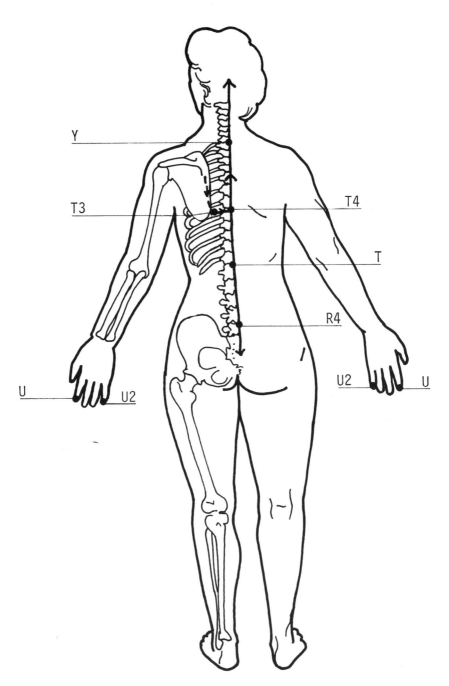

SPIRITUAL UNREST MUDRA (left-back)

Y

T3

T4

T

R4

U2

U

U

U2

Step	Place your left hand on your:	Place your right hand on your:
8		left U
9		touch thumb to right U2
10		touch thumb to right U
11		I
12		T4*
13		T
14	A	R4

TO ASSIST A FRIEND

Sit on her or his right side and place your hands as you would on yourself. Points U and U2 may be held in the usual manner rather than with the thumb.

TIME

The flow of energy illustrated on the preceding pages is produced temporarily by use of this mudra.

USES

This mudra may assist when meridians are blocked at or near their intersection at point C1. These meridians may include the heart, kidney, liver, lung, middle belt, penetrating vessel, small intestine, spleen, stomach, triple warmer, and ventral linking meridians. Its primary function is to assist you in understanding and dealing with problems of spiritual unrest which frequently seem to have the effect of producing tension, pains, etc. at or near point C1. It also may be of use in helping you to accept, relax, cleanse away, and/or discover the causes of tensions encountered in meditation and daily life in the forms of:

Physical: tension, pain, stiffness, etc. in the areas through which energy passes when this mudra is done, especially in the chest and armpit; difficulty in breathing due to tension in the muscles of the chest; tension related to difficulties of the sexual or other glandular organs, including menstrual tension; tension associated with problems of appetite, digestion, or elimination; and feelings of excessive cold. The mudra tends to have a generally relaxing and invigorating property.

Mental: general malaise and unrest, dullness or heaviness of mind, feelings of vulnerability or insecurity, sexual tension.

Karmic: karmic memories of having suffered or caused harm, in this or a previous life, by means of wounds along the path of flow diagrammed for this mudra, exposure, excessive cold, sexual abuse, or magic.

MUDRA ORIGIN

The spiritual unrest mudra was adapted from a release of Jin Shin Jyutsu.

TOP OF HARA MUDRA

LEFT MUDRA

Step	Place your left hand on your:	Place your right hand on your:
1	left G1	left C3
2		left C4 *or* C5
3		left G2
4		left I2
5		right Z1 *or* Z3
6	Place both hands on point G	

RIGHT MUDRA

Step	Place your left hand on your:	Place your right hand on your:
1	right G1	right C3
2		right C4 *or* C5
3		right G2

(continued)

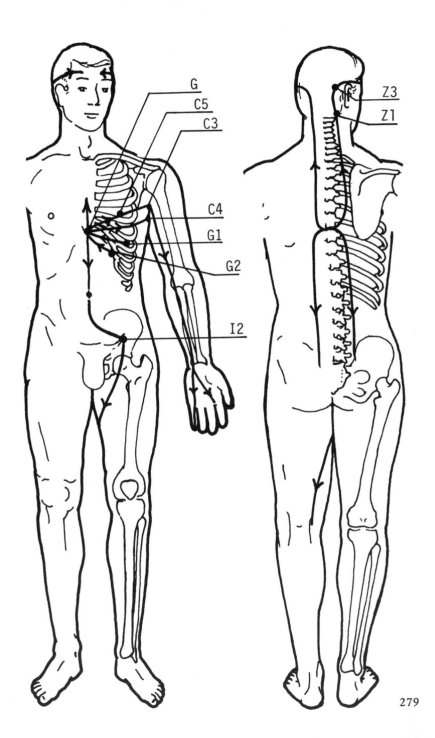

G
C5
C3
C4
G1
G2
I2
Z3
Z1

Step	Place your left hand on your:	Place your right hand on your:
4		right I2
5		left Z1 *or* Z3
6	Place both hands on point G	

The above points are approximate and may vary considerably with different people or occasions.

WARNING

This mudra can produce temporary physical exhaustion and stimulate dreaming to the point of producing restless sleep. It also has a substantial discovery property. Like the effects of any mudra, these effects are unlikely to occur unless you are meditating while doing the mudra. Since some people do this to a certain extent without knowing it, however, please pay attention to this warning regardless of whether or not you believe that you know how to meditate.

TO ASSIST A FRIEND

For the left mudra sit on his or her left side; for the right mudra sit on his or her right side. Place your hands as you would on yourself. *Step 6 should be done by your friend on him or herself.*

TIME

The energy pattern diagrammed here is temporarily created by use of the mudra.

USES

This mudra was created to help with problems of spiritual exhaustion. This is the state which arises when one has given all of one's energy to others without the opportunity to refresh one's spirit adequately through Zazen, rest, food, and fellowship. Sometimes this state of spiritual exhaustion is felt generally and sometimes it seems to focus in the chest area, causing pain, stiffness, and even difficulty in breathing (*pain in the chest and difficulty in breathing can, of course, be symptoms of serious physical disease; please consult your physician if you have reason to believe that this might be the case*). The top of the hara mudra can be used to help correct this exhaustion, but it is not a substitute for proper meditation, rest, nourishment, and companionship with fellow trainees. This mudra also has a mild tendency to relax the mind so that forgotten memories may come into awareness; it can thus be used as a discovery mudra. In addition to these uses it may be helpful for the following conditions:

Physical: tension, pain, stiffness, etc. along the lines of the path of the energy flow produced by this mudra, general tension or exhaustion, and tension which is concomitant with difficulties in breathing, especially those related to spasm or stiffness of the muscles of the chest wall.

Mental: exhaustion, overstimulation, inability or lack of opportunity to give to others or to love them (this is the inverse of spiritual exhaustion, in which one has given so much that there seems to be nothing left to give), or timidity.

Karmic: karmic memories of having suffered or caused harm, in this or a previous life, by means of wounds along the pathway established by this mudra, suffocation, exhaustion, abandonment, lack of love, or refusal of assistance.

MUDRA ORIGIN

This mudra was derived intuitively from meditation.

TRUTH-LIE MUDRA

Affects the Lung Meridian

LEFT MUDRA

Step	Place your left hand on your:	Place your right hand on your:
1	[optional: H3]	left X1
2	[optional: H]	
3	left C2	
4		left D1
5		left E
6		left D
7		left D3 & W
8		left E3
9	left C1	
10		left U3

(continued)

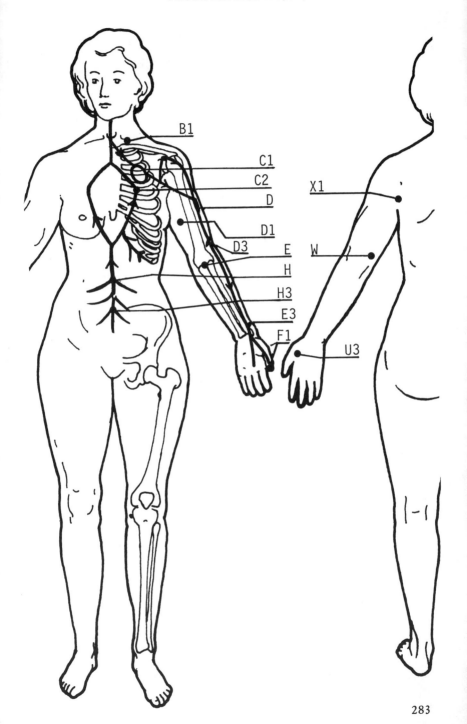

B1

C1
C2
D
X1
D1
D3 E W
H
H3
E3
F1 U3

Step	Place your left hand on your:	Place your right hand on your:
11	left B1	↓
12	↓	left F1

RIGHT MUDRA

Step	Place your left hand on your:	Place your right hand on your:
1	[optional: H3]	right X1 *or* touch right middle finger to right F1
2	[optional: H]	
3	right C2	
4	right C1	
5	right B1	↓
6	↓	touch right middle finger to right F1

TO ASSIST A FRIEND

For the left mudra sit on her or his left side and place your hands as you would on yourself. For the right mudra sit on her or his right side and place your hands as follows:

RIGHT MUDRA

Step	Place your left hand on her:	Place your right hand on her:
1	[optional: H3]	right X1
2	[optional: H]	
3	right C2	
4		right D1
5		right E
6		right D
7		right D3 & W
8		right E3
9	right C1	
10		right U3
11	right B1	
12		right F1

TIME
The lung meridian has maximum energy flow during the hours of 4 A.M. to 6 A.M., standard time.

USES
The truth-lie mudra may assist you in accepting, relaxing, cleansing away, and/or discovering the causes of tensions encountered in meditation and daily life in the forms of:

Physical: tension, pain, stiffness, etc. along the pathway of the lung meridian; tension, pain, etc. in the anatomical lung area.

Mental: depression (especially the tense, agitated variety), anguish, sadness, guilt, feelings that one is unable to express oneself completely, obsessions with past deceptions, fears of asphyxiation or of being in closed places, loneliness, and alienation.

Karmic: karmic memories of having suffered or caused harm, in this or a previous life, by means of wounds in the lung area or along the lines of the meridian, illness in the lung area, suffocation, lies or deceptions, slander, and abandonment.

BENEFICIAL INFLUENCES
The lung meridian may be benefitted by the exercise of Right Speech on the Eightfold Path, by the practice of the paramita of skill in means (how to act within the Truth to lead all beings towards Enlightenment), and the cultivation of truthfulness in all things. On the physical level it may be aided by supplementing your balanced diet with extra tomatoes, onions, garlic, and vinegar (especially cider, wine, or other undistilled natural vinegars).

HARMFUL INFLUENCES
The meridian may be harmed by attachment to getting what one wants, by the poison of greed, and by breaking the Precepts against untruthfulness, speaking against others, and defaming the Three Treasures of Buddha, Dharma, and Sangha. Fears of suffocation, feelings of depression or guilt, and being unable to tell the truth fully are also damaging.

MUDRA ORIGIN
The truth-lie mudra was derived from the lung meridian through meditation.

VENTRAL LINKING MUDRA

Affects the Ventral Linking Meridian

LEFT MUDRA

Step	Place your left hand on your:	Place your right hand on your:
1	left M1	left J1
2	left O2	
3	left P	
4		left I2
5	left J1	
6		left H1
7		left G2
8		left C2
9		left B2
10		B

RIGHT MUDRA

Step	Place your left hand on your:	Place your right hand on your:
1	right M1	right J1
2	right O2	
3	right P	
4		right I2
5	right J1	
6		right H1
7		right G2
8		right C2
9		right B2
10		B

TO ASSIST A FRIEND

Sit on his or her left side and place your hands as you would on yourself.

VENTRAL LINKING MUDRA(right)

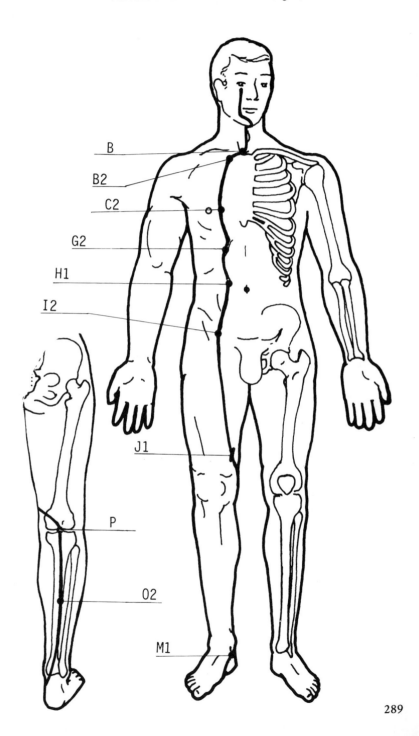

B

B2

C2

G2

H1

I2

J1

P

O2

M1

TIME

The ventral linking mudra has energy passing through it intermittently as needed.

USES

This meridian ascends the body on the ventral side, linking and harmonizing the interaction between the following meridians: lung, heart, conception vessel, pericardium, spleen, kidney, and liver. Its effect is strongest on the first three. The ventral linking mudra may be of use whenever blocks are encountered in any of these meridians or there is a disequilibrium among them. The mudra may also be of use for tensions in the following forms:

Physical: tension, pain, stiffness, etc. along the path of the meridian, especially at the waist or around the heart (*please see the caution statements given under the life-death mudra before using any mudra when pain is present around the heart*), tension in the back or genital area, and tension which is related to indigestion, problems of bowel function (especially constipation), problems of water elimination, sexual dysfunction, or menstrual difficulties.

Mental: lassitude, fatigue, fears, anxiety, timidity, sadness or depression, uncontrollable laughter, nightmares, sexual tension or absence of sexual pleasure, and weakness of memory.

Karmic: karmic memories of having suffered or caused harm, in this or a previous life, by means of wounds in the path of the meridian, starvation, sexual abuse, or mental illness.

MUDRA ORIGIN

The ventral linking mudra was derived from the meridian through meditation.

WILL-DESPAIR MUDRA

Affects the Kidney Meridian

LEFT MUDRA

Step	Place your left hand on your:	Place your right hand on your:
1	left N4	I
2	left M1	
3	left P1	
4	I	R
5	right H1	
6	right G2	
7	right S2	
8	right C1	
9	right A2	
10	right Z5	
11	right X1	

RIGHT MUDRA

Step	Place your left hand on your:	Place your right hand on your:
1	right N4	I
2	right M1	
3	right P1	
4	I	R
5	left H1	
6	left G2	
7	left S2	
8	left C1	
9	left A2	
10	left Z5	
11	left X1*	

WILL-DESPAIR MUDRA (right)

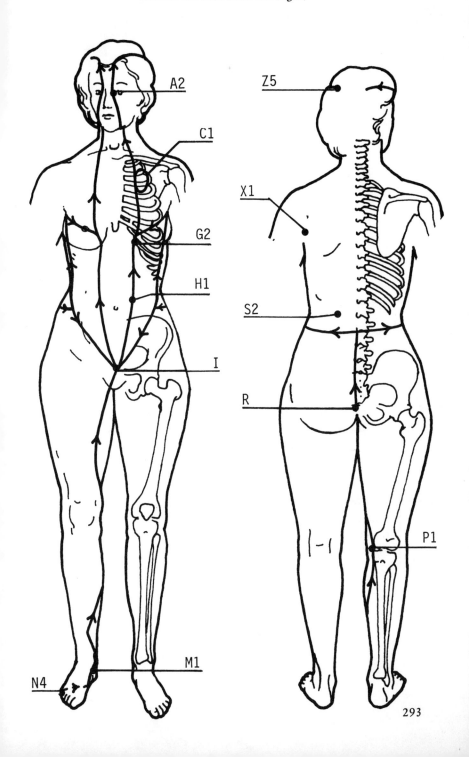

293

TO ASSIST A FRIEND

For the left mudra sit on her or his right side; for the right mudra sit on her or his left side. Place your hands as you would on yourself.

TIME

The kidney meridian has maximum energy flow from 6 P.M. to 8 P.M., standard time.

USES

The will-despair mudra may assist you in accepting, relaxing, cleansing away, and/or discovering the causes of tensions encountered in meditation and daily life in the forms of:

Physical: tension, pain, stiffness, etc. along the path of the kidney meridian; tension, pain, etc. in the area of the anatomical kidney; tension associated with metabolic and related disturbances, with problems of water elimination, and with sensitivity to cold.

Mental: deep fear (panic, terror), despair, alienation, distrust, pride, inadequacy, boredom, and lack of energy.

WARNING

The will-despair mudra has a substantial discovery property and may tend to increase the likelihood of your uncovering traumatic memories or feelings of deep fear or despair any time up to 72 hours after having used the mudra. As always, the effects of the mudra depend upon your meditation but, since people sometimes meditate without knowing that they are doing so, please heed this warning whenever you use this mudra, regardless of whether or not anything seems to happen at the time.

Karmic: karmic memories of having suffered or caused harm, in this or a previous life, by means of wounds in the kidney area or along the lines of the meridian, illness in the kidney area, extreme cold or exposure, despair, fear, treachery, magic, or deception.

BENEFICIAL INFLUENCES

The kidney meridian may be benefitted by the exercise of Right Effort on the Eightfold Path, by the practice of the paramita of vigor, and by the development and proper use of will. On the physical level, it may be assisted by supplementing your balanced diet with extra celery, carrots, fresh (not dry) peas and beans, sage, and thyme.

HARMFUL INFLUENCES

This meridian may be harmed by attachment to a false notion of self or of existence, by the poison of delusion, and by breaking the Precepts against defaming the Three Treasures of Buddha, Dharma, and Sangha and against being proud of oneself and devaluing others. Mental states of despair, fear, pride, and inadequacy are also detrimental.

MUDRA ORIGIN

The will-despair mudra was derived from the kidney meridian through meditation.

ANNOTATIONS.

The following abbreviations are used:

ZEL   —*Zen is Eternal Life* by Rōshi Jiyu Kennett (Emery-ville, CA: Dharma Publishing, 1976).

HGLB   —*How to Grow a Lotus Blossom or How a Zen Buddhist Prepares for Death* by Rōshi Jiyu Kennett (Mt. Shasta, CA: Shasta Abbey, 1977).

ZM   —*Zen Meditation* (Mt. Shasta, CA: Shasta Abbey, Revised Edition, 1978).

J   —Japanese
C   —Chinese
S   —Sanskrit

1. *The Practice of Chinese Buddhism, 1900-1950* by Holmes Welch (Cambridge: Harvard University Press, 1967).

2. Tathagata (S), Nyorai (J). Another word for Buddha.

3. Cosmic Buddha. The Buddha Shakyamuni said, "There is an Unborn, Uncreated, Undying, Unchanging." A term for the Dharmakaya, Eternal Nature, Buddhahood or Amitabha Buddha. The Buddha who appears in every place and time and in all beings; also called by various other names such as Vairocana Buddha, Amitabha Buddha, Dharmakaya, Buddha Nature, Lord of the House. It can be revealed by genuine training but It cannot be explained as existing or not existing, or in any other dualistic way.

4. Buddha Nature, Busshō (J), Buddhata (S). That which is shared by oneself with the Cosmic Buddha. One's own True Nature, True Self. After Shakyamuni Buddha was enlightened He said, "All beings without exception have the Nature of Buddha." One's own Buddha Essence.

5. Trikaya (S), Sanshin (J). The Three Bodies of the Buddha which are unified throughout the universe as well as

in one's own body. "I am not Buddha and there is nothing in me that is not of Buddha."

6. Precepts, kai (j), sila (S). The ways of living that are in accordance with the Dharma. The second Paramita. One of the fundamental practices of the Bodhisattva training along with meditation, compassion and wisdom. The Precepts include the Three Refuges (I take refuge in the Buddha, I take refuge in the Dharma, I take refuge in the Sangha), the Three Pure Precepts (cease from evil, do only good, do good for others) and the Ten Great Precepts (do not kill, do not steal, do not covet, do not say that which is not true, do not sell the wine of delusion, do not speak against others, do not be proud of yourself and devalue others, do not be mean in giving either Dharma or wealth, do not be angry, do not defame the Three Treasures).

7. The reader should be aware that this statement, like all statements about the operation of the Law of Karma, is an oversimplification and an approximation. The full scope and operation of this Law is so vast and complex that it can be understood fully only by the Mind of a Buddha. Thus it is possible to trace back your own karmic history and learn from it what to do in order to clean it and set the residues of old karma to rest, but it is not possible to predict with absolute accuracy and detail the exact karmic consequences of any act. It is, however, possible to give a general idea thereof, and this is what I am doing in this book. The reader should also be aware that karma is not a substance which has a physical location and the use of the words "sparks" or "karmic residues" does not imply a material existence for them although they can be recognised through meditation.

8. Bodhisattva (S), bosatsu (J), pu-sa (C), "enlightened (bodhi) being (sattva)." A person who seeks enlightenment not only for himself but for all living beings as well, devoting himself to the Precepts, Four Wisdoms and Six Paramitas. One who undertakes training to become a fully enlightened Buddha for the benefit of all beings including himself. The

Bodhisattva ideal is the central aspect of Mahayana Buddhism. Bodhisattvas come forth for many reasons other than those given in the text at this point.

9. Skhandas (S), "aggregates," that of which a human or other living being is composed, i.e. (1) form or matter; (2) sensation or feelings; (3) thoughts or perceptions; (4) impulses or activity; (5) consciousness. When human skhandas are viewed through ignorance the false notion of a separate, individual self is created. When seen through the eyes of meditation, the five skhandas are recognised as "void, empty or pure, unstained and clean."

10. Fukanzazengi (Zazen Rules). See ZEL, pp. 287-91.

11. Corpse pose. Meditating whilst lying on one's back with one's feet together and hands in Shashu (see illustration on facing page).

12. Kanzeon Scripture. See ZEL, pp. 274-7.

13. Sandokai. See ZEL, pp. 279-80.

14. Hōkyozammai. See ZEL, pp. 280-83.

15. Scripture of Great Wisdom. See ZEL, pp. 277-8.

16. Litany of the Great Compassionate One. See ZEL, pp. 292-5.

17. Makura Om Dharani. "Peace upon the pillow." See ZEL, p. 295.

18. Birushana Buddha, also Birushanofū (J), Birushanabutsu, or Dainichi Nyorai (J), Vairocana Buddha (S). The Illuminator. He represents the Dharmakaya or pure Buddha Mind. He is the central figure in the Kegon Scriptures and considered to be the essence of the universe by the Shingon School. See footnotes 3, 4 and 5 which also apply.

CORPSE POSE

19. Dharmakaya (S), Hosshin (J), "Law (dharma) Body (kaya)." The highest of the Three Bodies (Trikaya) of the Buddha, representing Absolute Truth, Buddha Mind. The Dharmakaya is one's own True Nature and can be realised directly for oneself through one's own training. See also footnotes 3, 4, 5 and 18; all explanations in the foregoing apply here also in various aspects.

20. Nirmanakaya (S), Ōjin (J), "transformation body." The first of the Three Bodies (Trikaya) of the Buddha; the physical Shakyamuni who is seen in the world. The Nirmanakaya is also our own True Body, thus our own physical bodies become our Nirmanakaya after enlightenment, i.e. rebirth either here (see *How to Grow a Lotus Blossom*) or after death. See also footnotes 3, 4, 5, 18 and 19, all of which apply here in varying aspects.

21. Kwatz (J). A loud cry uttered at funerals by a Zen Master to get the attention of the released consciousness of the deceased in order to assist it to make the right decisions.

22. Asura (S), "without wine." Occupant of one of the Six Worlds or Lokas; the world of fighting, anger and dissension. Titan, a rebel god; one who tries to storm Heaven.

23. Sesshin (J), "to search the heart." An intensive week of meditation usually held four times a year in Zen monasteries. The week includes not only many hours of meditation but also ceremonies, lectures, sanzen and manual work. A Sesshin usually lasts seven days and commemorates Shakyamuni Buddha's week of sitting under the Bodhi Tree. It was during this week that He gained enlightenment. (Sanzen is spiritual counseling.)

24. Funeral Ceremony of a Priest. See ZEL, pp. 362-72.

BOOK TWO:

25. Veith, I. (transl.) *The Yellow Emperor's Classic of Internal Medicine* (Berkeley: University of California Press, 1972).

26. Jin Shin Jyutsu is the corporate name of Jin Shin Jyutsu, Inc. of Scottsdale, Arizona, where this art is taught.

27. Masunaga, S. and Ohashi, W. *Zen Shiatsu* (Tokyo: Japan Publications, 1977).

28. Kōan. (1) A word used to describe the second and third of the Four Noble Truths, the finding of suffering's cause and the cessation of suffering. The fourth of the Four Noble Truths, the Eightfold Path, causes the prevention of a recurrence of the kōan. The Four Noble Truths, suffering exists (which is the reason for training), suffering's cause, the cessation of suffering, and the Noble Eightfold Path are the four stages of Shakyamuni Buddha's kōan and are the basis of His Teaching for the alleviation of the sufferings of mankind. (2) In modern times the word "kōan" has come to mean a statement or story used by a Zen Master as a teaching device to help a disciple realize his True Nature. By extension, it means any spiritual barrier or fundamental problem in one's training which one needs to face, penetrate, clarify and transcend. A kōan must never be understood as a philosophical, intellectual or metaphysical question; it is often a matter of spiritual life or death. In Rinzai formal kōans are used in Zazen; however, in Sōtō, the emphasis is on the Genjo-kōan, the naturally arising kōans of everyday life. In Sōtō, the old kōan collections are not studied in their entirety; when situations arise appropriate illustrations are used.

29. This was observed by Rōshi Jiyu-Kennett in Chinese Zen temples in Malaysia, where she found in at least one case an entire clinic staffed by monks, the head of the clinic

being a monk-doctor trained in China. Holmes Welch reports in *The Practice of Chinese Buddhism* (Cambridge, MA: Harvard University Press, 1967) that in mainland China the tradition of monastic medicine had largely disappeared in recent years, with the use of moxa being limited to the burning of small cones of the herb on the head at the time of ordination. Welch does report, however, (pp. 124 and 125) the case of a Chinese monk telling him how to assist his wife's back trouble by allowing the spirit of the Buddhas to flow through his fingers into her back by touching her and reciting a mantra.

30. Sato, G. and Nishimura, C. *Unsui: A Diary of Zen Monastic Life* (Honolulu: University Press of Hawaii, 1973, p. 46).

31. Suzuki, D.T. *The Zen Monk's Life* (New York: Olympia Press, 1972, Plate 17 and pp. 52 and 53).

32. See his "Gyakudo-yōjinshu" in ZEL, pp. 123-38.

33. See his "Fukanzazengi" in ZEL, pp. 287-91.

34. Saunders, E. *Mudra* (New York: Pantheon, 1960).

35. Teeguarden, I. *Jin Shin Do: Acupressure Way of Health* (Tokyo: Japan Publications, 1978).

36. In ZEL, p. 278.

37. The traditional term for this "energy" is *chi* or *ki* and is a recognized entity in Eastern physiology. I follow current usage in translating this as "energy," but I do not intend to imply by this translation that I believe that it is an energy in the physicist's definition of the term. *Something* is discernible to the trained observer; as to what it is in the scientific sense, I cannot say. In the religious sense, it is Pure Love or the Blood of the Buddhas as discussed in Chapter III.

38. See Kennett, J. "The Necessity of Zazen" in ZEL. See also "Sitting Place" in ZM, pp. 40-45.

39. Referred to in Rahula, W. *What the Buddha Taught* (New York: Grove Press, 1959, pp. 2 and 3).

40. See Dōgen Zenji, "Bendohō," "Tenzo-kyokan," and "Fukanzazengi," ZEL, 1976, pp. 113, 186, 190 and 287.

41. Eightfold Path. The way to transcend suffering as taught by Shakyamuni Buddha is the fourth Noble Truth. The eight stages are right understanding, right thought, right speech, right action, right livelihood, right effort, right mindfulness, and right concentration. Zen training is the practice of the Eightfold Path in daily life. See also footnote 28.

42. See footnote 33.

43. "Zen Meditation," *Journal of Shasta Abbey*, 1976, 7, nos. 9 and 10. Available by mail from the Gift Shop of Shasta Abbey, P.O. Box 478, Mt. Shasta, CA, 96067. Price at the time of this printing: $2.50, postpaid, within North America.

44. See HGLB, pp. 186-95.

45. See HGLB, pp. 74-80, and Sannella, L., *Kundalini— Psychosis or Transcendence?* (San Francisco: Dakin, 1976).

46. Should this happen, the person who is depleted and exhausted might be helped by having someone use the following mudras with him: offering, dynamo, top of hara, life-death, fountain rim, fountain screen, and/or good digestion. Such a situation is spiritually serious and should not be allowed to persist chronically.

47. As related in Narada Thera, *A Manual of Buddhism* (Kuala Lumpur: Buddhist Missionary Society, 1971, p. 13).

48. For the four vows of the Bodhisattva see p. 226.

49. Including Duke, M. *Acupuncture* (New York: Pyramid House, 1972); Manaka, Y. and Urquhart, I. *The Layman's Guide to Acupuncture* (New York: Weatherhill, 1972); Mann, F. *Acupuncture* (New York: Random House, 1962); and Teeguarden, I. *Jin Shin Do: Acupressure Way of Health* (Tokyo: Japan Publications, 1978).

50. Vajrasattva (S), "Diamond Being." Vajrasattva is believed to have received the teaching of Shingon Buddhism directly from Vairocana Buddha and in turn handed it to Nagyaarajuna. In Zen, however, Vajrasattva is used as an image for the Iron Man, the indestructible Buddha within.

51. For a more complete discussion of the origins of this mudra see Saunders, E. *Mudra* (New York: Pantheon, 1960).

52. For illustrations of meditation positions see ZM, pp. 25-37.

53. See footnote 51.

54. See footnote 51.

55. See footnote 51.

56. ZEL, pp. 292-94.

57. For a detailed discussion of the Spiritual Fountain consult HGLB.

58. See footnote 57.

59. See footnote 57.

60. See footnote 51.

61. Hara (J). Triangle formed from the base of the sternum, down the sides of the rib cage extending downwards to the navel.

62. For a further discussion see HGLB.

63. Sannella, L. *Kundalini—Psychosis or Transcendence?* (San Francisco: Dakin, 1976).

64. See HGLB.

APPENDIX A:

TABLES OF MUDRA INFORMATION.

Table I: Mudras and meridians classified by spiritual properties.

Subtable I-A: Mudras relevant to aspects of spiritual development.

All of the mudras in this book are of use in religious development by virtue of their ability to assist you to understand, accept, and harmonize your body and mind. The mudras listed below are those which, when used in conjunction with meditation and daily training, may be of particular value in helping you find or strengthen certain aspects of spiritual development.

AWARENESS
Discovery
Dynamo
Fountain screen
Karma
Karmic assistance
Meditation
Reverence
Top of hara
Will-despair

ENERGY
Dynamo
Fountain rim
Good digestion
Life-death
Meditation
Offering
Relaxation
Spiritual defense
Spiritual unrest
Top of hara

Ventral linking
Will-despair

EQUILIBRIUM
Earth witness
Fearlessness
Fountain spray
Meditation
Reverence
Spiritual unrest

FAITH
Faith-doubt
Fearlessness
Meditation
Reverence

FEARLESSNESS
Fearlessness
Meditation
Offering

JOY
Fountain screen
Joy-sadness
Lightness-heaviness
of spirit
Meditation
Offering

LOVE
Fountain screen
Life-death
Meditation
Offering
Spiritual bathing
Top of hara

MEDITATION
Earth witness
Fearlessness
Fountain
Meditation
Offering
Spiritual bathing

OFFERING
Earth witness
Fearlessness
Offering

PEACE
Discovery
Earth witness
Good digestion
Karma
Karmic assistance
Meditation
Peace-worry
Relaxation
Relief-frustration
Security-vulnerability

Sexual peace
Spiritual cleansing
Spiritual unrest

PROTECTION
Diamond
Earth witness
Spiritual defense

REFRESHMENT
Balancing
Dynamo
Good digestion
Meditation
Relaxation
Spiritual bathing
Spiritual unrest
Top of hara

REVERENCE
Meditation
Offering
Reverence

SPIRITUAL BATHING
Fearlessness
Fountain
Fountain rim
Fountain screen
Fountain spray
Junction Z1
Meditation
Spiritual bathing
Spiritual junction

STEADFASTNESS
Earth witness
Fearlessness
Meditation

STILLNESS	WILL
Dynamo	Dynamo
Meditation	Fearlessness
Peace upon the pillow	Meditation
Reverence	Will-despair
Spiritual unrest	

Subtable I-B: Meridians particularly benefitted by steps on the Noble Eightfold Path.

Step	Meridians most benefitted
Right Understanding	Spleen and stomach
Right Intention or Thought	Bladder
Right Speech	Lung
Right Action	Pericardium and triple warmer
Right Livelihood	Heart and small intestine
Right Effort	Kidney
Right Mindfulness	Gall bladder and liver
Right Concentration	Large intestine

Subtable I-C: Meridians particularly benefitted by the practice of the paramitas.

Paramita	Meridians
Giving	Heart and small intestine
Precepts	Large intestine and triple warmer
Patience	Gall bladder and liver
Vigor	Kidney
Meditation	All equally
Wisdom	All equally
Skillful means	Lung
Commitment	Bladder and heart
Strength	Heart and pericardium
Knowledge and understanding	Spleen and stomach

Subtable I-D: Meridians particularly damaged by the Three Poisons.

Poison	Meridians
Greed	Heart, large intestine, lung, pericardium, small intestine, spleen, stomach, triple warmer
Anger	Gall bladder and liver
Delusion	Bladder and kidney

Subtable I-E: Meridians particularly damaged by the Eight Attachments.

The Eight Attachments or Eight Miseries are the primary causes of human suffering when they are the object of cravings either to avoid them or hold on to them. Buddhism teaches their transcendence through non-duality and all-acceptance.

Object of attachment	Meridians
Birth	Small intestine
Old age	Large intestine and pericardium
Decay or illness	Large intestine, spleen, stomach
Death	Heart and small intestine
Separation from loved ones	Heart, pericardium, small intestine
Being with those whom one dislikes	Gall bladder and liver
Being unable to get what one wants	Lung and triple warmer
False notions of self and/or existence	Bladder, kidney, pericardium

Subtable I-F: Meridians particularly damaged by breakage of the Precepts.

Precept Against	Meridians Damaged by Its Breakage
Killing	Heart and small intestine
Stealing	Spleen and stomach
Coveting (including indulgent sexuality)	Large intestine, pericardium, triple warmer
Lying	Lung
Selling the wine of delusion	Spleen and stomach
Speaking against others	Lung
Being proud of self and devaluing others	Bladder and kidney
Being mean in giving Dharma or wealth	Heart and small intestine
Anger	Gall bladder and liver
Defaming the Three Treasures of Buddha, Dharma, and Sangha	Bladder, heart, kidney, lung

Subtable I-G: Mudras classified by karmic memory.

The following mudras may be relevant to the karmic memories under which they are listed. For karmic memories associated with a particular part of the body or mental state, please also consult Tables II and III.

ABANDONMENT
  Dorsal linking
  Fountain rim
  Joy-sadness
  Life-death
  Lightness-heaviness of
    spirit
  Offering
  Spiritual bathing
  Top of hara
  Truth-lie

ANGER (including hatred)
  Compassion-anger
  Relief-frustration

ASSISTANCE, refusal of
  Joy-sadness
  Offering
  Top of hara

BLEEDING, severe (see also
location of bleeding in
Table II)
  Joy-sadness
  Karma
  Life-death

CHILDBIRTH, problems of
  Fountain rim
  Good digestion
  Karma
  Sexual peace

COLD, excessive
  Dorsal linking
  Fountain rim
  Karma
  Spiritual bathing
  Spiritual unrest
  Will-despair

DECEPTION
  Faith-doubt
  Joy-sadness
  Peace-worry
  Truth-lie
  Will-despair

DISINTEGRATION, bodily
  Mudra specific to the area
    of disintegration, if there
    is one
  Fountain rim
  Fountain screen
  Fountain spray
  Spiritual bathing

DOUBT
  Faith-doubt
  Will-despair

ELECTROCUTION
  Joy-sadness
  Life-death
  Spiritual bathing
  Special procedures may
    be necessary

EXPOSURE (see "cold" and
"vulnerability")

FAITH, loss of (see "doubt")

HEAT, excessive
  Karma

ILLNESS (see also "infec-
tion")
  Karmic memories of ill-
    ness in specific areas may
    be benefitted by mudras
    listed for those areas in
    Table II.

INADEQUACY
  Faith-doubt

INFECTION, systemic (see
also "illness")
  Joy-sadness

JEALOUSY
  Cleansing-stagnation

KARMIC MEMORIES,
mudras to assist generally
  Discovery
  Fountain screen
  Karma
  Karmic assistance
  Relaxation

KILLING OTHERS, regardless of means or motive
Life-death
Lightness-heaviness of
spirit
Offering

LOVE, lack of
Fountain rim
Joy-sadness
Life-death
Offering
Top of hara

MAGIC (see also "deception" and "doubt")
Faith-doubt
Joy-sadness
Karma
Life-death
Spiritual unrest
Will-despair

MENTAL ILLNESS
Faith-doubt
Peace-worry
Ventral linking

POISONING (see also the place of action of the poison in Table II)
Compassion-anger
Joy-sadness
Lightness-heaviness of
spirit

PRIDE
Faith-doubt

SADISM
Karma
Life-death

SEXUAL ABUSE
Cleansing-stagnation
Faith-doubt
Fountain rim
Joy-sadness
Karma
Lightness-heaviness of
spirit
Security-vulnerability
Sexual peace
Spiritual cleansing
Spiritual unrest
Ventral linking

SLANDER
Peace-worry
Truth-lie

STARVATION
Dorsal linking
Fountain rim
Good digestion
Lightness-heaviness of
spirit
Spiritual bathing
Ventral linking

SUFFOCATION
Dynamo
Fountain screen
Karmic assistance
Life-death
Top of hara
Truth-lie

TERROR
Good digestion
Joy-sadness
Life-death
Will-despair

THEFT
Peace-worry

TORTURE
Karmic memories of
tortures which affect
specific areas of the body
may be benefitted by
mudras listed for those
areas in Table II.
Memories of tortures
which involve particular
means and/or motives may
be benefitted by mudras
listed elsewhere in this
table under those means
and/or motives.

VULNERABILITY
Security-vulnerability
Spiritual unrest
Will-despair

WOUNDS
Karmic memories of
wounds in specific areas
may be benefitted by
mudras listed for those
areas in Table II.

Table II: Mudras classified by physical location of tension.

The following mudras may be relevant to tension located in the physical areas under which they are listed.

ABDOMEN
Almost all mudras are relevant to the abdomen in some way. Please see specific organs or functions or examine the mudra illustrations.

ANKLE (see "foot")

APPETITE (see also "digestion" and "weight regulation")
Compassion-anger
Discovery
Good digestion
Karma
Lightness-heaviness of
  spirit
Peace-worry
Relaxation
Spiritual bathing
Spiritual unrest

ARM, back of
Cleansing-stagnation
Ease
Fountain
Karma
Karmic assistance
Lightness-heaviness of
  spirit

ARM, front of
Balancing
Cleansing-stagnation
Discovery
Dynamo
Earth witness
Ease
Fearlessness
Fountain
Joy-sadness
Karmic assistance
Life-death
Offering
Relaxation
Reverence
Spiritual junction
Spiritual unrest
Top of hara
Truth-lie

ARMPIT
Balancing
Discovery
Dorsal linking
Earth witness
Ease
Faith-doubt

315

Fearlessness
Fountain
Fountain screen
Joy-sadness
Karmic assistance
Life-death
Offering
Relaxation
Relief-frustration
Reverence
Spiritual junction
Spiritual unrest
Top of hara
Will-despair

BACK, lower
Balancing
Discovery
Dorsal linking
Faith-doubt
Fountain
Fountain rim
Good digestion
Junction Z1
Meditation
Peace upon the pillow
Peace-worry
Relaxation
Security-vulnerability
Sexual peace
Spiritual bathing
Spiritual junction
Spiritual unrest
Top of hara
Will-despair

BACK, upper
Abdominal tension
Balancing

Discovery
Dorsal linking
Dynamo
Faith-doubt
Fountain
Fountain screen
Junction Z1
Karmic assistance
Life-death
Meditation
Peace upon the pillow
Peace-worry
Relaxation
Security-vulnerability
Sexual peace
Spiritual bathing
Spiritual cleansing
Spiritual junction
Spiritual unrest
Top of hara

BLADDER (see also "water elimination")
Dorsal linking
Ease
Good digestion
Faith-doubt
Fountain rim
Fountain screen
Fountain spray
Junction Z1
Spiritual junction

BOWEL FUNCTION (see also "intestines, large and small")
Abdominal tension
Cleansing-stagnation
Fountain rim
Good digestion

Lightness-heaviness of
  spirit
Peace-worry
Spiritual cleansing
Spiritual unrest
Ventral linking

**BREATHING (see also
"lung")**
Balancing
Discovery
Fountain
Fountain screen
Junction Z1
Karmic assistance
Meditation
Offering
Relaxation
Spiritual bathing
Spiritual unrest
Top of hara

BUTTOCKS
Discovery
Dorsal linking
Faith-doubt
Fountain
Relief-frustration
Sexual peace
Spiritual junction
Top of hara

CHEST
Almost all mudras are
  relevant to the chest in
  some way. Please see
  specific organs or functions or examine the
  mudra illustrations.

**CIRCULATION (see also
"heart")**
Balancing
Fountain rim
Good digestion
Joy-sadness
Junction Z1
Life-death
Spiritual cleansing

**COLD, feelings of excessive
(see also "temperature regu-
lation")**
Dorsal linking
Fountain rim
Karma
Spiritual bathing
Spiritual unrest
Will-despair

**DIGESTION (see also
specific organs and
"bowel function")**
Abdominal tension
Balancing
Cleansing-stagnation
Compassion-anger
Fountain rim
Good digestion
Lightness-heaviness of
  spirit
Peace-worry
Relief-frustration
Security-vulnerability
Spiritual cleansing
Spiritual unrest
Ventral linking

Ventral linking
Will-despair

GALL BLADDER
Dorsal linking
Ease
Fountain rim
Fountain screen
Fountain spray
Good digestion
Junction Z1
Relief-frustration
Spiritual cleansing
Spiritual junction

GENITALS (see also "men-struation" and "pelvis")
Compassion-anger
Discovery
Fountain rim
Good digestion
Joy-sadness
Karma
Peace upon the pillow
Relaxation
Sexual peace
Spiritual bathing
Spiritual cleansing
Spiritual junction
Spiritual unrest
Ventral linking
Will-despair

GLANDS
Spiritual unrest

HAND
Balancing
Cleansing-stagnation
Diamond

Discovery
Earth witness
Ease
Fearlessness
Fountain
Joy-sadness
Karma
Karmic assistance
Life-death
Lightness-heaviness of
 spirit
Offering
Relaxation
Reverence
Spiritual junction
Spiritual unrest
Top of hara
Truth-lie

HEAD, back of
Abdominal tension
Balancing
Discovery
Dorsal linking
Dynamo
Faith-doubt
Fountain
Fountain spray
Junction Z1
Meditation
Peace upon the pillow
Relaxation
Relief-frustration
Sexual peace
Spiritual bathing
Spiritual cleansing
Spiritual junction
Spiritual unrest
Top of hara

Fountain rim
Fountain screen
Fountain spray
Good digestion
Spiritual junction

INTESTINE, small (see also "bowel function")
Dorsal linking
Ease
Fountain rim
Fountain screen
Fountain spray
Good digestion
Lightness-heaviness of spirit
Spiritual junction
Spiritual unrest

ITCHING (see also location of the itching)
Discovery

KIDNEY (see also "water elimination")
Abdominal tension
Fountain rim
Fountain screen
Fountain spray
Good digestion
Spiritual cleansing
Spiritual junction
Spiritual unrest
Ventral linking
Will-despair

KNEE, back of
Balancing
Compassion-anger

Discovery
Dorsal linking
Dynamo
Ease
Faith-doubt
Fountain
Fountain rim
Junction Z1
Karmic assistance
Relaxation
Relief-frustration
Security-vulnerability
Sexual peace
Spiritual cleansing
Spiritual junction
Ventral linking
Will-despair

KNEE, front of
Abdominal tension
Discovery
Dynamo
Fountain
Fountain rim
Peace-worry
Security-vulnerability
Spiritual cleansing
Spiritual junction

LEGS, back of
Balancing
Discovery
Dorsal linking
Dynamo
Ease
Faith-doubt
Fountain
Junction Z1
Karmic assistance

Relaxation
Relief-frustration
Sexual peace
Spiritual cleansing
Spiritual junction
Ventral linking

LEGS, front of
Abdominal tension
Compassion-anger
Discovery
Dynamo
Ease
Fountain
Karmic assistance
Peace-worry
Relief-frustration
Security-vulnerability
Spiritual cleansing
Spiritual junction
Ventral linking
Will-despair

LIVER
Abdominal tension
Balancing
Compassion-anger
Fountain rim
Fountain screen
Fountain spray
Good digestion
Spiritual cleansing
Spiritual junction
Spiritual unrest
Ventral linking

LUNG (see also "breathing")
Balancing
Ease

Fountain rim
Fountain screen
Good digestion
Spiritual junction
Spiritual unrest
Truth-lie
Ventral linking

MENSTRUATION (see also "genitals" and "pelvis")
Fountain rim
Good digestion
Sexual peace
Spiritual unrest
Ventral linking

METABOLISM (see also "digestion")
Security-vulnerability
Will-despair

MOUTH
Cleansing-stagnation
Compassion-anger
Good digestion
Life-death
Meditation
Peace upon the pillow
Peace-worry
Relaxation
Security-vulnerability
Sexual peace
Spiritual bathing
Spiritual junction
Spiritual unrest
Ventral linking
Will-despair

NECK, back or side of (for neck, front of, see "throat")
Abdominal tension
Cleansing-stagnation
Discovery
Dorsal linking
Dynamo
Ease
Faith-doubt
Fountain
Junction Z1
Karma
Lightness-heaviness of spirit
Peace upon the pillow
Peace-worry
Relaxation
Relief-frustration
Sexual peace
Spiritual bathing
Spiritual cleansing
Spiritual junction
Spiritual unrest
Top of hara

NOSE (see also "breathing")
Balancing
Cleansing-stagnation
Ease
Karma
Karmic assistance
Lightness-heaviness of spirit
Meditation
Peace upon the pillow
Peace-worry

Relaxation
Spiritual bathing
Spiritual junction
Spiritual unrest
Will-despair

PANCREAS (see "spleen")

PELVIS & PUBIC AREA (see also "genitals" and "menstruation")
Abdominal tension
Compassion-anger
Discovery
Dorsal linking
Dynamo
Ease
Faith-doubt
Fountain
Fountain rim
Good digestion
Junction Z1
Karma
Karmic assistance
Peace upon the pillow
Peace-worry
Relaxation
Relief-frustration
Security-vulnerability
Sexual peace
Spiritual bathing
Spiritual cleansing
Spiritual junction
Spiritual unrest
Top of hara
Ventral linking
Will-despair

PERICARDIUM (see cautions under life-death mudra; see also "heart")
Balancing
Ease
Fountain rim
Fountain screen
Good digestion
Joy-sadness
Ventral linking

POSTURE, poor
Meditation
Spiritual bathing

RIGIDITY, general
Spiritual bathing

SHOULDER
Balancing
Cleansing-stagnation
Discovery
Dorsal linking
Dynamo
Ease
Faith-doubt
Fountain
Fountain rim
Joy-sadness
Junction Z1
Karma
Karmic assistance
Life-death
Lightness-heaviness of
    spirit
Peace-worry
Relief-frustration
Security-vulnerability
Sexual peace

Spiritual junction
Spiritual unrest
Truth-lie

SPLEEN (and pancreas)
Abdominal tension
Fountain rim
Fountain screen
Good digestion
Security-vulnerability
Spiritual cleansing
Spiritual defense
Spiritual junction
Spiritual unrest
Ventral linking

STOMACH (see also "digestion")
Abdominal tension
Dorsal linking
Ease
Fountain rim
Fountain screen
Fountain spray
Good digestion
Peace-worry
Spiritual cleansing
Spiritual defense
Spiritual junction
Spiritual unrest

TEMPERATURE REGULA-TION (see also "cold" and "heat")
Dorsal linking
Fountain rim
Karma
Relief-frustration
Spiritual bathing

**TENSION, general physical
(see also "tension" in the
mental table)**
Balancing
Ease
Relaxation
Spiritual bathing
Spiritual cleansing
Spiritual junction
Spiritual unrest
Top of hara

**THROAT (see also
"neck")**
Balancing
Cleansing-stagnation
Compassion-anger
Fountain
Good digestion
Karmic assistance
Life-death
Peace upon the pillow
Peace-worry
Relaxation
Relief-frustration
Security-vulnerability
Sexual peace
Spiritual bathing
Spiritual junction
Spiritual unrest
Truth-lie
Ventral linking
Will-despair

TOE, great
Compassion-anger
Dynamo
Fountain
Junction Z1
Peace-worry

Relief-frustration
Security-vulnerability
Spiritual cleansing
Spiritual junction

TOE, second
Dynamo
Junction Z1
Security-vulnerability
Spiritual cleansing

TOE, third
Peace-worry
Spiritual cleansing

TOE, fourth
Relief-frustration
Spiritual cleansing

TOE, fifth
Discovery
Faith-doubt
Relief-frustration
Spiritual cleansing
Will-despair

**WATER ELIMINATION (see
also "bladder" and "kidney")**
Faith-doubt
Lightness-heaviness of
spirit
Ventral linking
Will-despair

**WEAKNESS, general (see
also "energy" and "weak-
ness" in mental table)**
Discovery
Dorsal linking
Fountain rim

Table III. Mudras classified by mental state.

The following mudras may be relevant to the mental states under which they are listed.

ALIENATION (see also "loneliness")
Joy-sadness
Truth-lie
Will-despair

ANGER (see also "frustration")
Compassion-anger
Earth witness
Faith-doubt
Relief-frustration

ANXIETY (see also "fear," "terror," and "worry")
Discovery
Earth witness
Good digestion
Life-death
Peace-worry
Relaxation
Security-vulnerability
Spiritual bathing
Ventral linking

BOREDOM
Will-despair

COMPLACENCY (see "pride")

CONFUSION
Earth witness
Karma
Reverence
Ventral linking

COORDINATION, lack of
Lightness-heaviness of spirit

DEPRESSION (see also "sadness")
Cleansing-stagnation
Compassion-anger
Discovery
Peace-worry
Relief-frustration
Truth-lie
Ventral linking
Will-despair

DISTRACTIONS
Earth witness
Reverence
Spiritual defense

DISTRUST
Lightness-heaviness of spirit
Peace-worry
Will-despair

INSECURITY (see also "vulnerability")
Fearlessness
Karma
Security-vulnerability
Spiritual defense
Spiritual unrest

INSOMNIA
Balancing
Compassion-anger
Dorsal linking
Dynamo
Fountain rim
Good digestion
Peace upon the pillow
Peace-worry
Relaxation
Relief-frustration
Security-vulnerability

JEALOUSY
Lightness-heaviness of spirit

LASSITUDE (including flaccidity and inertia)
Cleansing-stagnation
Karma
Lightness-heaviness of spirit
Ventral linking

LAUGHTER, uncontrollable
Joy-sadness
Ventral linking

LIGHTHEADEDNESS
Discovery

LONELINESS (see also "alienation")
Fountain screen
Joy-sadness
Truth-lie

LOVE, inability to give enough
Life-death
Offering
Top of hara

MALAISE, general (see also "tension")
Discovery (or any other mudra having a discovery property)
Joy-sadness
Spiritual unrest

NIGHTMARES
Discovery (or any mudra having a discovery property)
Ventral linking

OBSESSION
Security-vulnerability
Truth-lie

OVERSENSITIVITY
Fountain spray
Peace-worry
Security-vulnerability

OVERSTIMULATION
Fountain spray
Relaxation

Spiritual bathing
Top of hara

PLEASURE, inability to enjoy or to distinguish from pain
Karma
Ventral linking

POWER, lust for
Compassion-anger

PRIDE (including complacency)
Faith-doubt
Will-despair

PROTECTION, mudras for
Diamond
Earth witness
Spiritual defense

RESTLESSNESS
Good digestion
Karma
Relief-frustration

SADNESS, including grief (see also "depression")
Faith-doubt
Fountain screen
Joy-sadness
Life-death
Offering
Truth-lie
Ventral linking

SEXUAL TENSION (see also "genitals" in physical table)
Fountain rim

Good digestion
Karma
Sexual peace
Spiritual cleansing
Spiritual unrest
Ventral linking

TALKATIVENESS, excessive
Discovery

TENSION, general mental (see also "tension" in the physical table)
Balancing
Dorsal linking
Dynamo
Ease
Fountain
Fountain rim
Fountain spray
Good digestion
Junction Z1
Life-death
Relaxation
Spiritual bathing
Spiritual junction
Spiritual unrest

TERROR (see also "fear")
Life-death
Will-despair

TIMIDITY
Fearlessness
Relief-frustration
Top of hara
Ventral linking

**VULNERABILITY (see
also "insecurity")**
  Relaxation
  Security-vulnerability
  Spiritual bathing
  Spiritual defense
  Spiritual unrest

**WEAKNESS, general (see
also "energy," "exhaustion,"
and "fatigue," and see
"weakness" in the physical
table)**
  Dorsal linking
  Fountain rim
  Fountain screen
  Joy-sadness
  Karma
  Lightness-heaviness of
    spirit
  Relaxation

**WORRY (see also
"anxiety")**
  Balancing
  Joy-sadness
  Life-death
  Peace-worry
  Spiritual defense

Table IV: Mudras for assistance in discovery.

The following mudras have been found to be particularly helpful in relaxing one in such a way that one may become more aware of oneself. Whether or not anything of significance comes to mind during or following their use depends upon the state of one's meditation and upon whether there is something just beyond awareness which can be accepted and assimilated once the added relaxation provided by the mudra is present. The results of using these mudras are therefore quite unpredictable and they should be used by mentally mature individuals with good judgment.

MUDRAS

Discovery	Karmic assistance
Fountain screen	Top of hara
Karma	Will-despair

Table V: Mudras classified by the meridians which they use.

The mudra which is primarily associated with each meridian is given in italics.

BLADDER MERIDIAN
  Doubt-faith
  Relaxation
  Sexual peace

CONCEPTION VESSEL
  Fountain
  Meditation
  Peace upon the pillow
  Relaxation
  Spiritual bathing
  Spiritual junction

DORSAL LINKING MERIDIAN
  Dorsal linking

GALL BLADDER MERIDIAN
  Relief-frustration

GOVERNING VESSEL
  Fountain
  Meditation
  Peace upon the pillow
  Relaxation
  Spiritual bathing
  Spiritual junction

HEART MERIDIAN
  Life-death
  Offering

Spiritual unrest
Top of hara

HEEL VESSELS
  Ease
  Fountain
  Karmic assistance

KIDNEY MERIDIAN
  Abdominal tension
  Ease
  Karmic assistance
  Will-despair

LARGE INTESTINE MERIDIAN
  Cleansing-stagnation

LIVER MERIDIAN
  Abdominal tension
  Compassion-anger
  Dynamo
  Spiritual cleansing
  Spiritual junction

LOWER BELT MERIDIAN
  Fountain rim
  Junction Z1

LUNG MERIDIAN
Balancing
Truth-lie

**MIDDLE BELT
MERIDIAN**
Fountain screen

**PENETRATING
VESSEL**
Good digestion

**PERICARDIUM
MERIDIAN**
Balancing
Discovery
Earth witness
Ease
Fearlessness
Joy-sadness
Offering
Relaxation
Reverence
Spiritual junction

**SMALL INTESTINE
MERIDIAN**
Ease
*Lightness-heaviness of
spirit*

SPLEEN MERIDIAN
Dynamo
Security-vulnerability
Spiritual cleansing

STOMACH MERIDIAN
Peace-worry
Spiritual cleansing

**TRIPLE WARMER
MERIDIAN**
Ease
Karma

**UPPER BELT
MERIDIAN**
Fountain spray
Junction Z1

**VENTRAL LINKING
MERIDIAN**
Ventral linking

Table VI: Mudras and Meridians classified by time of maximum activity.

Hours of Maximum Energy Flow (Standard Time)	Meridian	Primary Associated Mudra
Midnight-2 A.M.	Gall bladder	Relief-frustration
2 A.M.-4A.M.	Liver	Compassion-anger
4 A.M.-6 A.M.	Lung	Truth-lie
6 A.M.-8 A.M.	Large intestine	Cleansing-stagnation
8 A.M.-10 A.M.	Stomach	Peace-worry
10 A.M.-Noon	Spleen	Security-vulnerability
Noon-2 P.M.	Heart	Life-death
2 P.M.-4 P.M.	Small intestine	Lightness-heaviness of spirit
4 P.M.-6 P.M.	Bladder	Doubt-faith
6 P.M.-8 P.M.	Kidney	Will-despair
8 P.M.-10 P.M.	Pericardium	Joy-sadness
10 P.M.-Midnight	Triple warmer	Karma
Continuous	Conception vessel	Spiritual bathing
	Governing vessel	Spiritual bathing
	Lower belt	Fountain rim
	Middle belt	Fountain screen
	Upper belt	Fountain spray

Table VII: Meridians classified by food preference.

Preferred Food	Meridians
Asparagus	Spleen and stomach
Beans (fresh)	Bladder and kidney
Carrots	Bladder and kidney
Celery	Bladder and kidney
Eggs	Gall bladder and liver
Fruit (sweet ripe)	Spleen and stomach
Greens (leafy)	Heart and small intestine
Honey	Spleen and stomach
Margarine	Gall bladder and liver
Mayonnaise	Gall bladder and liver
Mint	Spleen and stomach
Oils	Gall bladder and liver
Onions	Large intestine and lung
Parsley	Spleen and stomach
Peas (fresh)	Bladder and kidney
Sage	Bladder and kidney
Thyme	Bladder and kidney
Tomato	Large intestine and lung
Vinegar	Large intestine and lung

Table VIII: Mudra Points and their notations in other anma systems.

MUDRA POINT	ACUPUNCTURE NOTATION[1]	JIN SHIN DŌ NOTATION[2]	G-JO NOTATION[3]
A	––	––	––
A1	G14	1	––
A2	B1	––	80A
A3	G1	––	––
A4	Li20, S2 & 3	2	112
A5	––	––	49
A6	S5	––	––
B	Cv22	––	––
B1	S11	––	––
B2	K27	––	––
B3	S13	3	87
C	Cv19	––	––
C1	K24 & 25; S15 & 16	4	22
C2	K23	––	55
C3	H1	––	110
C4	G22	––	––
C5	Cx1	––	––
D	L3 & 4	––	78
D1	kong chung	––	––
D2	H2	––	––
D3	L5, Li11	25	2, 11
E	Cx3	28	44
E1	H3	––	37
E2	Cx6	27	10
E3	L7 & 8	––	18
E4	H4-6	––	15, 79
E5	Cx7	––	40
F	Cx8	––	––
F1	L11	––	12
F2	––	––	––
F3	––	––	––
F4	Cx9	––	––

MUDRA POINT	ACUPUNCTURE NOTATION[1]	JIN SHIN DŌ NOTATION[2]	G-JO NOTATION[3]
G	Cv15	——	31
G1	Lv14	——	——
G2	G24	5	86
G3	Lv13	——	——
H	Cv10	——	——
H1	S24	——	——
H2	Cv8	——	——
H3	Cv5	——	6
I	Cv2	——	54
I1	G27 & 28	——	——
I2	Sp 12 & 13	6	——
I3	Lv12, S30	——	——
J	S32	——	——
J1	Lv9, Sp10	7	——
K	S35	——	——
K1	Sp9	8	57
L	Sp8	——	111
L1	Lv5	——	36
L2	Sp6	——	7
L3	G40	——	50
M	B62	12	20
M1	K6	9	——
M2	K2	——	58
M3	G41	11	43
M4	G43	——	92
N	Sp2	——	——
N1	Lv1, Sp1	——	68
N2	——	——	——
N3	G44	——	64
N4	B67	——	75
O	B60	——	5
O1	B59, G39	——	——
O2	B57	——	——
O3	Lv7	——	——
O4	G34	13	62
P	B54	——	3
P1	Lv8	——	73

MUDRA POINT	ACUPUNCTURE NOTATION[1]	JIN SHIN DŌ NOTATION[2]	G-JO NOTATION[3]
P2	B53	––	––
P3	G33	––	––
Q	G31	14	––
R	Gv1	––	––
R1	B50	––	––
R2	G30	––	41
R3	midway between B47 & B48	15	––
R4	Gv3	––	26
S	Gv4	––	59
S1	Gv5	––	––
S2	B46	––	83
S3	G25	––	93
T	Gv6	––	––
T1	Gv8	––	––
T2	B42	17	––
T3	B40	––	45
T4	Gv10	––	––
U	Li1	––	56
U1	T1	––	––
U2	H9, Si1	––	76
U3	Li4	––	13
V	Li5	––	1
V1	T9	––	––
W	T10	––	––
W1	Li13	––	––
W2	T12	––	––
X	Gv12	––	––
X1	Si9	23	––
X2	Si11	––	––
X3	B37	18	82
Y	Gv14	––	23
Y1	Si12	––	21
Y2	G21, T15	20, 19	29, 103
Y3	Si15	––	––
Y4	Si16	––	––
Y5	B10	––	60

MUDRA POINT	ACUPUNCTURE NOTATION[1]	JIN SHIN DŌ NOTATION[2]	G-JO NOTATION[3]
Y6	Gv15	––	100
Z	Gv16	––	98
Z1	G20	22	106
Z2	Gv17	––	108
Z3	G19	––	––
Z4	G8	––	90
Z5	B8, G18	––	––
Z6	B7, G17	––	––
Z7	Gv21	––	99

1. Acupressure notations following the College of Chinese Medicine of Peking, *Practical Acupuncture* (Copenhagen: FADL Publishing, 1973).
2. Jin Shin Dō notation following Teeguarden, I., *Acupressure Way of Health: Jin Shin Do* (Tokyo: Japan Publications, 1978).
3. G-Jo notation following Blate, M., *The G-Jo Handbook* (Davie, FL., Falkynor Books, 1976).

APPENDIX B:

Oral Traditions Concerning the Transmission of Mortal Illness.

Translated from the *Taisodaisokyo,* Vol. 78, papers 2507 and 2508, by Rev. Mokurai Cherlin. The *Taisodaisokyo* is the equivalent of the Bible to Mahayana Buddhists. It is edited and with an introduction and commentaries by Rev. Daizui MacPhillamy.

Introduction.

The text of the two papers translated here was evidently written down from verbal discourses, presumably between master and disciple. While some of the segments date back to the twelfth century A.D., the papers in their present form may have been written as late as the eighteenth century. Because of the rambling and fragmented style of the original, a literal translation would have been confusing to the reader. Rōshi Jiyu-Kennett therefore worked with Rev. Cherlin's exact translation so as to clarify the meaning of the passages, researching any questionable areas herself. Unfortunately a large number of passages had to be omitted owing to the unreadability of the text. The resulting translation was then edited extensively by me so as to bring together sections of the text which covered the same subject and to delete fragmentary and questionable passages. I also interpolated the commentaries to be found in italic type and deleted a few sections devoted to herbal preparations and curing ceremonies which are outside the scope of this book. The resulting work is to be found below, followed by the original Chinese text.

—D. MacPhillamy

The Spiritual Illness which Leads to All Mortal Illnesses.

Concerning the Fundamental Matter.

Q. Why should we search for the cause of illness?

A. It is a matter of training.

Q. To what Teaching shall we refer?

A. Consider the matter explained in the Way of the Eighteen (the Five Buddhas and Four Bodhisattvas in the centers of the Vajradhatu and Garbhadhatu Mandalas).

> *These are the two primary mandalas of the esoteric schools of Buddhism. They symbolize the direct Teachings of Vairocana Buddha (the Cosmic Buddha or Dharmakaya) and thus represent the direct experience of the Supreme Enlightenment.*

Q. What is the core of this Teaching?

A. The whole of the Vajradhatu is the core; the Sanskrit syllable ﾐ is Its symbol.

> *The Vajradhatu is the Wisdom of the Cosmic Buddha, Which destroys all delusion.*

Q. Where does the Buddha's Wisdom teach that we should look to find the explanation for the cause of suffering and illness?

A. Look to the three parasites. They are congenital to the human body and are firmly established at birth. The desires of one's previous life come together at birth and, within seven days, these parasites are born. They are the karmic consequence of errors and the breakage of the Precepts, according to the Laws of the Universe. Every being who is born can investigate this matter and prove it true.

—Written in the third year of Jōan (1173 or 1198 A.D.), tenth month, eighteenth day, and recorded by Shomon Kaihan [*date unknown*].

The Three Parasites.

The "Filial Son Keeps the Raising of the Seed to Prolong Life Scripture" says, "All parasites live in men's bellies. The

342

three are as generals of an army that is invading man's five-fold treasury [*i.e. the aggregates which compose a man's body and mind*]. The higher one likes chariots, horses, and fine clothes. The middle one similarly leads men to like delicious food. The lowest leads men to prefer sexual pleasure. These three parasites are the roots of the three poisons [*greed, anger, and delusion*]. The three parasites lead men to careless and reckless enjoyment, always looking for what can be turned to their own advantage.

These parasites are as ghosts, which can travel unimpeded through heaven and earth. They lead men constantly to do evil, seldom to do good. Cruel people have a great many of these parasites [*i.e. are strongly attached to these desires*], which are called demons in other religions. The Taoist Scriptures say that these three are spirits which act materially upon the body and have form but yet are still a type of spirit or ghost. They wish to lead all men to an early death.

Q. What are the names of these spirits?

A. The "Scripture of the Great Essence" says that the highest one is called Peng chu, the middle one Peng chih and the lowest Peng chao.

Q. What do they look like?

A. This scripture says that, in form, they may resemble a man three *ts'un* [*roughly three inches*] in height. It also says that the highest one is black in colour and has the shape of two hands, the middle one is white with the form of a chicken. Master Chao said that the form resembled that of a body or a great horse with head and tail. It was three or four ts'un long. Ch'ien Chin Fang says that the form was that of a thin muscle.

Q. Where do these three spirits reside in a human body?

A. The "Scripture of the Great Essence" says that the first lives in the head and is therefore called the upper spirit; the second lives in the throat and is called the middle spirit, whilst their third relative lives in the feet and is called the lower spirit. This last is also said to live in the belly. The Taoist Scriptures say that these three spirits, when inhabiting the body, may bring disharmony to the heart as a result of a multitude of desires, lusts and greeds. They lead the poor and needy to cruelty and murder.

Q. Why do these parasites tend to lead people to an early death?

A. They desire to remain unconverted, with free access to all of a man's energy. Therefore they wish followers of the Way to die quickly.

Q. By what means do these parasites attempt to get people to die quickly?

A. When a man has reached the night of *genshen*, they are exhausted and so try to go to the Ruler of Heaven to tell Him of all the wrongdoing of this follower of the Way. Thus they try to cut short his registered period of life and cause his spirit to be reborn in an animal form, leaving themselves free reign on the earth.

> *Genshen means literally "to change, or come, to a new era in the depth of the night." In one sense, it refers to that state which Christian mystics have called the Dark Night of the Soul, a period of spiritual aridity, torment, and questioning in which faith is strengthened and one's attachments are weakened so that one may be drawn into closer union with the Infinite. The three lusts of mind, appetite, and sexuality, in imminent danger of being curbed, are most violent at such a time. They try to cause the trainee to judge himself as worthless and evil and hence lead him to abandon his efforts at training, sink into dejection, and give in to their demands.*

Q. Do the three parasites have other ways of harming people in particular parts of their bodies besides leading them into lusts, desires, enjoyments, and rage?

A. Peng chu, in the head, attacks the eyes, which go dim; the face becomes wrinkled, the breath stinks, and the teeth fall out. Peng chih, in the throat or belly, attacks the five organs and makes the breath short. The man thus attacked likes to do wrong and even dares to eat human flesh. Peng chao, in the feet, leads a man to involvement in disorder and rebellion. In such a man the five desires [*gain, sexuality, food and drink, fame, and sleep*] are rampant.

Characteristics of the Spiritual Illness.

All diseases are mild at first, only later becoming serious; one gradually becomes completely debilitated and wastes away. One is as a fish in a river that is drying up; there is no realisation that death is imminent.

If one has good intentions in the morning but loses them by noon it will be a long time before these intentions show any results. Body and mind will wither if inflamed by anxiety. Disease will arise if one tries to dwell with right thought but is lazy, has no appetite and always wants to sleep. Disease will arise if, in trying to raise the Way-Seeking Mind at the wrong time, one cries rudely from anger and frustration at not being able to do so; conversely, disease will arise if one gives oneself over to debauchery, scornfulness or anger towards others at the right time for raising the Way-Seeking Mind, or if, at such a time, one brings up the passions or breaks off one's training. At the time of the important thing [*when the Spirit rises to greet the Lord*] one should lie down on the left side if one wishes to die; at the time of dying one should sit.

Even at the time of kenshō (when the Spirit arises)
one can create spiritual illness unless one keeps up
one's meditation and training; this is true also at
the time of physical death.

The Physical Mortal Illnesses.

After the above mentioned disease has taken hold the following physical symptoms occur. The human body is weak and frightened and subject to many dangers. The heart beats against the ribs in fright. The palms of the hands and the soles of the feet get hot. The face is always flushed. In the beginning it seems that one will soon be completely well but then there is a relapse that causes one to spit and there are also many hallucinations.

The point that indicates the beginning of mortal illness is located below the left nipple; when the pain from this point moves round to a similar point below the right nipple one must die. After death one can still see one's body; it appears to one as did rats' flesh when one was alive. In the beginning a man suffering from this disease will not transmit it to others but, when he dies, he will infect myriads for, when his organs decompose, their water will scatter in all directions. At a later date it may perhaps completely enter into another. At the time of death will not this wildly disordered one be disappointed? At the time of the death of such a one the feet gradually swell and the breath is hot. This is a four-fold disease of delusion which is marked by a swollen belly as well as by the marrow in the bones being painful. All the above are varieties of transmissible mortal illness.

The Cure.

Control of the Three Parasites.

Ssŭ ming said, "The purpose of disease is to make you become more virtuous."

The "Filial Son Three Spirits Book" says, "The upper parasite is humbled through training; the middle parasite is controlled by not sleeping at genshen; the lower parasite is killed by being baited with good medicine."

Q. What is permissible to do at genshen [*the time of spiritual trial; the Dark Night of the Soul*] ?
A. The Taoist Scriptures state, "Do not lie down during the night of genshen. After midnight, bow twice facing due south."

The mantra says, "Son of Marquis P'eng, Son of the Yellow Emperor, let the child enter completely inside the guest of the house that the latter may leave my body."

The child is the Child of Buddha, the Buddha Nature within; the mantra seeks the conversion of the parasites ("guests" in the house of one's body) from within.

Repeat three times. As soon as this is completed, bow. To get the parasites to leave a man, this must be used at every fourth hour until they are exhausted, at which point it is precisely genshen [*here literally meaning "the moment of coming to a new era in the depth of the night"*].

The "Filial Son Three Spirits Scripture" says, "Keep genshen seven times and the three spirits will be cut off for a long time." Also if toward dawn one is aware of tiredness, it is essential not to lie down and sleep. As long as one can stay awake, they cannot ascend to speak to the Lord of Heaven. Whenever the Raising of the Seed time [*raising the Seed of Bodhi; the time of spiritual awakening*] arrives the parasites are helpless if one stays awake both day and night. If they are unable to escape for three years, as a result of this watchfulness, they will destroy themselves.

The (Tendai) Chih kuan states, "If it is necessary to cure the two diseases caused by demons, one must journey until the power of the great spiritual mantra is reached, then there will be a change. If it is a disease of karma, then one must use the power of joy inwardly whilst outwardly one must do sange [*an act which combines contrition for wrongdoing with acceptance of karmic consequence*], then there will be a change. This is not the same as a cure. One ought to understand this point absolutely; if one cannot restrain this force [*of karma, it is like*] embracing a sword and destroying oneself.

The above was recorded by Sramanera Ch'ing.

Points Used in the Curing of Disease.

Wind Gate Cave or Big Push Cave.

Find this point above the first vertebra at the nape of the neck or between the first and second [*cervical*] vertebrae [*mudra points Z and Y6*].

This is a very extensive cave.

Altar Mirror.

This point is located in the center of the nipple [*mudra point C5*].

Upper and Lower Altar Mirrors.

The Altar is the heart within the breast. A little over one ts'un above the Upper Altar Mirror Point is the first place to burn moxa (hereafter, if holding, and not burning, hold actual points). A little over one ts'un below the Lower Altar Mirror is the last point to treat. This treatment is called the 'Upper and Lower Altar Mirror.' The measure of a ts'un must be that of the sick person. Its length begins at the tip of the left middle finger and extends down to the [first] joint.

Heart Treasury.

This point is one ts'un above the navel, less 1/100th.

Cinnabar Field.

This is the pubic region. The moxa or holding point is situated two and a half ts'un below the navel.

Twelve diseases come forth from the Cinnabar Field.

Wind City Cave.

Let the left and right arms hang down, with the fingers between the thighs.

Shoulder Well.

This is found inside the shoulder at the top.

Strong Force Cave.

This point is below the protruding bone on the inner side of the left and right ankles. For a man the moxa, or holding, point is the left cave; for a woman it is the right one. Both caves bear the same name and number [*mudra point M1*].

Burn moxa once for each year of age.

Benevolence Cave.

The spine at the level of the heart is the point [*mudra point T1*].

Benevolence means humanity. This is the very center of the lotus position.

Back of the Head Cave.

This point is below the protruding bone on the back of the head [*mudra point Z2*].

The Tendai teaching of the 'Harmony of Body and Mind' (or composure and attention) states, "After treatment do not sleep in the daytime and do not moan. Think often of the King of Universality, [*the Cosmic Buddha*], for purification is the purpose of healing; think of Shining White Light, the Nyoi Wheel of Kanzeon [*the Wheel of the Law*] and Yakushi Nyorai [*the Buddha of Healing*]."

Altar Back.
    This is in the center of the Altar at the back of the head.

Outside Boundary Cure.
    Hold the shoulder at its beginning and give a big push in the center.

Points and Mantras.

    If there is no change, one should burn moxa on the sick person on these moxa points:—

1. Top Ten Character Center, whilst reciting the Hūm phat mantra [*Hūm is the symbol of the Essence of Truth and the Source of all virtue*] five or seven times (this brings together all the merit of the King of Universally Shining Pure Light, the Cosmic Buddha),

2. Wind Gate Cave Center, whilst reciting the Hūm phat mantra five or seven times,

3. Altar Mirror, whilst reciting the Hūm phat mantra five or seven times,

4. Heart Treasury, whilst reciting the Hūm phat mantra five or seven times,

5. Cinnabar Field, whilst reciting the Hūm phat mantra five or seven times,

6. Left and Right Wind City, whilst reciting the Hūm phat mantra five or seven times,

7. Left and Right Peng Chao Cave [*referred to above as the Strong Force Cave*]. Do not burn moxa on the Chao Cave as it will be extremely debilitating. This cave is like bamboo; hold the point whilst reciting the Hūm phat mantra five or seven times.

    One can also use the back, the Shoulder Well and the Benevolence Cave in the same way as the above, making thirteen points in all. One can also add the Head Back Cave.

When burning moxa on these points chant the Body Mantra seven times before each. During genshen [*the Dark Night of the Soul*] take the Three Refuges and the Five Precepts and then burn moxa for the illness. This must be done thoroughly.

After this moxa cure, do not sleep during the day and do not moan and mope. Think constantly of the King of Universally Shining Pure Light [*the Cosmic Buddha*] , of the Nyoi Wheel of Kanzeon [*the Wheel of the Law*] and of Yakushi Nyorai [*the Buddha of Healing*] .

❶傳屍病灸治

第二肋間乳上三寸自中骨
左右一寸五分

乳中間骨上一寸

第二肋間乳上三寸
左右一寸五分

胸ノ骨ノ下
五分許サゲテ

胸崎ヨリ一寸
下左右三寸ノキヨ

膝節ノカワラ
キハ也

章門穴
腹デ左當レリ

ツフミノ　ヒヲ
ヒヲノ　トロ　ヒヲ
ノヒロ　□□クロ
ト　ワヒタチ

默心

入リ三寸
三合ト　御際ヨリ
五合　一寸五分可ハ

肩上一肋ノ分内ハ入
眉ノ際ョリ六肋右五合ノキヨ

一肋ト龜尾中心
サ（クラフヘシ

陳ノイタノキハ
ヨリ五合ニアシ
腹ノホネ

❷僞書論一卷

恭提 ❸逃十三條

僞書之目錄先年雖令書寫之、今度重祖師
之勘文少少書拔而授與、努努不可有他見
而已、僞是破邪顯正之謂歟、傍流之族不得
正流之師傳故、多端以如是之僞書爲賞養、
太以不可也、不可不慎、不可不慎能知其趣
而守惜可眼貯莫使他披露矣
一三千事、于本房云定位謀作也、一圓房
淨發律師相傳重書令傳持之間、定位雖有
懇望不評用之間、號故樂嶐法親王御傳之
重書、以彼三盻一四仁、與之云。自他爲無隔
心之前方便之斷云、就中以彼三盻御稱之
親王爲御相承之重書之由、定位白稱之間
深以一圓上人令信仰六云、隨而榮海僧正以
此書按或仁之時奧書云、遍智院宮御宇一
本有之、其外全無除所極秘書也謂如之
一、寶❹陀羅尼經事、師主云、故極樂房
僧正語云、覺禪阿闍梨、ニクシツク之善、
眞言師也、但一心劣事在之云、寶❺悉陀羅尼
經文ヲ今書裏
一、堀出經云、世間流布敢諸家、目錄所不載
也云云
一、或泚云、濟朝開梨軌、六字軌愛王軌、
多本八萬茶羅軌、光明眞言軌、本等僞書也
也云云
共中愛染王軌宜書有一本云

❶鷹島田乾、三郎氏ニ傳寫本。❷傳高山寺謙寫本、無長谷狩獲秀氏傳寫本、僞書論二僞書目錄ナリ。❸〔逃十三條〕一勢 ❹僞書乃差如左十五行甲本ニ無之 ❺悉十（地）勢＊ ❻甲本傍註曰憲深 ❼僞二論一勢 ❽堀二窟勢 ❾云十（傳祕決）一勢 ❿（一或一云云）四十七字一勢

沙門慶口記

止觀云若鬼魔二病此須除親行及大
神呪力乃得差耳若藥病者當内用
歟力外須懺悔乃可得差對治不同
宜普得其意不可操力抱刀而自發

傷文

瘦病治方依青色大金剛童子
治此病時誦前大身呪三七遍以右手
把白芥子誦前身呪三七遍散打其病
人額面其鬼身碎裂如火可燒失
或抱楊柳枝誦前身呪三七遍打其病
人

或以柘榴枝誦前身呪三七遍打其病
人如此三日其鬼退散其病即愈若猶不
差應灸其病人灸右□處

一者頂十字中
二者風門穴中　[梵字]　吽發吒五七反
三者墳鍩　[梵字]　吽發吒五七反
四者心藏　[梵字]　吽發吒五七反
五者丹田　[梵字]　吽發吒五七反
六者左右風市　[梵字]　吽發吒五七反

七者左右彭矯穴　[梵字]　吽發吒五七反

或加重背肘井仁穴成以庚申日受三
處時誦前身呪各七遍以十三處若灸此
歸五戒應灸此病必得其驗
已上以前根本印加持其灸處是灸
猫鬼兜羅羅鬼障難之處誦前身呪
以沈香白檀香等入銅器中誦前身呪
三七遍加持其香水入病處楊柳柘榴湯
中應浴洗其病人灸病處傳屍病止息
灸治已後勿勿寢眠又勿愁吟常念百光
遍照王及如意輪觀世音并藥師如來

云云

茵草者鬼ノヤカラトイフ草也或
猫鬼者說二ハキレキレト云云也
墳鬼者ネコノ形鬼也
墳背者墳中ノトヲリノ背獄
屏井者在屑上陷中外境治之肩端與
大推中央也
仁穴者跌ノ中心也
彭矯穴者左右内踝下傍出骨下也
惱時者男左女右灸也其人生年之數灸
也
風市者垂下左右手股中指充所也
丹田者又名丹心臍下二寸半也從
丹田出生十二病云云
心藏者臍上一寸不足程也
坩鍩者乳ノ中心也
風門穴者大推穴也項ノ第一骨上也
或第一第二ノ骨間也

十字者蹇スヘヲ以額頭測四折髮
際頂充彼ノ蹇スヘノ至ル所ニ灸ル也
灸時指案寸法取ノ寸法取折四寸五分用之
節指案寸法取男左女右中指外下
阿多婆狗大神
瘦病治方以撰出之

❶以下象書

問。開・立戚指有何意歟　師云。□就意歟
云々

問。可依何法歟　答。十八道有何耶歟
問。種子何　答。⿱字也。金剛部通種子故也
問。三昧耶形輪云々　見。何文歟　答

三尸者

彭涅尸。彭質尸矯尸

修行事

　　　　書寫交合畢　理眞記

　　　　　　　　沙門慶範記之

貞應第三秋九月十三日夜書寫了但書云々
本以假字書寫之常地下。今被書云々　今爲易
者以異字書之了爲思思相州沙門慶
寫了

承安三年十月十八日以乘房御書本書

若是歟可尋之
蟲爲報人罪過申二天帝釋歟。俱生神者
往生要集。人生有七日二蟲生者若是歟此
已上人身。始出生。蟲名也尸者固也

篤尾桷口傳

❖孝子守庚申求長生經

〇凡人腹中有諸蟲。三尸乃爲將軍屬
人五藏。上尸好二車馬衣裳。中尸亦令入
好五味飲食。下尸令人好色。是三尸亦
三毒之根。殺之者壽百二十也。三尸者
令人怡悅無所畏慢。天地帶令入造諸惡
事不可爲善。每庚申日出於上界。告二人
〇其蟲精靈能通天聽。明胞波悅

惡事不論善功。每至庚申日晝夜不眠
則不得出矣。〇經三年不出自滅〇凶惡
之人其蟲最多。而實魂鬼神之威而人
三尸爲物雖有形而名尸〇上尸彭涅中尸彭
俱生經曰上尸名彭涅中尸彭質下尸彭
太清經曰上尸好二車馬衣裳。問其名色如何答
矯。問。其形色如何。答同經曰三尸其形
顏似人長三寸許又曰。上尸色黑形如手。
中尸色青形如〇下尸色白形如鷄子。又趙
先生曰形似小兒二足。或如二大馬有肖尾長
三四寸。又合金曰。形如薄筋。問。此三
尸人身中居何處。答。大清經曰。彭涅居
頭故名二上尸彭質居喉中故名二中尸又
脊彭矯居足故名下尸二又云尸居腹〇仙經
曰三尸在人身中。或亂人心。多嗜欲令
飲食五味。令人好婬欲。又令貪躬
好殺害。〇問。令人早死乎。答
此尸常得作白放縱行饕食人祭醮故欲
令人早死。問。三尸欲令人早死乎。何業
謀計。答。三尸每到六申夜中二辄上天白司
命道人罪過奢人化三百小日也失籌人算
也。一〇月晦弦望庚申夜必曰入罪過〇
矯。三尸於人一端令多嗜欲喜怒〇
問。三尸於人一端令多嗜欲喜怒
外又有所害哉答。彭涅在頭令伐入眼。
目暗面皺口臭齒落彭質在腹令伐入五
藏〇少樂□好作惡事敢食二眾生。彭矯
在足令關格擾亂。五情躁動不能白禁〇

曰。上士修□以伏之。中士每夜二庚申二
以守之二下士伺良藥以殺之〇問。凡可
庚申守二事如何答。仙經曰。庚申夜不
寢。夜半之後向正南專拜。呪曰。彭侯子
三尸亦身。尸去尸當用六甲□□。即
庚申足也〇孝子守尸經二曰二守二庚申二尸
長絕〇又若向曉覺疲倦者。宜不可伏。
而眠每令數覺即不得上告二天帝二
同經問云
諸案孝子三尸經曰。夫人生也。持寄形
於父母抱殼之精。是以人形中盡有三尸
爲人之大害也。常庚申之夜。上告二天帝
記〇唯三尸絕人生籍欲令速死魄三於
泉。唯三尸獨治在地上。此此相承日鬼。四
時祀爲人。痛癢竹伐之性命〇此三
形似人小兒或如似馬。皆有肖尾。長二三寸
在人身中。卒後後遂號□鬼似人生時形像
呪曰。彭涅尸詳尸。今悉入家賓去離我
身。

厄花文陽

之時叩。齒三七反。左手撫心。三呼二尸名二
即不得〇大白山。人楊遇相含〇
山中得此本。傳揚雀睒雀睒季芳庚申
卽〇爲二害矣〇大白山人楊遇芳庚申
靈也。且三尸九蟲種類群多〇每夜欲臥
衣服長短視人謂是死人遲〇賓非人之
呪曰。彭涅尸詳尸。今悉入家賓去離我
已上
此經被無此法中仍疎一見之時□□
了

❶後註日外封歟

●傳屍病口傳

病相（凡此病始而後直，耳漸就で沈滯，如水潤而不盛也、此性素）

朝心地好午剋已後不快。是似發心地云

或身心熱惱漸漸乾瘦。

或住「正念惰人身」「或不喫病常好眠

　云、或非時發道心疎愛、或

時起瞋恚云、或時發興、或時止息、及大事

之時好で左而臥、赤死而坐、而死云

此病始左乳下跼也、移「右乳下」之肉必死耳

死去し後見し之、有似鼠之肉云々又

此病始一人患之時不傳于人、病者逝去時

移萬人、器破之時、其水如散治也云々

或時絶入也コトハ失意狂亂者若是歟云

又死期足漸腫云

又此病從風熱而發云

先身易怖搜多。心驚、脇下痛、手足裏熱。

時赤如膿疾治、而後發好吐唾、又

夢想常多云。又云此鬼有九萬春屬住哀

山云山「日日喫」人精氣并血肉名「阿梨多夜

又「此鬼出」彼山「超曠野時、阿多婆拘大神

來降伏云。汝喫人血肉、我喫汝血肉

于、時悶絕躄地而出血云、我佛末法顧勿食。今日以後長不

食、血肉顧勿食、此大神過去空王佛

時長者。其佛末法飢渴人多死。哀之捨妻

子荷諸食施衆生。依此功德今得攝「預

諸鬼神之威德云々

治病事

千手千眼觀世音治病合藥經云。燒で揹具羅

香、薰入傳屍病人鼻孔中治之、輕時其病

人差（文取意縷、正縷文云涌于手々　足

此經西天竺國沙門伽梵達譯也

揹具羅香者安悉香是也

十字

頂十字ワラス「ヲ「用額、頭週四折愛

際、頂充也彼ワラスヘノ至ル所炙也

大推穴也頂第一骨中也

埴鋭上下

埴者乳中心也。埴鋭上一寸餘登炙也。埴

下一寸餘下炙也。是謂埴鋭也。埴鋭

一寸者病者一寸歟。左中指半、下指出節。

至也。コシヲ撃、指出節也。是五寸歟。

是五折「一分「爲一寸也。或左頭指半。下

文至「是口寸」也。是手、而方「左五寸手裏方

餘二二三分許歟

臍下二寸半炙也從「丹田出生十二病」云云

臍上一寸、不足程歟

丹田

准醫者可知

彭嬌穴

風市

左右內踝下、傍出「骨下也」男、

時可、投火爐中、歟

左穴炙也。其人生年之數炙也。女右穴、炙

也。其數同前

問本發誓可用之歟　答爾也

頭背穴

頭後「出骨下炙也

止觀云、上氣胸滿一左右脇病三、背竦念四

左右脅「病五六心熱懊病七、不能飲食、心

下冷上熱八下冷上熱十下冷陰陽不和十一

氣弱疎十三炙治已後勿卦眼、又勿愁吟、常

念百光遍照王、及如意輪觀音、并藥師如來、

云々

脈蝶腹連骨蒸

脈蝶者四枝「迷之病也

腹連者。腹服之病也

骨蒸者骨中膸痛之病也

是皆傳屍病流類也

鬼ノヤカラトイフ草也

莪草。是三尸口歟之草也

莪草。是三尸口口也。孝子守庚申求長生經云、又

莪草。是三尸口口、姝之草、煮湯沐浴で三尸

去炙

如灾佛部金剛部蓮花部等事

問以藥師口口爲金剛部其心何　答

造三鬼像「入鋼鏡器油中事

問三鬼形如何　答、如六字法三類形歟

問護摩色所入鋼器油、先煮之、其後護摩之

時可、投火爐中、歟　答、爾也

讚獄四句事

問本發誓可用之歟　答爾也

肩井　如常

仁穴

仁者人也趺中心炙也

（●島田乾三郎氏藏寫本　②傍註曰或書云）

The Traditional Points for Curing
Mortal Illness by Cauterization (front).

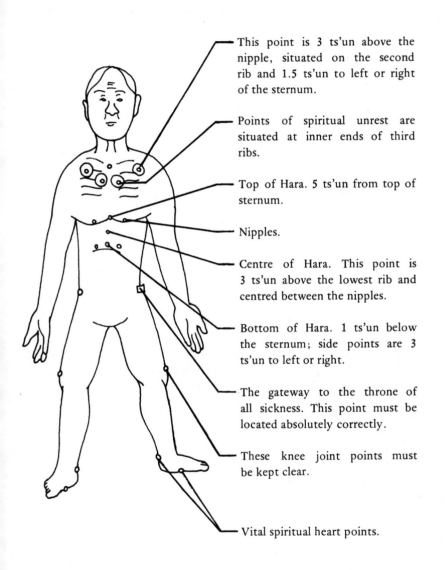

This point is 3 ts'un above the nipple, situated on the second rib and 1.5 ts'un to left or right of the sternum.

Points of spiritual unrest are situated at inner ends of third ribs.

Top of Hara. 5 ts'un from top of sternum.

Nipples.

Centre of Hara. This point is 3 ts'un above the lowest rib and centred between the nipples.

Bottom of Hara. 1 ts'un below the sternum; side points are 3 ts'un to left or right.

The gateway to the throne of all sickness. This point must be located absolutely correctly.

These knee joint points must be kept clear.

Vital spiritual heart points.

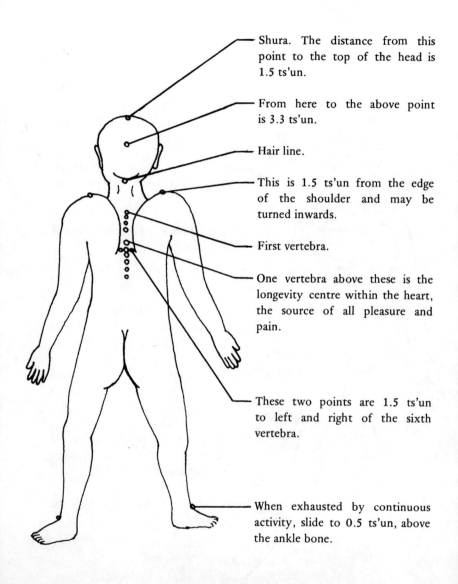

Shura. The distance from this point to the top of the head is 1.5 ts'un.

From here to the above point is 3.3 ts'un.

Hair line.

This is 1.5 ts'un from the edge of the shoulder and may be turned inwards.

First vertebra.

One vertebra above these is the longevity centre within the heart, the source of all pleasure and pain.

These two points are 1.5 ts'un to left and right of the sixth vertebra.

When exhausted by continuous activity, slide to 0.5 ts'un, above the ankle bone.

ABOUT THE AUTHORS.

Rōshi Jiyu-Kennett is a Zen Master trained in the Sōtō Zen tradition and is the Abbess and Spiritual Director of Shasta Abbey, a Zen seminary and training monastery at Mt. Shasta, California. Born in 1924, in England, Rōshi Kennett became a Buddhist in the Theravādin tradition. She was later introduced to Rinzai Zen by D.T. Suzuki in London where she held membership in, and lectured at, the London Buddhist Society. She received her formal education at Trinity College of Music, London, where she was awarded a Fellowship as well as obtaining the degree of Bachelor of Music from Durham University.

In January, 1962, Rōshi Kennett was ordained in the Chinese Rinzai tradition in Malacca, Malaysia, and then continued on to Japan to study Sōtō (Ts'ao Tung) Zen at Dai Hon Zan Sōji-ji Temple, one of the two head temples of the Sōtō Zen school of Japan where she became the personal disciple of the Chief Abbot, the Very Reverend Chisan Kōhō Zenji. After several years of training she became head of the Foreign Guest Department being in charge of instructing the many Westerners who came to the temple. Rōshi Kennett was Transmitted by Kōhō Zenji and was installed as Abbess of Unpuku-ji Temple, in Mie Prefecture, Japan, where she taught her own Western disciples. She also earned the Sei Degree (a priesthood degree that requires at least five years of continuous study, roughly equivalent to a Christian Doctor of Divinity) whilst at Dai Hon Zan Sōji-ji and was granted a Sanzen License.

In November, 1969, accompanied by two Western disciples, Rōshi Kennett came to San Francisco on a lecture tour. The Zen Mission Society was founded the following year and moved to Mt. Shasta for the founding of Shasta Abbey.

In addition to being Abbess of Shasta Abbey, Rōshi Kennett has been an instructor at the University of California Extension, in Berkeley, since 1972, is on the faculty of the California Institute of Transpersonal Psychology and has lectured at universities throughout the world. She has founded numerous Zen temples and meditation groups throughout the United States, Canada and England. She has also authored *Zen is Eternal Life* (Dharma Publishing, 1976), formerly published as *Selling Water by the River* (Pantheon, 1972), a manual of Zen Buddhist training; *How to Grow a Lotus Blossom or How a Zen Buddhist Prepares for Death* (Shasta Abbey, 1977); and *The Wild, White Goose, Vols. I and II* (Shasta Abbey, 1977 & 1978), the diaries of her years in Japan.

Rev. Daizui MacPhillamy was born in New Jersey in 1945. He attended Amherst College, from which he received a B.A., *magna cum laude*, in psychology and anthropology in 1967. His graduate work was done at Stanford University (M.A. in education) and the University of Oregon, where he received an M.A. and a Ph.D. in clinical psychology. He served as a Fellow in Medical Psychology at the Neuropsychiatric Institute of the University of California at Los Angeles during 1972-73, and is the author of several articles on psychological measurement.

Rev. MacPhillamy became a Buddhist in 1968 under the guidance of Rev. J. Eugene Wagner of the American Buddhist Order. In 1973 he entered Shasta Abbey, from which he graduated in 1976 as a full priest and in 1978 as a Teacher of Buddhism. He received the Transmission from Rōshi Jiyu-Kennett and was named by her as a Rōshi in 1978. Rev. Mac-Phillamy was prior of the Berkeley Buddhist Priory, Oakland, California, in 1976 and was appointed to the faculty of Shasta Abbey in 1978, where he currently serves as the chief assistant to Rōshi Jiyu-Kennett. He has provided seminars on Zen meditation to psychological groups and is engaged in research on the long-term effects of Zen meditation and monastic training on the personality.

ABOUT SHASTA ABBEY.

Shasta Abbey, headquarters of the Order of Buddhist Contemplatives of the Sōtō Zen Church, is a seminary and training monastery for the Zen Buddhist priesthood. Located on fifteen acres of forest land north of the city of Mt. Shasta, California, the Abbey was established in November, 1970, by Rōshi Jiyu-Kennett who is the Abbess and Spiritual Director. The Abbey provides training for both members of the priesthood and lay students; there is no discrimination with regard to sex; both men and women may enter the priesthood and become full priests and teachers. At the time of going to print, January, 1979, there are fifty priests and priest-trainees in residence. The priest training program is approved by the California Department of Education, approved for Veterans Administration and Social Security benefits and for attendance by foreign students.

The Abbey's lay training program is open to serious lay students who wish to undergo Zen Buddhist training for any period of time; there are week-long sesshins, introductory and advanced weekend retreats throughout the year. In addition to the above there are the following religious services:— reception into the Buddhist Church (lay ordination), naming ceremonies for children, weddings, funerals and memorial services; the Abbey has a cemetery available to members and other Buddhists. Private spiritual direction (sanzen) is available at all times; all letters concerning serious religious questions are answered.

Shasta Abbey publishes a monthly magazine, the *Journal of Shasta Abbey,* which includes articles by Rōshi Kennett, priests of the Abbey and others on various aspects of Zen training. The Abbey also publishes special booklets from time to time; these include "Zen Meditation" and "Becoming a Buddhist."

Branch communities and affiliated meditation groups are located in Eureka, Los Angeles, Oakland, Ojai, and Sacramento, California; Eugene and Portland, Oregon; Seattle, Washington; Bigfork, Montana; Edmonton, Toronto, and Vancouver, Canada; and Hexham, England.

For more information please contact Shasta Abbey, Mt. Shasta, California, 96067; telephone (916) 926-4208.